# AAT

## Qualifications and Credit Framework (QCF)
## LEVEL 4 DIPLOMA IN ACCOUNTING

TEXT

Budgeting

2012 Edition

First edition July 2010
Third edition June 2012

ISBN 9781 4453 9464 0
(Previous edition 9780 7517 9736 7)

*British Library Cataloguing-in-Publication Data*
A catalogue record for this book is available from the
British Library

Published by

BPP Learning Media Ltd
BPP House
Aldine Place
London
W12 8AA

www.bpp.com/learningmedia

Printed in the United Kingdom

# CONTENTS

Introduction

BPP Learning Media's AAT materials      v

A note on terminology      vii

Assessment strategy      ix

AAT unit guide      xi

1    Cost classification      1

2    Budgetary control systems      35

3    Forecasting      55

4    Budget preparation      103

5    Preparing cash budgets      135

6    Budget preparation – limiting factors      165

7    Flexed budgets and variances      179

8    Performance indicators      211

Answers to chapter tasks      227

Test your learning – answers      245

Index      275

# A NOTE ABOUT COPYRIGHT

Dear Customer

What does the little © mean and why does it matter?

Your market-leading BPP books, course materials and e-learning materials do not write and update themselves. People write them: on their own behalf or as employees of an organisation that invests in this activity. Copyright law protects their livelihoods. It does so by creating rights over the use of the content.

Breach of copyright is a form of theft – as well being a criminal offence in some jurisdictions, it is potentially a serious breach of professional ethics.

With current technology, things might seem a bit hazy but, basically, without the express permission of BPP Learning Media:

- Photocopying our materials is a breach of copyright

- Scanning, ripcasting or conversion of our digital materials into different file formats, uploading them to facebook or emailing them to your friends is a breach of copyright

You can, of course, sell your books, in the form in which you have bought them – once you have finished with them. (Is this fair to your fellow students? We update for a reason.)

And what about outside the UK? BPP Learning Media strives to make our materials available at prices students can afford by local printing arrangements, pricing policies and partnerships which are clearly listed on our website. A tiny minority ignore this and indulge in criminal activity by illegally photocopying our material or supporting organisations that do. If they act illegally and unethically in one area, can you really trust them?

## BPP LEARNING MEDIA'S AAT MATERIALS

Since July 2010 the AAT's assessments have fallen within the **Qualifications and Credit Framework** and most papers are now assessed by way of an on demand **computer based assessment**. BPP Learning Media has invested heavily to ensure our ground breaking materials are as relevant as possible for this method of assessment. In particular, our **suite of online resources** ensures that you are prepared for online testing by allowing you to practise numerous online tasks that are similar to the tasks you will encounter in the AAT's assessments.

The BPP range of resources comprises:

- **Texts**, covering all the knowledge and understanding needed by students, with numerous illustrations of 'how it works', practical examples and tasks for you to use to consolidate your learning. The majority of tasks within the texts have been written in an interactive style that reflects the style of the online tasks we anticipate the AAT will set. Texts are available in our traditional paper format and, in addition, as ebooks which can be downloaded to your PC or laptop.

- **Question Banks**, including additional learning questions plus the AAT practice assessment and a number of other full practice assessments prepared by BPP Learning Media Ltd. Full answers to all questions and assessments, prepared by BPP Learning Media Ltd, are included. Our question banks are provided free of charge in an online environment containing tasks similar to those you will encounter in the AAT's testing environment. This means you can become familiar with being tested in an online environment prior to completing the real assessment.

- **Passcards**, which are handy pocket-sized revision tools designed to fit in a handbag or briefcase to enable you to revise anywhere at anytime. All major points are covered in the Passcards which have been designed to assist you in consolidating knowledge.

- **Workbooks**, which have been designed to cover the units that are assessed by way of project/case study. The workbooks contain many practical tasks to assist in the learning process and also a sample assessment or project to work through.

- **Lecturers' resources**, providing a further bank of tasks, answers and full practice assessments for classroom use, available separately only to lecturers whose colleges adopt BPP Learning Media material. The practice assessments within the lecturers' resources are available in both paper format and online in e format.

This Text for Budgeting has been written specifically to ensure comprehensive yet concise coverage of the AAT's new learning outcomes and assessment criteria. It is fully up to date as at June 2012 and reflects both the AAT's unit guide and the practice assessments provided by the AAT.

Each chapter contains:

- Clear, step by step explanation of the topic

- Logical progression and linking from one chapter to the next

- Numerous illustrations of 'how it works'

- Interactive tasks within the text of the chapter itself, with answers at the back of the book. In general, these tasks have been written in the interactive form that students will see in their real assessments

- Test your learning questions of varying complexity, again with answers supplied at the back of the book. In general, these test questions have been written in the interactive form that students will see in their real assessments

The emphasis in all tasks and test questions is on the practical application of the skills acquired.

If you have any comments about this book, please e-mail paulsutcliffe@bpp.com or write to Paul Sutcliffe, Senior Publishing Manager, BPP Learning Media Ltd, BPP House, Aldine Place, London W12 8AA.

# A NOTE ON TERMINOLOGY

On 1 January 2012, the AAT moved from UK GAAP to IFRS terminology. Although you may be used to UK terminology, you need to now know the equivalent international terminology for your assessments.

The following information is taken from an article on the AAT's website and describes how the terminology changes impact on students studying for each level of the AAT QCF qualification.

**What is the impact of IFRS terms on AAT assessments?**

The list shown in the table that follows gives the 'translation' between UK GAAP and IFRS.

| UK GAAP | IFRS |
|---|---|
| Final accounts | Financial statements |
| **Trading and profit and loss account** | **Income statement or Statement of comprehensive income** |
| Turnover or Sales | Revenue or Sales revenue |
| Sundry income | Other operating income |
| Interest payable | Finance costs |
| Sundry expenses | Other operating costs |
| Operating profit | Profit from operations |
| Net profit/loss | Profit/Loss for the year/period |
| **Balance sheet** | **Statement of financial position** |
| Fixed assets | Non-current assets |
| Net book value | Carrying amount |
| Tangible assets | Property, plant and equipment |
| Reducing balance depreciation | Diminishing balance depreciation |
| Depreciation/Depreciation expense(s) | Depreciation charge(s) |
| Stocks | Inventories |
| Trade debtors or Debtors | Trade receivables |
| Prepayments | Other receivables |
| Debtors and prepayments | Trade and other receivables |
| Cash at bank and in hand | Cash and cash equivalents |
| Trade creditors or Creditors | Trade payables |
| Accruals | Other payables |

| UK GAAP | IFRS |
| --- | --- |
| Creditors and accruals | Trade and other payables |
| Long-term liabilities | Non-current liabilities |
| Capital and reserves | Equity (limited companies) |
| Profit and loss balance | Retained earnings |
| Minority interest | Non-controlling interest |
| **Cash flow statement** | **Statement of cash flows** |

This is certainly not a comprehensive list, which would run to several pages, but it does cover the main terms that you will come across in your studies and assessments. However, you won't need to know all of these in the early stages of your studies – some of the terms will not be used until you reach Level 4. For each level of the AAT qualification, the points to bear in mind are as follows:

### Level 2 Certificate in Accounting

The IFRS terms do not impact greatly at this level. Make sure you are familiar with 'receivables' (also referred to as 'trade receivables'), 'payables' (also referred to as 'trade payables'), and 'inventories'. The terms sales ledger and purchases ledger – together with their control accounts – will continue to be used. Sometimes the control accounts might be called 'trade receivables control account' and 'trade payables control account'. The other term to be aware of is 'non-current asset' – this may be used in some assessments.

### Level 3 Diploma in Accounting

At this level you need to be familiar with the term 'financial statements'. The financial statements comprise an 'income statement' (profit and loss account), and a 'statement of financial position' (balance sheet). In the income statement the term 'revenue' or 'sales revenue' takes the place of 'sales', and 'profit for the year' replaces 'net profit'. Other terms may be used in the statement of financial position – eg 'non-current assets' and 'carrying amount'. However, specialist limited company terms are not required at this level.

### Level 4 Diploma in Accounting

At Level 4 a wider range of IFRS terms is needed, and in the case of Financial statements (FNST), are already in use – particularly those relating to limited companies. Note especially that an income statement becomes a 'statement of comprehensive income'.

**Note:** The information above was taken from an AAT article from the 'assessment news' area of the AAT website (www.aat.org.uk).

# ASSESSMENT STRATEGY

The assessment for Budgeting is normally a two hour 30 minutes computer based assessment (CBA), which will include extended writing tasks.

The assessment consists of two sections relating to Planning (Section 1) and Control (Section 2).

Section 1 consists of five tasks covering the research of available data, forecasting, production scheduling, financial budgeting and splitting plans and budgets into accounting periods. It also tests relevant communication.

Section 2 consists of three tasks covering revisions to budgets, budget flexing, variance analysis and reporting plus relevant communication. The focus of this section is on understanding and communicating the significance of results.

As the CBA will require both computer and human marking, results will normally be available approximately 6 weeks after the assessment (this timing is provisional and may be subject to change).

## Competency

Learners will be required to demonstrate competence in both sections of the assessment. For the purpose of assessment the competency level for AAT assessment is set at 70 per cent. The level descriptor in the table below describes the ability and skills students at this level must successfully demonstrate to achieve competence.

| QCF Level descriptor | **Summary** |
|---|---|
| | Achievement at level 4 reflects the ability to identify and use relevant understanding, methods and skills to address problems that are well defined but complex and non-routine. It includes taking responsibility for overall courses of action as well as exercising autonomy and judgement within fairly broad parameters. It also reflects understanding of different perspectives or approaches within an area of study or work. |
| | ### Knowledge and understanding |
| | ■ Have practical, theoretical and technical understanding to address problems that are well defined but complex and non-routine |
| | ■ Analyse, interpret and evaluate relevant information and ideas |
| | ■ Be aware of the nature and approximate scope of the area of study or work |
| | ■ Have an informed awareness of different perspectives or approaches within the area of study or work |
| | ### Application and action |
| | ■ Address problems that are complex and non-routine while normally fairly well defined |
| | ■ Identify, adapt and use appropriate methods and skills |
| | ■ Initiate and use appropriate investigation to inform actions |
| | ■ Review the effectiveness and appropriateness of methods, actions and results |
| | ### Autonomy and accountability |
| | ■ Take responsibility for courses of action including, where relevant, responsibility for the work of others |
| | ■ Exercise autonomy and judgement within broad but generally well-defined parameters |

# AAT UNIT GUIDE

## Introduction

The Budgeting learning and assessment area (LAA) comprises two units:

- Principles of Budgeting
- Drafting Budgets

For assessment purposes the two units are combined. The information below should be read in conjunction with the standards for the two units.

## The purpose of the units

The creation of these two core units at level four recognises the importance of financial planning in every organisation. Budgets are an essential tool for planning, coordinating, authorising, and cost control. Much of the Principles of Budgeting unit consolidates knowledge required at level three. However, Drafting Budgets requires new skills to create appropriate forecasts and budgets for a wide range of activities and circumstances; to agree the budgets with other functional managers, to monitor results against budget and trigger suitable management interventions.

## Learning objectives

In the Principles of Budgeting unit, learners develop an understanding of how and why budgets are prepared. Assessment candidates need to display the necessary knowledge to prepare revenue forecasts and a range of budgets for different circumstances, and be able to tailor them to meet organisational requirements.

In the Drafting Budgets unit, learners develop their forecasting and budgeting skills. Assessment candidates need to demonstrate their ability to prepare forecasts and budgets, to analyse variances and to make recommendations for improving operational performance. They must also be able to guide managers in planning and control.

The computer based assessment (CBA) covers a broad range of skills and knowledge:

- Management accounting practice, and related techniques
- Understanding of the management of operational performance (cost control, efficiency, effectiveness and utilisation of resources)
- Data collection from internal and external sources
- Creation of forecasts, plans and budgets
- Adaptation of budgets in response to changing circumstances
- Communication of plans and actual results
- Analysis of historical data and variances from budget
- Providing guidance to management

## Learning outcomes

Each unit includes three learning outcomes comprised of a number of assessment criteria.

### Principles of Budgeting (Knowledge unit)

1. Demonstrate an understanding of the impact of internal and external business factors on budgets

2. Understand why budgets are used

3. Understand the skills needed in budget preparation

### Drafting Budgets (Skills unit)

1. Prepare forecasts and budgets

2. Understand the impact that changes in the economic environment will have on the budget

3. Use budgetary control to ensure organisational targets are met

## Delivery guidance

The table below summarises where to find the topics tested in this learning area. The full explanation of the delivery guidance is given below the tables.

### Principles of Budgeting

**1    Demonstrate an understanding of the impact of internal and external business factors on budgets**

| | |
|---|---|
| 1.1  Explain the structure of the organisation; responsibility centres and the relationships between the departments and functions | **Chapter 1** |
| 1.2  Identify internal and external sources of information on costs, prices, demand, availability of resources and availability and cost of finance, to include Government statistics, trade associations, financial press quotations and price lists | **Chapter 3** |
| 1.3  Describe the impact of the external environment and any specific external costs on budgets | **Chapter 3** |
| 1.4  Describe the internal charges made to attribute indirect costs to production | **Chapter 1** |

**2    Understand why budgets are used**

| | |
|---|---|
| 2.1  Explain the behavioural aspects of budgeting | **Chapter 2** |
| 2.2  Justify the uses of budgetary control for planning, co- | **Chapter 2** |

| | | |
|---|---|---|
| | ordinating, authorising and cost control | |
| **2.3** | Identify the correct budget to prepare according to the organisational requirements | **Chapters 3 & 5** |
| **2.4** | Explain the relationship between budgetary control, product life cycles, and forecasts and planning | **Chapter 3** |
| **2.5** | Explain the significance of budget variances | **Chapter 7** |
| **2.6** | Recognise the effect that capacity, production and sales constraints have on budgets | **Chapter 6** |

## 3    Understand the skills needed in budget preparation

| | | |
|---|---|---|
| **3.1** | Explain the principles of standard costing | **Chapters 4 & 7** |
| **3.2** | Describe the purpose of revenue and cost forecasts and how they link to budgets | **Chapters 2 & 3** |
| **3.3** | Identify when to use the following techniques: Indexing, Sampling, Moving Averages, Linear Regression and Seasonal Trends | **Chapter 3** |
| **3.4** | Recognise expenses as different types of costs | **Chapter 1** |
| **3.5** | Identify the sources of relevant data used in budget proposals | **Chapter 3** |

## Drafting Budgets

## 1    Prepare forecasts and budgets

| | | |
|---|---|---|
| **1.1** | Identify relevant data for forecasting income and expenditure from internal and external sources | **Chapter 3** |
| **1.2** | Correctly code, classify and allocate cost and revenue data to responsibility centres | **Chapter 1** |
| **1.3** | Forecast future income from relevant internal and external data | **Chapter 3** |
| **1.4** | Schedule the required production resources to meet forecasts | **Chapter 4** |
| **1.5** | Budget in accordance with the organisation's costing systems, stating any assumptions made | **Chapter 4** |
| **1.6** | Prepare accurate cash flow forecasts to facilitate the achievement of organisational objectives | **Chapter 5** |
| **1.7** | Prepare draft budgets from forecast data | **Chapter 4** |

| | | |
|---|---|---|
| **1.8** | Break down budgets into time periods according to organisational needs | **Chapter 2** |
| **1.9** | Plan and agree draft budgets with all parties involved | **Chapter 4** |

**2   Understand the impact that changes in the economic environment will have on the budget**

| | | |
|---|---|---|
| **2.1** | Calculate the effect that variations in capacity on costs, production and sales will have on budgeted costs and revenues | **Chapter 6** |
| **2.2** | Prepare an accurately flexed budget | **Chapter 7** |
| **2.3** | Analyse critical factors affecting costs and revenues and draw clear conclusions | **Chapter 6** |
| **2.4** | Identify and evaluate options and solutions to increase profitability or reduce financial losses or exposure to risk | **Chapter 6** |

**3   Use budgetary control to ensure organisational targets are met**

| | | |
|---|---|---|
| **3.1** | Set clear targets and performance indicators to enable the budgets to be monitored | **Chapter 8** |
| **3.2** | Check and reconcile budget figures on an ongoing basis | **Chapters 4 & 7** |
| **3.3** | Review and revise the validity of budgets in the light of any significant anticipated changes | **Chapters 4 & 7** |
| **3.4** | Identify variances between budget and actual income/expenditure | **Chapter 7** |
| **3.5** | Analyse the variances and explain the impact that this will have on the organisation | **Chapter 7** |
| **3.6** | Inform management of any significant issues arising from budgetary control | **Chapter 7** |
| **3.7** | Present any recommendations with a clear rationale to appropriate people | **Chapter 7** |

**Delivery guidance: Principles of budgeting**

**1.   Demonstrate an understanding of the impact of internal and external business factors on budgets**

**1.1. Explain the structure of the organisation; responsibility centres and the relationships between the departments and functions**

Candidates must understand that the structure of a budget needs to be appropriate to the organisation. For instance, if there is a production

department, a marketing department and an administration department, the organisation's budget will need to include a production budget, a marketing budget and an administration budget. Appropriate profit centres, cost centres and investment centres will need to be defined and the budget must be structured accordingly. The budget responsibility of managers must be consistent with their authority. Candidates can be assessed on their ability to propose or critique the structure of a budget; to describe the purpose of departments and functions and to describe the responsibility of senior managers for preparing budgets and delivering performance.

1.2. **Identify internal and external sources of information on costs, prices, demand, availability of resources and availability and cost of finance, to include Government statistics, trade associations, financial press quotations and price lists**

Budget data is drawn from a wide variety of sources within the organisation and externally. Candidates must be able to suggest an appropriate, reliable source for each piece of information required in budget construction. They will not be expected to have a detailed knowledge of, for instance, government statistical publications, but must be able to demonstrate that they know which external source, or which member of the organisation, to go to for any specified data.

1.3. **Describe the impact of the external environment and any specific external costs on budgets**

The external environment has a direct impact on sales demand, prices, availability of resources and costs. Some costs, including taxes, are not within the organisation's control. Even material and labour costs are subject to economic pressures that may not be quantifiable when budgets are constructed. Realistic budgets have to be prepared in this context. Candidates must be able to review budget proposals, comment on their achievability and identify inherent risks.

1.4. **Describe the internal charges made to attribute indirect costs to production**

Indirect costs (overheads) may be attributed to production through apportionment to departments and the use of overhead recovery rates, or through activity based costing, etc. The budget needs to be consistent with the method of attribution that will be employed to calculate the actual results. Candidates need to be able to identify appropriate methods of attribution and recognise the distortions that can be created by inappropriate methods.

2. **Understand why budgets are used**

2.1. **Explain the behavioural aspects of budgeting**

The purpose of a budget is to drive improved performance for the organisation. It should be motivational. Poor budgeting can be extremely de-motivational. A budget is both a plan and a performance measure. Each element of a budget must be owned by an appropriate responsible manager. Candidates must be able to describe the relationships between budgets and accountability, between authority and responsibility, and between planning and control, and be able to make recommendations to ensure that budgets promote the right behaviour and inspire the management team to achieve the corporate goals.

2.2. **Justify the uses of budgetary control for planning, co-ordinating, authorising and cost control**

Budgetary control fulfils these four apparently diverse functions and a balance must be maintained. For instance, over-emphasis on cost control can constrain business growth. Also, high level planning targets can conflict with detailed co-ordination activity. Candidates must be able to describe each of these functions and demonstrate an understanding of the potential for conflict.

2.3. **Identify the correct budget to prepare according to the organisational requirements**

Candidates must know the purpose and content of each of the following budgets: Income and expenditure, Production, Material and Labour (employees and other resources). They must also be able to explain the distinction between Capital and Revenue. They must be able to describe the circumstance under which flexible budgets are appropriate and when it is better for budgets to be fixed. Finally they need to be able to explain the purpose and construction of a Cash Forecast and how it is constructed and updated.

2.4. **Explain the relationship between budgetary control, product life cycles, and forecasts and planning**

Many organisations prefer the term financial plan to budget. The budget is an integral part of an overall plan for the business. Forecasting is an essential element of determining realistic data and assumptions upon which the plan is based. Statistical projections are useful aids to forecasting (see assessment criterion 3.3 below) but judgement and knowledge of the market and the products is essential. In particular, sales revenue forecasts must recognise market trends, promotional activity and the product lifecycle. The control element of budgetary control includes monitoring actual results against budget, analysing variances and taking appropriate management action. Candidates must be able to describe budgetary control, product lifecycles, and forecasts and to make appropriate recommendations to ensure that the planning process is coordinated and soundly based.

2.5. **Explain the significance of budget variances**

Variances can be caused by better or worse than expected performance within the organisation or by unforeseen external factors. They can also be due to unrealistic or inaccurate budgeting. A significant variance requires a management response. This could be, for example, to investigate poor performance and take corrective action. Candidates need to be able to demonstrate an understanding of how variances should be investigated and of the range of management actions that could be appropriate.

2.6. **Recognise the effect that capacity, production and sales constraints have on budgets**

To be realistic budgets have to be based on what is practically possible. Every business has a budget factor (limiting factor), which could, for instance, be a production bottleneck, possible market share or access to finance. Candidates must be able to identify budget factors and describe how to create a budget that maximises the potential contribution.

3. **Understand the skills needed in budget preparation**

3.1. **Explain the principles of standard costing**

Standard costing and budgetary control are powerful management tools that can be used separately but naturally combine into a seamless system of planning and control. They share the approach of setting targets, measuring actual performance, analysing variances and initiating management action to correct or improve future performance and set new targets. This creates a cycle of continuous improvement. Candidates must be able to describe the principles of standard costing and variance analysis, explain the main material and labour variances and identify possible causes of each. They should be able to place this in the context of budgetary control and explain how an integrated standard costing system provides the data for budget preparation and variance analysis.

3.2. **Describe the purpose of revenue and cost forecasts and how they link to budgets**

Some aspects of business performance are within the control of the organisation and can be planned. Others are subject more or less to external factors that must be forecast. For example, budgeted sales revenue may be calculated from forecasts of market demand and market share. Cost budgets may be influenced by forecasts of world markets and national inflation. These forecasts are used to develop the planning assumptions on which budgets are based. These assumptions must be clearly stated so that variances from budget can be analysed and understood. Candidates must be able to distinguish between forecasts and plans, and describe how each forecast fits into the planning process. They must also be able to recommend techniques for dealing with the uncertainty inherent in forecasts. These techniques include planning models, regular re-forecasting, re-budgeting and flexible budgets.

3.3. **Identify when to use the following techniques: Indexing, Sampling, Moving Averages, Linear Regression and Seasonal Trends**

These techniques have been learned in previous units. Detailed explanations of each technique are not required at this level but candidates must be able to recognise the circumstances in which each technique could be appropriate, explain why, and describe limitations to their use.

3.4. **Recognise expenses as different types of costs**

Cost budgets include both direct and indirect (overhead) costs (see assessment criterion 1.4 above) and the budget construction must be consistent with the organisation's costing and financial reporting systems. Candidates must be able to describe the appropriate accounting methodology for raw materials, direct labour and other direct costs. They must also be able to explain how to budget for underlying indirect costs and for their attribution into product costs (cost objects).

Various cost behaviours are recognised such as variable, semi-variable and stepped. Not all costs fit these textbook profiles, of course. Labour is usually described as variable when, in practice, basic wages are often a fixed cost and overtime is a variable at a higher rate that only applies when basic hours are utilised. Candidates need to be able to recognise cost behaviours and recommend appropriate methods of budget calculation and performance measurement.

### 3.5. Identify the sources of relevant data used in budget proposals

Budgets are compiled from a wide range of sources: market forecasts, current performance data and planning assumptions. Candidates must be able to clearly state these sources in appropriate footnotes to the budget or covering correspondence.

## Delivery guidance: Drafting budgets (skills)

### 1. Prepare forecasts and budgets

#### 1.1. Identify relevant data for forecasting income and expenditure from internal and external sources

Candidates must be able to recognise the relevance of data available for forecasting and extract the appropriate items.

#### 1.2. Correctly code, classify and allocate cost and revenue data to responsibility centres

The creation of an appropriate accountability structure (investment centres, profit centres and cost centres) is fundamental to planning, coordination and control. Candidates must be able to recommend suitable structures and to classify and allocate cost and revenue data accordingly.

#### 1.3. Forecast future income from relevant internal and external data

Candidates must be able to prepare sales revenue forecasts from relevant internal and external data using appropriate forecasting techniques and judgement and present the results clearly, stating assumptions.

#### 1.4. Schedule the required production resources to meet forecasts

Candidates must be able to prepare the underlying 'physical' plans upon which budgets are calculated. This involves calculating the production plan and the resource plans for materials, labour and production facilities and making appropriate adjustments for inventory levels, wastage, available staff hours and production facility hours, etc.

#### 1.5. Budget in accordance with the organisation's costing systems stating any assumptions made

Candidates must be able to prepare budgets for production costs (consistent with the organisation's costing systems) based on 'physical plans' for materials, labour and other production facilities. They must be able to present the results clearly, stating assumptions and sources of information.

#### 1.6. Prepare accurate cash flow forecast to facilitate the achievement of organisational objectives

Cash flow forecasts must be consistent with all other aspects of the budget. Candidates must be able to prepare a cash flow forecast from the budget data and update it as actual performance results become available. Forecasts must be presented clearly, stating assumptions and sources of information.

### 1.7. Prepare draft budgets from forecast data

Candidates must be able to prepare budgets for sales revenue, material costs, labour (employees and other resources), other production facilities, other overheads (including depreciation) and capital expenditure and assemble these results into a master budget. Budgets must be presented clearly, stating assumptions.

### 1.8. Break down budgets into time periods according to organisational needs

Candidates must be able to break down budgets into weeks, months or quarters, etc, to facilitate regular reporting and monitoring of performance.

### 1.9. Plan and agree draft budgets with all parties involved

Communication is a key requirement of the budgeting process and candidates must be able to demonstrate their ability to read and understand the planning data available; check their understanding with appropriate managers; set out the results of their work in a clear, understandable and professional manner; understand the impact of these results on the organisation and provide management with clear written explanation and advice. Draft budgets should be presented to the appropriate executive(s) for approval.

## 2. Understand the impact that changes in the economic environment will have on the budget

### 2.1. Calculate the effect that variations in capacity on costs, production and sales will have on budgeted costs and revenues

Candidates need to be able to recognise budget limiting factors (constraints in capacity and limitations on costs and sales) and to prepare or revise a budget to fit within such a constraint.

### 2.2. Prepare an accurately flexed budget

Candidates must be able to flex a budget, adjusting each element of the budget correctly according to the original budget data and stating assumptions about cost behaviour. They must also be able to present the flexed budget clearly and explain the changes from the original.

### 2.3. Analyse critical factors affecting costs and revenues and draw clear conclusions

Candidates must be able to identify critical factors affecting costs and revenues, such as market conditions, staffing levels, material availability, etc, and explain their impact on the budget. They must be able to advise on the consequences of changes to key planning assumptions.

2.4. **Identify and evaluate options and solutions to increase profitability or reduce financial losses or exposure to risk**

Candidates must be able to calculate the impact on the budget of alternative strategies and provide sound advice based on their evaluation of profitability and exposure to risk

3. **Use budgetary control to ensure organisational targets are met**

3.1. **Set clear targets and performance indicators to enable the budgets to be monitored**

Candidates must be able to identify suitable physical and financial measures, consistent with the key planning assumptions, to use as performance measures. They must be able to calculate these measures for the budget and for actual performance and provide clear advice to enable budgets to be achieved. Examples of physical measures include quality indicators such as reject rates; efficiency indicators such as the number of products made per labour hour or idle time ratios, and capacity measures, such as machine utilisation ratios. Simple financial measures include average selling price, profit percentage of sales revenue, material cost per unit of purchase, labour rate per hour, cost per unit of production and, of course, sales and cost variances.

3.2. **Check and reconcile budget figures on an ongoing basis**

Candidates must ensure that budget data is reported accurately and consistently.

3.3. **Review and revise the validity of budgets in the light of any significant anticipated changes**

Budgets need to be reviewed regularly in the light of actual performance and by updating the underlying forecasts. Candidates need to be able to review the planning assumptions, recalculate budgets and offer appropriate guidance to management. Volume changes can often be dealt with by budget flexing but significant changes in business strategy must be evaluated and the budget amended accordingly. Candidates must recognise the limitations of budget flexing.

3.4. **Identify variances between budget and actual income/expenditure**

Candidates must be able calculate variances in absolute and percentage terms, accurately comparing like with like and present the results clearly.

3.5. **Analyse the variances and explain the impact that this will have on the organisation**

Candidates must be able to analyse variances, in the context of any operational information available, to identify possible causes and provide suitable management advice. This advice might explain how performance could be improved or suggest appropriate further investigation. Candidates also need to explain how any variance impacts on overall performance and the possible consequences for the organisation.

3.6. **Inform management of any significant issues arising from budgetary control**

Issues that arise can include changes in planning assumptions or underlying forecasts; significant variance from budget; inaccuracies in the budget; organisational issues and problems with accountability or motivation. Candidates must be able to clearly describe the issue to the appropriate manager(s) and offer constructive advice.

3.7 **Present any recommendations with a clear rationale to appropriate people**

Communication is a key constituent of an effective budgetary control system. Candidates must be able to present forecasts, budgets and control reports clearly, highlighting key issues for attention and providing relevant and focused recommendations to initiate management action.

# chapter 1:
# COST CLASSIFICATION

---
**chapter coverage** 📖
---

In this chapter, we will look at costs, as an understanding of these will be crucial to the preparation of budgets. Specifically, we will consider how costs can be classified, allocated and attributed to different responsibility centres in an organisation, and how this determines the structure of budgets.

The topics that are to be covered are:

- ✍ Organisational structure in terms of responsibility centres, and the impact on budget structure

- ✍ The classification of cost and revenue data to responsibility centres

- ✍ Direct and indirect costs

- ✍ Cost behaviours such as variable, semi-variable, stepped and fixed

- ✍ The attribution of indirect costs to production

## RELEVANCE OF COSTS WHEN BUDGETING

A budget is a numerical plan for a business, covering a future period.

The structure of a budget will vary from one organisation to the next, as it must be appropriate for the activities of that organisation, reflecting the income generated and the costs incurred.

This chapter looks at the costs incurred by different areas of a business, and how they should be allocated to different departments or 'responsibility centres' within an organisation, such that they can be considered in a meaningful manner when constructing a budget.

To construct a budget, the nature of these costs must be understood in terms of whether they are direct (relating to specific units of product made, or services delivered) or indirect (costs which cannot be attributed directly to a cost unit). The costs must also be understood in terms of their behaviour as variable, semi-variable, fixed and stepped. Once these aspects of costs are known, it is possible for managers to construct forecasts of future costs, from which budgets are formed.

## ORGANISATIONAL STRUCTURE

Different organisations will be arranged into different departments depending on the activities of that business. For example, a manufacturing business may have production departments (arranged by way of activity such as cutting, finishing, assembling), a maintenance department, and a purchasing team. In common with service businesses, there may also be administration, finance, IT, Human Resources ('HR', also known as Personnel), sales and marketing departments.

The structure of a budget must be appropriate for the organisation to which it relates so for example, the existence of a marketing team means there should be a marketing budget, a production department requires a production budget etc.

## HOW IT WORKS

A firm of solicitors may have several departments based on their activities eg corporate law, private client advice, litigation etc, but will also have service functions which may include a finance team, office administration, IT, HR (Personnel) and marketing.

The firm's budget will then include separate budgets for each of these departments, which include the costs and income (where appropriate) incurred and generated by those departments.

A firm's sales and marketing functions may exist as one department, or may be separate if some activities are directly concerned with making sales eg a salesperson on commission in a showroom, and other activities involve, say, raising brand awareness in the market place eg with an advertising campaign.

## Task 1

Match the functions listed below to the departments:

**Functions**

- Buys raw material for use in production

- Finds and secures new customers

- Ensures employees have the appropriate computer hardware and software

- Promotes the organisation's name, brand, products or services

- Manufactures products for sale

**Choose from these departments**

- IT
- Marketing
- Production department
- Sales department
- Purchasing department

## RESPONSIBILITY CENTRES

To structure an overall budget, the various department and functions within an organisation can be classified, in terms of their purpose and responsibilities, into responsibility centres. These can be cost centres, profit centres or investment centres.

This means that each centre has responsibility for the costs or revenues in its budget, and actual results will then be compared to budgets for each centre, to monitor and control performance.

A COST CENTRE is an area of a business, maybe a department such as the factory or canteen, for which costs are incurred.

There are two types of cost centre. Those that are directly involved in the production or provision of the cost unit, such as the factory, are known as production cost centres. There are also cost centres that, while not actually producing the cost unit, do provide a service to the production cost centres such as the canteen. These are known as service cost centres.

A PROFIT CENTRE is an area of the business which not only incurs costs but also earns revenue, for example a sales department in an organisation which earns revenue from sales but incurs costs such as a salesperson's salary and commission.

An INVESTMENT CENTRE is an area of the business which not only incurs costs and earns revenues but also accounts for its own capital employed. An example might be a separate division of the organisation which has a factory from which it produces goods, sells and despatches them.

It is important that managers are only allocated the task of preparing, and answering to, a budget over which they have control ie they only include costs and revenues relevant to their responsibility centre. We consider these responsibilities in further detail when comparing budgeted and actual performance in later chapters.

When the budgets for each of these centres are combined, a full budget is produced. We consider the specific preparation of these budgets in later chapters.

## HOW IT WORKS

In the example of the solicitors' firm above, each of the Corporate Law, Private Client and Litigation departments would be considered profit centres, as they incur costs, such as the salaries of the solicitors employed in each centre, but also generate income from charging work to clients.

The IT, HR (Personnel), Finance teams etc, would be considered service cost centres, incurring their own costs such as staff salaries but not raising income for the firm.

If the firm had two different offices, incurring the above costs and generating income, but each office was responsible for the costs of its own building for example, then the separate offices would each be considered investment centres.

## Task 2

An organisation owns a factory manufacturing and bottling a soft drink, which it sells to a variety of customers, delivering the product across the UK. The business purchases raw materials and uses extensive machinery in the production process, which requires regular maintenance. The business also sells merchandise relating to the drink over the internet.

On the basis of the activities described, identify the departments which may exist within the organisation, classifying them as cost centres or profit centres.

## Task 3

Allocate the following costs and revenues to the responsibility centres in a business (as listed below).

- Client entertaining at horse racing
- Repair of security alarm system in offices
- Sick pay for production manager
- Bonus for sales managers
- Depreciation of production equipment

Select from:

- Production department
- Marketing department
- Administration department
- Sales team
- HR (Personnel) department

## DIRECT AND INDIRECT COSTS

We have discussed various costs, and how they should be allocated to different profit centres, cost centres and investment centres according to the activities of an organisation. These responsibility centres then each have a budget associated with them, from which a master budget for the whole organisation is prepared.

To prepare a budget, costs must be classified into types such that we can work out how to forecast them. Here, we look at how costs can be classified as direct or indirect costs, and also how costs behave with varying activity (or quantity of units produced) – as variable, semi-variable, fixed and stepped. You will have learnt about such costs in previous studies.

Costs in both manufacturing and service industries are traditionally split between:

- material costs
- labour costs
- overheads (or expenses)

These costs in turn can be described as DIRECT costs or INDIRECT costs. This analysis depends upon whether the cost in question can be directly attributed to a unit of production or unit of service. The first stage in the cost allocation process then is to determine the cost units of the business.

In a manufacturing business the COST UNIT may be each unit of production or each batch of production. In a service business the identification of the cost unit may not be quite so straightforward but, for example, in a transport business the cost unit might be each lorry mile travelled or, in a restaurant, it might be each meal served. Note that sometimes the cost unit may be referred to a 'cost object', which is the generic term for anything for which a separate measurement of cost is needed. However we will continue to refer to 'cost units' as we progress through this Text.

Any material cost or labour cost or expense that can be directly related to the cost unit is a DIRECT COST of that cost unit. However many costs of the business cannot be directly attributed to a cost unit. These costs are known as INDIRECT COSTS or overheads.

Later in this chapter we will look at how we can include indirect costs in a cost per unit and why this is needed in budgeting, but firstly we will consider cost behaviours so that we can forecast costs at different activity levels.

# CLASSIFICATION OF COSTS BY BEHAVIOUR

In order to be able to correctly deal with all of these different types of cost you must be able to recognise that different types of cost behave in different ways when the levels of activity in the organisation change. This is known as classification of costs by behaviour and the main classifications are:

- variable costs
- fixed costs
- semi-variable costs
- stepped costs

## Variable costs

VARIABLE COSTS are costs that vary directly in line with changes in the level of activity. Direct materials are often viewed as variable costs. For example if 0.5kg of a material is needed for each cost unit then 50,000 kg will be required if the budget requires 100,000 units of production and 250,000 kg if 500,000 units of production are budgeted.

The total variable cost can be expressed as:

Total variable cost = Variable cost per unit × number of units

A graph can be used to illustrate the total variable cost as activity levels change.

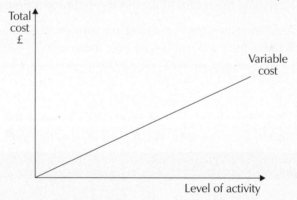

Direct costs such as materials costs may not always be true variable costs. For example, if a supplier offers a bulk purchasing discount for purchases above a certain quantity, then the cost per unit will fall if orders are placed for more than this quantity, and the budget should take account of this.

**Fixed costs**

A FIXED COST is one which does not change as activity levels alter. An example often used is that of the rent and rates of the factory. This will remain the same cost whether 100,000 units are produced or 500,000 units. The behaviour of fixed costs can be shown graphically:

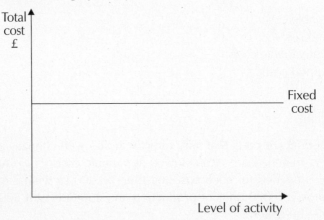

In practical terms fixed costs are only truly fixed over the RELEVANT RANGE. For example, the rent of the factory will only remain constant provided that the level of activity is within the production capacity of the factory. If production levels increase above the capacity of the current factory then more factory space must be rented thus increasing the rent cost for this level of production.

As the activity level increases the fixed cost remains fixed in total but the fixed cost per unit will fall as the total cost is split over more units.

## Task 4

A business expects to incur fixed costs of £100,000. Complete the table below showing the budgeted fixed cost per unit at each production level.

| Production level | Budgeted fixed cost per unit £ |
|---|---|
| 20,000 units | |
| 40,000 units | |
| 80,000 units | |

## Stepped costs

STEPPED COSTS are costs which are fixed over a relatively small range of activity levels but then increase in steps when certain levels of activity are reached. For example, if one production supervisor is required for each 30,000 units of a product that is made, then three supervisors are required if the budget is for production of 90,000 units, four for production of up to 120,000 units, five for production up to 150,000 units and so on.

Stepped costs can be illustrated on a graph:

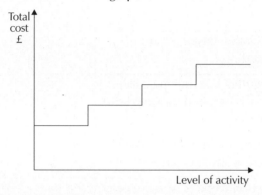

Stepped costs are really a fixed cost with a relatively short relevant range.

## Semi-variable costs

SEMI-VARIABLE COSTS are costs which have a fixed element and also a variable element. For example, the telephone bill includes a fixed element, being the fixed line rental for the period, and a variable element which will increase as the number of calls increase.

The total of a semi-variable cost can be expressed as:

Total cost = Fixed element + (variable cost per unit x number of units)

A semi-variable cost can be illustrated on a graph as follows:

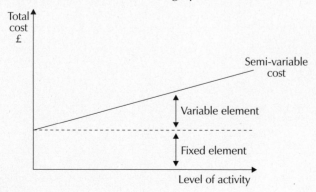

## Task 5

Choose from the list below to show how each of the following costs would be classified according to their behaviour.

| Cost | Behaviour |
|------|-----------|
| Stores department costs which include £5,000 of insurance premium and an average of £100 cost per materials receipt or issue | ▼ |
| Machinery depreciation based upon machine hours used | ▼ |
| Salary costs of lecturers in a training college where one lecturer is required for every 200 students enrolled | ▼ |
| Buildings insurance for a building housing the stores, the factory and the canteen | ▼ |
| Wages for production workers who are paid per unit produced with a guaranteed weekly minimum wage of £250 | ▼ |

**Picklist**

Variable
Fixed
Semi-variable
Fixed, then semi-variable
Stepped

## HOW IT WORKS

Here is a comprehensive example of the use of all the cost behaviour principles described above to forecast production costs.

Cameron Ltd will produce one product, which requires the following inputs, in the forthcoming quarter:

| | |
|---|---|
| Direct materials | 1 kg @ £3.50 per kg |
| Direct labour | 1 hour @ £6.00 per hour |
| Rent | £4,000 per quarter |
| Leased machines | £1,500 for every 4,000 units of production |
| Maintenance costs | £1,000 per quarter plus £1.00 per unit |

Calculate the budgeted total cost of production and the budgeted cost per unit for each of the following production levels for the coming quarter:

- (a) 4,000 units
- (b) 10,000 units
- (c) 16,000 units.

**Direct materials** – these are a variable cost with a constant amount per unit (1kg × £3.50 = £3.50) therefore the total cost is found by multiplying the number of units by the unit cost:

| | | |
|---|---|---|
| £3.50 × 4,000 units | = | £14,000 |
| £3.50 × 10,000 units | = | £35,000 |
| £3.50 × 16,000 units | = | £56,000 |

**Direct labour** – another variable cost, with a unit cost of 1hr x £6 = £6:

| | | |
|---|---|---|
| £6.00 × 4,000 units | = | £24,000 |
| £6.00 × 10,000 units | = | £60,000 |
| £6.00 × 16,000 units | = | £96,000 |

**Rent** – this is a fixed cost and therefore, provided we are still operating within the relevant range, will remain at £4,000 whatever the production level.

**Leased machines** – this is a stepped cost and the number of machines leased will depend upon the quantity of production.

| | | | | |
|---|---|---|---|---|
| 4,000 units | = | 1 machine | = | £1,500 |
| 10,000 units | = | 3 machines | = | £4,500 |
| 16,000 units | = | 4 machines | = | £6,000 |

**Maintenance costs** – this is a semi-variable cost with a fixed element of £1,000 and a variable cost of £1 per unit. The total cost for each activity level is:

| | | | | |
|---|---|---|---|---|
| 4,000 units | = | £1,000 + (4,000 × £1.00) | = | £5,000 |
| 10,000 units | = | £1,000 + (10,000 × £1.00) | = | £11,000 |
| 16,000 units | = | £1,000 + (16,000 × £1.00) | = | £17,000 |

Thus the total costs of production are:

| | Production level – units | | |
|---|---|---|---|
| | **4,000** | **10,000** | **16,000** |
| | **£** | **£** | **£** |
| Direct materials (variable) | 14,000 | 35,000 | 56,000 |
| Direct labour (variable) | 24,000 | 60,000 | 96,000 |
| Rent (fixed) | 4,000 | 4,000 | 4,000 |
| Leased machines (stepped) | 1,500 | 4,500 | 6,000 |
| Maintenance costs | 5,000 | 11,000 | 17,000 |
| Total cost | 48,500 | 114,500 | 179,000 |
| Number of units | 4,000 | 10,000 | 16,000 |
| Cost per unit | £12.13 | £11.45 | £11.19 |

The cost per unit will decrease if the production quantity increases. This is because the fixed cost and the fixed element of the semi-variable cost will then be spread over a larger number of units.

**Variable costs with a discount**

Suppose now that the supplier of the materials offers a bulk purchasing discount of 6% for all purchases if an order is placed for more than 8,000 kgs.

What is the direct materials cost in total and per unit at each level of production?

**4,000 units**

| | | | |
|---|---|---|---|
| Total cost | 4,000 × £3.50 | = | £14,000 |
| Cost per unit | £14,000/4,000 | = | £3.50 |

**10,000 units**

| | | | |
|---|---|---|---|
| Total cost | 10,000 × (£3.50 × 94%) | = | £32,900 |
| Cost per unit | £32,900/10,000 | = | £3.29 |

BPP
LEARNING MEDIA

## 16,000 units

| | | | |
|---|---|---|---|
| Total cost | 16,000 × (£3.50 × 94%) | = | £52,640 |
| Cost per unit | £52,640/16,000 | = | £3.29 |

The direct materials are now not a true variable cost as the cost per unit falls once production is in excess of 8,000 units.

Note that sometimes the term PRIME COST is used for the total direct costs, whereas the FULL PRODUCTION COST includes the overheads or indirect costs of production of the product. The prime cost for production of 4,000 units above would therefore be £38,000 with a full production cost of £48,500.

## Task 6

A salesperson will receive a fixed salary of £800 per month plus commission of £20 for each sale confirmed in the month.

Complete the table to show the salesperson's budgeted monthly salary for the month if their forecast level of sales are at each of the following levels.

| Sales | Monthly salary £ |
|---|---|
| 4 sales | |
| 8 sales | |
| 15 sales | |

### Practical limitations of cost classifications

As we have seen in this chapter so far, it can be useful to classify costs according to their behaviour. However in order to make these classifications we have assumed that the costs have a linear behaviour ie, are a straight line when drawn on a graph. This may not always be the case in practice.

For example, we saw in the example of Cameron Ltd above, that if a discount is given for purchases above a certain level then the materials purchases cost will not be a true variable cost. Thus unit variable costs may fall as economies of scale are achieved. Similarly although the direct labour cost is often viewed as a variable cost, there may be two elements to labour cost depending on the activity level: a core of labour costs may be fixed, and only when the basic hours are exceeded does overtime begin, so that element of the cost becomes variable.

The assumption is normally that variable costs, or the variable element of a semi-fixed cost, will increase as activity levels increase and fall as activity levels fall. However this may not always be the case. For example, an organisation's

telephone bill is normally assumed to have a fixed element, the line rental, and a variable element, call costs, which increase as activity levels increase. In this case the relevant activity level causing the call cost to vary is the number of calls made. If we look at the call costs in relation to the level of output, in some organisations it may instead be the case that the call costs increase as the activity levels in terms of units of output fall, because the sales team will be trying to boost sales and therefore production.

## ATTRIBUTION OF OVERHEADS

In the example of Cameron Ltd, we included overheads or indirect costs, such as rent, in the cost per unit calculation. This was a simple example in this respect as we effectively treated Cameron Ltd as having only one cost centre (and one product), which in practice would not usually be the case. As we discussed early in this chapter, an organisation will have several cost centres, categorised as both production and service cost centres. To determine a cost per unit of product, the overheads of these cost centres must somehow be assigned to the products produced, as they are part of the necessary cost of producing the cost units.

You will have seen different methods of attributing and absorbing overhead costs in earlier studies, and we will look at this below. While you may be required to answer numerical or descriptive questions on absorption of overheads, there will not be extensive examination of this. This assessment is not aiming specifically to test the absorption of overheads but instead to test that such activity is a tool in the preparation of budgets.

The reason that the absorption of overheads is important in budgeting is that the budget constructed must be consistent with the method of attribution of indirect costs used in reporting the organisation's actual results. Otherwise meaningful comparisons, which are required in order to fulfil the control aspect of a budget, cannot be drawn. You must therefore understand what is meant by the different absorption methods, as they will be referred to throughout this Text.

### Allocation and apportionment of overheads

You may recall from previous studies that this is done by the following process:

- allocation of overheads that relate to just one cost centre, such as the depreciation of the factory machinery, being allocated to the relevant cost centre eg the factory. We discussed the allocation of costs to cost centres at the start of this chapter.

- apportionment of overheads that relate to a number of cost centres to each relevant cost centre on some fair basis, such as the apportionment of the rent of the building to each cost centre in the building on the basis of floor space occupied.

- re-apportionment of service cost centre costs to the production cost centres, to ensure that all overheads are now included within the production cost centre costs.

- absorption of all of the overheads of each production cost centre into the cost of cost units on some fair basis, such as the number of labour hours or machine hours that each cost unit uses.

We can summarise this process in a diagram:

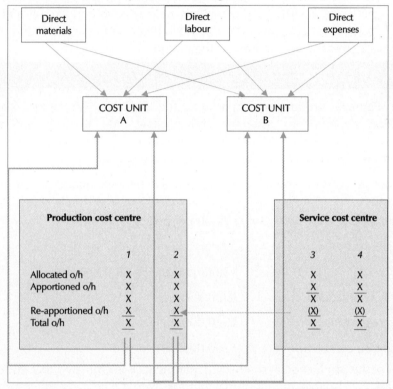

There are three main methods of calculating a cost per unit:

- **ABSORPTION COSTING** – under this costing method a 'full' production cost per unit is calculated by including in the cost of the cost unit a proportion of the production overheads from each of the production and service cost centres. This is done by allocating, apportioning and absorbing the overheads. Note that even when applying absorption costing it is usually only the production overheads of the production and service cost centres which are absorbed. Administrative overheads (eg the salaries of the finance team, the depreciation of the office building) or selling overheads (eg the cost of an advertising campaign) will remain outside the cost units.

- **ACTIVITY BASED COSTING** – this is a method of absorption costing which uses more sophisticated methods of allocating overheads to cost units than the normal methods of overhead allocation and apportionment. It does this by considering the activities that cause the overhead to be incurred and the factors that give rise to the costs (cost drivers).

- **VARIABLE OR MARGINAL COSTING** – under this method only the variable costs (or marginal costs) of production are included in the cost per cost unit. The fixed overheads are treated as period costs and not as part of the cost unit. The fixed overheads are charged to the income statement as an expense for the period.

## HOW IT WORKS

Fenton Partners produce one product, the Fenton. The factory has two production departments, assembly and packing, and there is one service department, maintenance. 75% of the maintenance department's time is spent in the assembly department and the remainder in the packing department.

The expected costs of producing 100,000 units in the next quarter are as follows:

| | |
|---|---|
| Direct materials | £24.00 per unit |
| Direct labour | 2 hours assembly @ £7.00 per hour |
| | 1 hour packing @ £6.00 per hour |
| Assembly overheads | £320,000 |
| Packing overheads | £240,000 |
| Maintenance overheads | £200,000 |

In each of the production and service departments it is estimated that 40% of the overheads are variable and the remainder are fixed. Overheads are absorbed on the basis of labour hours.

Calculate the cost per unit using the following costing methods:

(a) absorption costing
(b) marginal costing

## Absorption costing

### Production overheads

|  | | Assembly | Packing | Maintenance |
|---|---|---|---|---|
|  | | £ | £ | £ |
| Allocated and apportioned | | 320,000 | 240,000 | 200,000 |
| Reapportioned – maintenance (75%/25%) | | 150,000 | 50,000 | (200,000) |
| Total overhead | | 470,000 | 290,000 | – |
| Total hours | 2 × 100,000 | 200,000 | | |
|  | 1 × 100,000 | | 100,000 | |
| Absorption rate | | $\dfrac{470,000}{200,000}$ | $\dfrac{290,000}{100,000}$ | |
| = | | £2.35 per labour hour | £2.90 per labour hour | |

Interpretation:

For every one hour that the product is worked on in the assembly department, it is charged with a £2.35 share of the overheads incurred.

For every one hour that the product is worked on in the packing department, it is charged with a £2.90 share of the overheads incurred.

### Unit cost

|  | £ |
|---|---|
| Direct materials | 24.00 |
| Direct labour – assembly 2 hours × £7.00 | 14.00 |
| Direct labour – packing 1 hour × £6.00 | 6.00 |
| Overheads – assembly 2 hours × £2.35 | 4.70 |
| – packing 1 hour × £2.90 | 2.90 |
| Unit cost (total absorption costing) | 51.60 |

## Marginal costing

In this method only variable overheads are included in the cost per unit, so these must be ascertained:

|  | Assembly | Packing |
|---|---|---|
|  | £ | £ |
| Total overhead | 470,000 | 290,000 |
| Variable element (40%) | 188,000 | 116,000 |
|  |  |  |
| Absorption rate | $\dfrac{188,000}{200,000}$ | $\dfrac{116,000}{100,000}$ |
| = | £0.94 per labour hour | £1.16 per labour hour |

### Unit cost

|  | £ |
|---|---|
| Direct materials | 24.00 |
| Direct labour – assembly | 14.00 |
| Direct labour – packing | 6.00 |
| Variable overhead – assembly (2 hours × £0.94) | 1.88 |
| – packing (1 hour × £1.16) | 1.16 |
| Unit cost (marginal costing) | 47.04 |

## Selection of appropriate attribution methods

The example above is comprehensive. You might not be tested on this subject in this manner (ie by having to perform the whole calculation, having been told how overheads are absorbed, but you do need a thorough understanding of the principles as you may be tested on parts of this, or be asked to complete a budget (which we consider later in this Text) based on either marginal or absorption costing). As an example, you may be asked to select appropriate methods of treating various costs in a budget.

## HOW IT WORKS

Richards Engineering Ltd has the following costs. Select, from the list below, the appropriate accounting treatments for these when constructing a budget.

**Costs**

Salaries of office staff

Maintenance of machinery

Depreciation of finance director's car

Depreciation of machinery

Packaging material for units of finished goods

**List of accounting treatments**

Direct cost

Allocate to marketing overheads

Allocate to administrative overheads

Charge to production using a machine hour overhead rate

**Salaries of office staff**

These are not production costs and so are charged directly to the income statement after gross profit ie **allocate to administrative overheads**.

**Maintenance of machinery**

This is a cost of production and is likely to depend on the use of the machinery, therefore **charge to production using a machine hour overhead rate**.

**Depreciation of finance director's car**

**Allocate to administrative overheads** – again, not a production cost. If this had been the sales director's car, then it may have been appropriate to allocate it to marketing overheads.

**Depreciation of machinery**

This does relate to production, like maintenance of machinery, and so **charge to production using a machine hour overhead rate**.

**Packaging material for units of finished goods**

This is a raw material cost of production – a **direct cost**.

If you are asked to consider on what basis a production overhead should be absorbed ie on the basis of units, labour hours or machine hours, you need to consider the nature of that specific business.

If the business is labour-intensive, involving many labour hours, then absorption on a labour hour basis is appropriate. Alternatively, if the production process involves the heavy use of machinery, then machine hours would be a more suitable absorption basis.

## Marginal and absorption costing, inventory levels and profit

As we have seen the unit cost is very different under marginal costing from that calculated under absorption costing. Under absorption costing the fixed overhead is absorbed into the units produced in the period, and therefore the full production cost of the units actually sold in the period is charged to the income statement as part of cost of sales. However under marginal costing a lower value is assigned to cost of sales as the cost per unit only includes variable costs. The fixed costs are then charged to the income statement as a period cost.

This difference is also reflected in the valuation of inventory. Under absorption costing, inventory is valued at full production cost, which includes the absorbed fixed overhead. However under marginal costing a lower value is assigned to the value of inventory, as the cost per unit only includes variable costs.

If the opening inventory and closing inventory levels are the same (so that sales = production) then when we include revenue per unit and in total into our calculations, profit shown under both absorption costing and marginal costing will be the same. However if opening and closing inventories are different, ie there has been an increase or decrease in inventories, then absorption costing and marginal costing will not produce the same profit figure, because of the differences in the treatment of fixed overhead and the valuation of inventory.

An important difference in this context between absorption and marginal costing is that in the latter we calculate and focus on contribution per unit, which is revenue less variable costs per unit.

You need to be able to prepare a budget including an operating statement under both marginal and absorption costing, so make sure you understand the following comprehensive example.

# HOW IT WORKS

Spa Ltd makes a single product and produces management accounts including a costing income statement each month. In both May and June 100,000 units of the product were produced.

The production costs in both May and June were:

|  | £ |
|---|---|
| Direct materials | 200,000 |
| Direct labour | 300,000 |
| Fixed overheads | 300,000 |
| Total production costs | 800,000 |

There were no opening inventories at the start of May and all of the production for May was sold. However in June only 75,000 units of production were sold, leaving 25,000 units in inventory.

Each unit is sold for £10.

    (a)   What is the cost per unit using:

        (i)    absorption costing
        (ii)   marginal costing?

    (b)   What is the profit for each month using:

        (i)    absorption costing
        (ii)   marginal costing?

## (a)  Unit cost

    (i)    Absorption costing:

        £800,000/100,000 = £8 per unit

    (ii)   Marginal costing:

        £500,000/100,000 = £5 per unit

**(b)** **Income statements**

    (i)    Absorption costing (AC):

| | *May* | | *June* | |
|---|---|---|---|---|
| | £ | £ | £ | £ |
| Sales | | 1,000,000 | | 750,000 |
| Less: cost of sales | | | | |
| Opening inventory | – | | – | |
| Cost of production | | | | |
| 100,000 units × £8 | 800,000 | | 800,000 | |
| | 800,000 | | 800,000 | |
| Less: closing inventory | | | | |
| 25,000 units × £8 | – | | (200,000) | |
| Cost of sales | | 800,000 | | 600,000 |
| Profit (AC) | | 200,000 | | 150,000 |

    (ii)   Marginal costing (MC):

| | *May* | | *June* | |
|---|---|---|---|---|
| | £ | £ | £ | £ |
| Sales | | 1,000,000 | | 750,000 |
| Less: cost of sales | | | | |
| Opening inventory | – | | | |
| Cost of production | | | | |
| 100,000 units × £5 | 500,000 | | 500,000 | |
| | 500,000 | | 500,000 | |
| Less: closing inventory | | | | |
| 25,000 units × £5 | – | | (125,000) | |
| Marginal cost of sales | | 500,000 | | 375,000 |
| Contribution to fixed costs | | 500,000 | | 375,000 |
| Less: fixed costs | | 300,000 | | 300,000 |
| Profit (MC) | | 200,000 | | 75,000 |

In May the profit is the same under both costing methods, £200,000. This is because there is no movement in inventory during the period, since all of the production is sold.

In June however profit under absorption costing is £150,000 whereas it is only £75,000 under the marginal costing method. The reason for the £75,000 difference in profit is that the closing inventory under absorption costing includes £75,000 (£300,000/100,000 × 25,000 units) of fixed costs that are being carried forward to the next accounting period, whereas under marginal costing they were all written off in June.

The rules are that:

(1) **if inventory levels are rising then absorption costing will give higher profits** (as the fixed overheads are being carried forward into the next accounting period)

(2) **if inventory levels are falling then absorption costing will give a lower profit figure** (as more fixed overheads from the previous period are charged to the income statement in this period)

(3) **where inventory levels are constant (provided that unit costs are constant), then absorption costing and marginal costing will give the same level of profit**

## Task 7

A business expects to produce 5,000 units of its single product in the next month with the following costs being incurred:

|  | £ |
|---|---|
| Direct materials | 12,000 |
| Direct labour | 15,000 |
| Variable overheads | 23,000 |
| Fixed overheads | 25,000 |

What is the budgeted cost per unit under both absorption costing and marginal costing methods?

| Costing method | Cost per unit £ |
|---|---|
| Absorption costing |  |
| Marginal costing |  |

## ACTIVITY BASED COSTING (ABC)

An alternative method of absorption costing is activity based costing or ABC.

Under basic absorption costing the production overheads of a cost centre are all absorbed on the same basis, usually labour hours or machine hours, no matter what the cause of the overhead. This could be viewed as quite an arbitrary approach to absorbing overheads particularly as overheads now tend to form a very large part of product costs.

The principle of Activity Based Costing (ABC) is to break down the overheads into their constituent elements, for example costs incurred due to receiving materials, costs incurred due to issuing materials to production, costs incurred due to setting up machines for a production run (production setups), costs incurred due to quality control procedures etc.

### Cost pools

Each of these elements that cause costs to be incurred are called ACTIVITIES and the costs associated with each activity are gathered together into COST POOLS. For each cost pool what must then be identified is the factor that causes or drives these costs to change. This is known as the COST DRIVER.

The total of the cost pool is then divided by the number of times the cost driver takes place and this gives an overhead rate per cost driver. The overheads from the cost pool are then allocated to different products depending upon their particular usage of the cost driver.

For example, a product that required frequent purchases of inventories and frequent production setups would have larger overheads allocated to it than a product that required few purchases and few production runs.

The diagram that follows illustrates in outline how ABC works:

| Identify activities causing overheads | Activity 1 | Activity 1 |
| --- | --- | --- |
| Gather all costs for each activity | Cost pool 1 | Cost pool 1 |
| Identify what causes the cost | Cost driver 1 | Cost driver 1 |
| Calculate cost driver rate | $\dfrac{\text{Cost pool 1 total}}{\text{No. of cost drivers}}$ | $\dfrac{\text{Cost pool 1 total}}{\text{No. of cost drivers}}$ |
| Apply to individual cost units | Use of cost driver × cost driver rate | Use of cost driver × cost driver rate |

## HOW IT WORKS

Caplan Ltd produces two products, the C and the P. The direct costs per unit of the two products are given below:

|  | C | P |
| --- | --- | --- |
| Direct materials | £3.50 | £4.80 |
| Direct labour | £2.00 | £1.20 |

The budgeted production is for 120,000 units of C and 50,000 units of P.

The two main activities identified for the fairly simple production process are materials handling and production setups.

C requires only large production runs and large transfers of materials from stores. However P is a more complex product with a number of different types of materials required and shorter and more frequent production runs.

The budgeted overheads for Caplan are £800,000 and they are made up as follows:

|  | £ |
| --- | --- |
| Materials handling cost pool | 300,000 |
| Production setup cost pool | 500,000 |
|  | 800,000 |

The use of these activities for each product is as follows:

|  | C | P | Total |
|---|---|---|---|
| Number of materials requisitions | 200 | 800 | 1,000 |
| Number of production setups | 100 | 400 | 500 |

Calculate the total costs incurred and the unit cost of each product using the costing method of Activity Based Costing. Also calculate the direct cost and the overhead cost per unit.

## Cost driver rate

| Materials handling | $\dfrac{£300,000}{1,000}$ | = | £300 per materials requisition |
|---|---|---|---|
| Production setups | $\dfrac{£500,000}{500}$ | = | £1,000 per production setup |

## Total production costs and cost per unit

|  | C £ | P £ |
|---|---|---|
| Direct materials |  |  |
| 120,000 × £3.50 | 420,000 |  |
| 50,000 × £4.80 |  | 240,000 |
| Direct labour |  |  |
| 120,000 × £2.00 | 240,000 |  |
| 50,000 × £1.20 |  | 60,000 |
| Materials handling overhead |  |  |
| 200 × £300 | 60,000 |  |
| 800 × £300 |  | 240,000 |
| Production setup overhead |  |  |
| 100 × £1,000 | <u>100,000</u> |  |
| 400 × £1,000 |  | <u>400,000</u> |
|  | <u>820,000</u> | <u>940,000</u> |

| Cost per unit | $\dfrac{£820,000}{120,000 \text{ units}}$ | $\dfrac{£940,000}{50,000 \text{ units}}$ |
|---|---|---|
|  | £6.83 per unit | £18.80 per unit |

## Analysis of cost per unit

|  |  | C | P |
|---|---|---|---|
|  |  | £ | £ |
| Direct costs | (3.50 + 2.00) | 5.50 |  |
|  | (4.80 + 1.20) |  | 6.00 |
| Materials handling overhead |  |  |  |
| 60,000/120,000 |  | 0.50 |  |
| 240,000/50,000 |  |  | 4.80 |
| Production setup overhead |  |  |  |
| 100,000/120,000 |  | 0.83 |  |
| 400,000/50,000 |  |  | 8.00 |
| Unit cost |  | 6.83 | 18.80 |

In this instance C is charged with £1.33 of production overhead whereas the more activity-intensive P is charged with £12.80 of production overhead. Given that the direct labour cost of product P is only £1.20 compared to the £2.00 labour cost of C, if the overheads had been apportioned according to labour hours, as with traditional absorption costing, then the picture would have been very different indeed.

## Task 8

The costs of the quality control department of a manufacturing business are estimated to be £74,000 for the next quarter. During that period it is estimated that there will be 370 quality inspections. Product A will require 25 inspections during the quarter and Product B 130 inspections.

Using Activity Based Costing, how much quality control overhead will be absorbed into Product A and Product B?

| Overhead included in Product A |  |
|---|---|
| Overhead included in Product B |  |

# CHAPTER OVERVIEW

- The structure of an organisation depends on its activities

- Different departments or functions can be classified, according to responsibility, as profit centres, investment centres or cost centres

- These responsibility centres each have a budget associated with them which are combined to form the organisation's budget

- Costs must be allocated and attributed to the relevant responsibility centre

- The nature of costs must be determined before budgets can be constructed

- Direct costs are costs that can be related directly to a cost unit, whereas indirect costs (or overheads) cannot be attributed directly to a cost unit and instead are initially allocated or apportioned to a cost centre

- Costs are often classified according to their behaviour as activity levels change – the main classifications are variable costs, fixed costs, stepped costs and semi-variable costs

- There are three main methods of attributing indirect costs to production units – absorption costing, marginal costing and activity based costing (ABC)

- Absorption costing is where the production overheads are included in the cost of each cost unit

- Under marginal costing only variable overheads are included in the cost of cost units with the fixed overheads being charged to the income statement as period cost

- Activity based costing (ABC) considers the activities that cause overheads to be incurred and the factors that give rise to costs (cost drivers). It is a method of absorbing overheads into products on the basis of the amount of each activity that the particular product is expected to use in the period

## Keywords

**Cost centre** – an area of the business for which costs are incurred

**Profit centre** – an area of the business which incurs costs, but also generates income

**Investment centre** – an area which incurs costs, generates income but also accounts for its own capital employed

**Direct cost** – cost that can be directly attributed to a cost unit

**Indirect cost** (overhead) – cost that cannot be attributed directly to a cost unit but is initially attributed to a cost centre

**Cost unit** – in a manufacturing business each unit of production; in service industries such as hospitality it may be for example, each meal served.

**Variable cost** – cost that increases/decreases directly in line with any change in activity level

**Fixed cost** – cost that remains constant as activity levels change

**Stepped cost** – cost which is fixed over a relatively short range and then increases in steps

**Semi-variable cost** – cost which has both a fixed element and variable element

**Relevant range** – the range of activity levels over which a fixed cost will not change

**Prime cost** – the total of all direct costs

**Full production cost** – prime cost plus indirect costs of production

**Absorption costing** – a costing method which includes all production overheads within the cost of the cost units

**Activity based costing (ABC)** – a more complex approach to absorption of overheads based on an analysis of the detailed causes of the overheads

**Marginal costing** – a costing method which includes only variable costs within the cost of the cost units with fixed costs written off as period costs

**Activities** – the elements of the overhead costs which cause costs to be incurred

**Cost pools** – costs that can be attributed to each activity

**Cost driver** – the factor that causes the costs for each cost pool

## TEST YOUR LEARNING

1   To which responsibility centre should these costs be allocated? Choose from the list below.

**Costs:**

Overtime costs of production workers

Depreciation of cars used by sales staff

Training course for sales director

Advertising posters

**Responsibility centres:**

HR (Personnel) department

Sales department

Marketing department

Production department

2   An organisation pays for annual computer support from an external firm. This costs £2,000 per annum plus £100 for each computer used in the company.

The cost behaviour demonstrated by this cost is

**Picklist:**
Variable
Semi-variable
Stepped
Fixed

3   A manufacturing company budgets for one supervisor at a cost of £20,000 for every 100,000 units produced annually. The company expects to make 270,000 units in the coming year.

The budgeted cost for supervisors is £ [          ]

This cost exhibits [          ] behaviour

**Picklist:**
Variable
Semi-variable
Stepped

4   The direct materials cost for 10,000 units is estimated to be £43,600 and for 12,000 is estimated to be £52,320.

This a purely variable cost. True or false?

5   A business expects to incur fixed costs of £64,000 in the next month. What are the budgeted total fixed cost and the budgeted fixed cost per unit if activity levels are:

|  | Fixed costs (£) | Cost per unit (£ to nearest 1p) |
|---|---|---|
| (a)  3,000 units? |  |  |
| (b) 10,000 units? |  |  |
| (c) 16,000 units? |  |  |

6   Select an appropriate accounting treatment for each of the following costs:

Cost of the production staff canteen ▽

Redecorating reception area ▽

Machine maintenance ▽

Sick pay for production workers ▽

**Picklist:**
Charge to production in a machine hour overhead rate
Allocate to administrative overheads
Charge to production in a labour hour overhead rate
Activity based charge to production cost centres

7   A department has the following indirect costs in its annual budget.

|  | £ |
|---|---|
| Management salaries | 55,000 |
| Depreciation | 26,000 |
| Heat, power and water | 85,000 |
| Machine maintenance | 14,000 |
| **Total** | **180,000** |

The budgeted production is 6,000 units, which will require 30,000 machine hours and 5,000 direct labour hours.

How should the indirect costs be absorbed (labour hours, machine hours or units produced), and what is the absorption rate?

**8** A business produces two products, the GH and the JK. There are two production cost centres, cutting and finishing, and one service cost centre, stores. It is estimated that 80% of the stores activity is for the cutting cost centre.

The expected costs for the next quarter for production are:

| Direct materials – | GH | £20.00 per unit |
| | JK | £12.00 per unit |
| Direct labour – | GH – cutting | 3 hours @ £8.00 per hour |
| | GH – finishing | 1 hour @ £6.40 per hour |
| | JK – cutting | 2 hours @ £8.00 per hour |
| | JK – finishing | 0.5 hours @ £6.40 |

| Cutting overheads | £225,000 |
| Finishing overheads | £180,000 |
| Stores overheads | £100,000 |

All overhead costs are expected to be fixed costs.

It is budgeted that 50,000 units of GH and 30,000 units of JK will be produced during the quarter.

The budget is to be constructed using total absorption costing.

Complete the following table:

| | Cutting | Finishing |
|---|---|---|
| Reapportioned store overheads (£) | | |
| Overhead absorption rate | | |

| Costs per unit | GH (£) | JK (£) |
|---|---|---|
| Direct materials | | |
| Direct labour | | |
| Overheads | | |
| Total cost per unit | | |

9  A business produces two products, the LM and the NP. The direct costs of the two products are:

|  | LM | NP |
|---|---|---|
| Direct materials | £2.60 | £3.90 |
| Direct labour | £3.50 | £2.70 |

The total overhead cost is made up as follows:

|  | £ |
|---|---|
| Stores costs | 140,000 |
| Production setup costs | 280,000 |
| Quality control inspection costs | 180,000 |
|  | 600,000 |

The budgeted production is for 50,000 units of LM and 20,000 units of NP.

Each product is expected to make the following use of the service activities:

|  | LM | NP | Total |
|---|---|---|---|
| Materials requisitions | 100 | 220 | 320 |
| Production setups | 80 | 200 | 280 |
| Quality control inspections | 30 | 60 | 90 |

Complete the following:

Overheads should be absorbed on an activity basis as follows:

Stores costs = £ [        ] per [            ]

Production setup costs = £ [        ] per [          ]

Quality control costs = £ [        ] per [            ]

The budgeted cost per unit of LM is £ [         ]

The budgeted cost per unit of NP is £ [        ]

# chapter 2:
# BUDGETARY CONTROL SYSTEMS

## chapter coverage 📖

In this chapter we will look at the purposes of budgeting and a high-level view of budget setting. In later chapters we will consider the detail of how budgets are prepared.

The topics that are to be covered are:

✍ The purposes of budgeting for planning, co-ordination, authorising, cost control and motivating

✍ The potential for conflicts between these purposes

✍ An overview of budget-setting within an organisation

✍ Time periods within a budget

✍ The purpose of forecasts in relation to budgeting

## PURPOSES OF BUDGETING

A BUDGET is a formalised, numerical plan of action for a business. It represents what the business wants to achieve in the forthcoming period, usually a year.

There are many reasons for a business to create and implement a budget:

- Planning
- Cost control
- Co-ordination
- Authorisation
- Motivation

We now look at these reasons in more detail. You might be asked to discuss the use of a particular budget in the written elements of the assessment.

### Planning

Planning is a primary purpose of a budget; as stated above, a budget is a plan. It allows a business to consider the revenue and costs in earlier periods, and plan its revenue and costs for future periods.

As we shall see shortly a budget reflects, and so enables, an organisation to implement its strategic plans.

### Control

The actual financial results achieved for a period can be compared to the budgets for that period and the differences can be calculated, investigated and reported to management. Variances or performance indicators are often used as analysis tools in this comparison. In this way, a budget allows management to control the business.

Chapters 7 and 8 of this Text examine this use of budgets to control and evaluate performance, by comparison against actual performance.

A budget is therefore both a plan for the future and a benchmark against which performance can be measured.

### Co-ordination

We saw in Chapter 1 that organisations consist of various departments and functions. For the successful delivery of the end product or service, the different departments must CO-ORDINATE their activities on a timely basis.

Each function will have individual aims but these must fit with the aims of the organisation overall. What is best for one department may impact adversely on another.

For example, a low-cost alternative material may appear a good option for the purchasing team but if this leads to say, more machine break-downs, this will impact adversely on the production or maintenance departments.

As we will examine in more detail in this and future chapters, different departments will have their own budgets which will then be combined in a master budget.

The process of constructing these budgets therefore allows management to co-ordinate departments by setting targets in each budget, which fit with other functions and which will promote the overall aims of the business. The targets should be such that individual functions and departments act in the interest of the organisation overall (known as GOAL CONGRUENCE).

## Authorisation

Agreeing a budget with each department's manager gives the responsibility to that manager for meeting the budget, by incurring costs within the agreed expenditure, and in some cases by achieving the expected income. As such a budget is often the authorisation to a manager to allow them to, for example, offer overtime to workers if the costs are within their wages budget, or invest in new equipment if they have a capital budget to spend.

Through a departmental budget, there is therefore a direct link between the manager's responsibility and authority; the budget gives and demands both.

## Motivation

We discussed above that a budget is used to monitor and evaluate performance, by comparing budgeted and actual performance, in order to drive improved performance across an organisation. Given that managers and their staff are judged on this comparison, that is, they are accountable for the actual performance compared with budgets, budgets can be used as tool to motivate. This is discussed later in this chapter.

## Potential for conflict

As there are a variety of uses of a budgetary control system, some of these may conflict.

The uses of a budget may conflict if attempts to control costs, or define and restrict authorities, act against attempts to achieve the company's strategic plan. Co-ordination between departments may limit cost control. Examples of such conflicts are given below.

## HOW IT WORKS

A sales director may be concerned about controlling the costs within her budget, and so limits the petrol costs of her sales team. This may mean potential customers at greater distances from the company's base are not visited, and the sales growth being sought is restrained. This is an example of cost control conflicting with planning.

---

### Task 1

A production manager does not invest in machinery to manufacture a new product as his capital budget limits his authorisation to purchase such equipment. This action risks sales falling if the organisation's competitors have made such investment. Sales growth is part of the organisation's strategic plan.

Which two purposes of budgeting are conflicting in this example?

---

## STRATEGIC PLANS

We discussed above that the primary purpose of a budget is planning, but where do the plans come from? Before budgets can be set for the next 12 months, the business must have an overall plan for where it is going in the longer term.

When a business is started, the management must determine a long -term plan of how the business is to be operated and where its future lies, which will then be reviewed on a regular basis. This will mean that the senior management of the business must determine the strategic objectives of the business. These may include any of the following:

- to increase market share
- to maximise profitability
- to develop new products
- to increase the quality of the products
- to expand the product range
- to expand production
- to acquire other businesses

These long-term plans for the business are known as its STRATEGIC PLAN. This lays out the overall strategy for the business for the next few years.

The strategic plan will remain in place for the life of the business but may be altered from time to time as circumstances change or opportunities become available.

## Identifying strategies

The strategic plan shows where the business is going but the next stage of the planning process is to determine how the business is going to get there. This will involve a detailed review of the business, from both an internal and external perspective, in order to decide what possible strategies there are to move the business closer to the strategic objective.

Information will need to be gathered about all of the resources of the business, the state of its products or services and the amount of finance that is available. External information about the market, competitors and the general economic environment will also be required.

This detailed review of the position of the business is often called a SWOT analysis as the review will cover the following areas for the business:

- **S**trengths
- **W**eaknesses
- **O**pportunities
- **T**hreats

Once the analysis has been carried out, the management will be in a position to identify the various strategies that are available to the organisation. These might include marketing a new product or concentrating on the production of its current products.

## Choosing a strategy

Once the various available strategies have been identified, management will be in a position to choose which strategy is the most suitable and has the greatest potential for achieving the overall strategic objective. When the strategies for the future have been chosen then they can be co-ordinated into the strategic plan for the business.

---

## Task 2

A business makes several high-technology products. One of these products uses old technology compared with competitors' products. The strategic plan of the business involves continuing to sell the old product while developing an updated replacement as soon as possible.

Suggest two ways in which this strategy may be reflected in the budget for the coming year.

---

## HOW IT WORKS

A professional Rugby Club has as its strategic objectives the aims of increasing its crowds for its weekly matches by 50% over the next three years and increasing the sales made in the club shop by the same percentage over the same period.

Its chosen strategies for this include:

- building a new covered stand
- finding a new sponsor
- refurbishing the club shop
- liaising with local rugby clubs to encourage attendance at matches

### Operational plans

Once the strategic plan is in place, then the management can look at shorter term plans necessary in order to meet the strategic objectives of the business.

These will take a variety of forms – there will be plans for the purchase of non-current assets, plans for the amount of production and plans for the financing of the business. All of these plans take the form of budgets.

In Chapter 1, we saw that costs and revenues can be allocated to different departments or responsibility centres in an organisation. Each centre will prepare a budget. The types of budget and how they are set are covered in detail in later chapters, but the process of co-ordinating the setting of these individual budgets is considered below.

## CO-ORDINATION OF THE SETTING OF BUDGETS

As we have seen in the previous paragraph there are many functional budgets that will have to be set and many of them are inter-related. This will all take place over a considerable period of time and will require the involvement of many managers and staff of all levels. Therefore it is important that the budget setting is co-ordinated if any meaningful budgets are to be produced.

### Budget manual

Many organisations will produce a BUDGET MANUAL which is a set of detailed instructions as to how the budget is to be prepared. The budget manual might typically include the following:

- the names of the budget holders – those responsible for producing each budget
- the manager to whom each budget holder reports

- an organisation chart
- the timescale for the production of each budget
- the procedures for preparing each budget
- the format of the budgets
- how and when actual performance is compared to budget

## Budget committee

Many organisations will also have a BUDGET COMMITTEE made up of senior executives who are responsible for co-ordinating and administering all of the individual budgets and who will review and authorise each individual budget. Each function of the business should be represented on the budget committee in order to ensure that there is full communication between all areas of the business. The budget committee will normally be assisted by an accountant known as the BUDGET OFFICER.

## Budget holders

The manager who is responsible for preparing a resource budget is known as the BUDGET HOLDER. In most cases the budget holder should be the manager who will also be responsible for ensuring that the activities meet the budget. For example, the production manager should be preparing the production budget and the purchasing manager should be preparing the materials purchasing budget. The involvement of the responsible manager in the preparation of the budgets is an important behavioural aspect of budgetary control and will be considered further later in the chapter.

Once the budget holder has drafted their budget then they will submit this to the budget committee. The budget officer will ensure that the budget is consistent with the other resource budgets, checking, for example, that the purchasing budget has been prepared in line with the production budget.

There will then frequently be negotiations between the budget committee and the budget holder regarding the detailed content of the budget. The manager might, for example, have built in an increase in costs over previous years which the budget committee does not agree with. The budget holder may well have to change their draft budget and re-submit it to the budget committee a number of times before the budget committee is satisfied with it.

## Master budget

Once the budget committee has agreed all of the resource budgets with the budget holders then they will be incorporated into the MASTER BUDGET which normally takes the form of a budgeted income statement, budgeted statement of financial position and a cash budget.

---

## Task 3

Who should sit on the budget committee?

---

## Rolling budgets

A ROLLING BUDGET is a budget that is continuously updated by adding a further accounting period each time the current accounting period is completed.

## HOW IT WORKS

A budget is set on a quarterly basis for the next year. The January to March budget is set in detail while the budget for the period from April to December is in less detail. At the end of March the detailed budget is created for April to June and an additional outline budget for January to March of the following year is added in.

This has the advantage of allowing budget holders and the budget committee the opportunity to react to changes in circumstances; however it also means that budgeting will tend to be done more frequently and take up more management time.

The break-down of budgets themselves into time periods is discussed further in this chapter.

## METHODS OF BUDGETING

In Chapter 4 we will look at the details of setting each of the budgets but in this chapter we will consider the overall methods that might be adopted to set the resource (or cost) budgets for each period.

You will not be asked simply to list the advantages and disadvantages of a particular method, although you do need to know them. You need to be able to identify the method being used in a particular scenario, and know and understand whether it is appropriate or not.

A task may present you with a budget prepared using one method (without necessarily naming the method used, but describing how the budget has been constructed). You may be asked to assess the suitability of the method applied, and suggest an alternative.

## Incremental budgeting

One of the most common methods of setting the budget for a period is INCREMENTAL BUDGETING. Under this method the budget for the forthcoming period is set by taking the previous period's budget and adding a percentage to reflect any increases in prices since the last budget was set or any changes in activity level.

The advantages of incremental budgeting are:

- it is a fairly simple procedure which will not require too much management time
- the budget is stable and changes are only gradual
- co-ordination of budgets is made easier

However the disadvantages are:

- any inefficiencies in the original budget are repeated each period
- there is no incentive to reduce costs or develop new ideas
- the budgets may become out of date
- there may be budgetary slack built into the budget, meaning that meeting the budget is easier for managers and this slack remains each year

# HOW IT WORKS

The Rugby Club's advertising budget last year was £100,000. This year it is anticipated that 20% more advertising will be made and that inflation has been 2%.

The advertising budget for this year would be:

£100,000 x 20% = £120,000 – for the additional advertising

£120,000 x 1.02 = £122,400 – for inflation

## Zero based budgeting (ZBB)

ZERO BASED BUDGETING, as the name implies, is a method of budgeting whereby the budget for each cost centre is looked at from scratch for each period.

BPP LEARNING MEDIA

43

The main point about zero based budgeting is that every item of expenditure must be justified before it can be included in the budget. This will often be approached from an activity-based perspective on the basis that, in general, it is activities that incur costs.

For each item of activity which causes an expense, a decision package is compiled in which the following questions must be asked and answered:

- is the activity necessary?
- are there alternatives to this activity (eg outsourcing)?
- what are the costs of the alternative?
- what would happen if the activity were not carried out?
- is the expense of the activity worth the benefit?

By asking such questions the activity and its related expenditure can be justified for inclusion in the budget or a cheaper alternative found.

ZBB is not particularly useful for production departments where costs are largely dependent upon the levels of production and sales. However it can be a useful technique for service department costs such as the maintenance or personnel departments. It can also be a useful method for discretionary costs such as advertising and training.

The advantages of zero based budgeting are:

- It challenges the *status quo* and forces an organisation to examine alternative activities and existing expenditure levels

- any inefficiencies in the budget in one period are not automatically reproduced in the budget for the next period

- inefficient practices can be removed

- the cost effectiveness of work practices and procedures is constantly being monitored

- budgetary slack should be eliminated

The disadvantages of the method are:

- it is time consuming, complex and costly

- short-term benefits are emphasised which may be detrimental in the long term

## Programme based budgeting

PROGRAMME BASED BUDGETING is a method of budgeting that is suitable for non-profit making organisations. It is a method whereby the work of the organisation is split into programmes which are designed to achieve the organisational objectives.

Different departments of the organisation may be involved in more than one programme but the funds for the business are allocated to the programmes rather than to the departments.

As there will usually not be enough funds to achieve all of the programmes, decisions must be made as to which programmes will be supported and at what level.

## Activity based budgeting

ACTIVITY BASED BUDGETING is a system of setting budgets based upon Activity Based Costing principles, which were considered in Chapter 1. The principle of both Activity Based Costing and Budgeting is that the costs of activities are caused (driven) by the cost drivers. For example, the costs of the works canteen will (largely) be driven by the number of meals served. When budgeting on this basis the numbers of each cost driver that will be incurred must be considered and the cost of that cost driver.

---

## Task 4

A charity carries out different projects each year, raising funds specifically to cover the costs of those projects. The finance office is preparing the budget for the coming year, by increasing all costs of the prior year to reflect current inflation.

Explain why this method of budgeting may not be appropriate for the charity, and suggest a suitable alternative.

---

## BUDGETING AND MOTIVATION

At the start of this chapter, we listed motivation as one of the purposes of budgeting, and consider this in more detail here.

For the budgetary control system to be at its most effective, employees and managers must be motivated to ensure that the budget is met. There have been a number of research projects on how this can be achieved and there are arguments for and against the different approaches. The key areas that a business should consider when setting up the budgetary system are:

- who sets the budgets – participation
- how achievable the budgets are
- goal congruence
- performance related pay

## Top down budgeting

TOP DOWN BUDGETING is a method of setting budgets where the senior management are solely responsible for the setting of the budgets and they are then imposed upon the managers, who are responsible for meeting the targets.

The advantages of this are:

- the senior management will incorporate the strategic plans in all of the budgets

- the resource (or cost) budgets will all be in harmony with each other

- senior management have an overview of all of the resources of the business

- the budget should be produced more quickly

- input from junior management who may not have the skills or knowledge necessary for the budgeting process is eliminated

The disadvantages are:

- managers may become de-motivated by the prospect of working to meet targets that someone else has set

- the manager's detailed knowledge of the resource concerned is ignored

- the initiative of lower level management may be stifled

## Bottom up budgeting

In BOTTOM UP BUDGETING the budgets are prepared by the functional managers based upon their detailed knowledge of the resource and the costs associated with it. In practice these budgets are then normally reviewed by the budget committee and a process of negotiation then takes place in which the requirements of the senior management are balanced with what the managers believe is possible.

The advantages of this method are:

- the budgets are based on the detailed knowledge of the managers

- the motivation of the managers to achieve the budget which they have set should be increased

- the managers commitment to the strategic plans should be increased

There are disadvantages though:

- the outcome of the negotiations with the budget committee may cause dissatisfaction

- managers may be tempted to introduce BUDGETARY SLACK in order to ensure that when the actual results are compared to the budget, the outcome is favourable

- the budgeting process will take more time and involve more personnel

- there may be a lack of co-ordination between resource budgets that must be corrected

## Task 5

A designer at a small website design company has been asked by the managing director to prepare a budget for the coming quarter. It usually takes him or his staff about two days to design a website, but in the budget he allows for 2.5 days per new website.

What problems might this lead to when assessing the performance of the design department?

### Attainable budgets

Budgets can be set in an ideal manner or in an attainable manner.

If a budget is seen as ideal and therefore impossible to achieve, this can have a de-motivating effect. The manager and the employees will perceive the budget as 'ridiculous' and not even attempt to achieve it. However if a budget is set at a level which is challenging but essentially attainable, then this can be motivating to the manager and the employees, who will set about trying to meet the budget figures.

### Goal congruence

The budgets for a business should be set within the context of the strategic plans of the business. The aim of the budget should be to move the business further towards its strategic goals, and the relationship between the strategic goals and the budget should be clear. If the managers of a business are personally motivated to meet the budgets and therefore to move towards the strategic goal, then there is said to be GOAL CONGRUENCE within the business.

This goal congruence of employees, managers and senior management is not easy to achieve within a business, particularly as the question of motivation of managers and employees is very dependent on the personalities of the individuals involved. However, it is possible to try to achieve goal congruence particularly if the employees' and managers' remuneration packages are set in such a way that the employee or manager is better off financially if they do work towards the corporate goal. For example, if the strategic goal is to increase sales quantity then the salespeople may be given a bonus if they achieve their weekly sales targets.

## Performance related pay

Remuneration can be a powerful motivator if there is a formal and communicated link between higher pay and achieving targets or budgets. However this is an area that has to be dealt with very carefully.

PERFORMANCE RELATED PAY is a method of remunerating employees or managers in such a way that their total remuneration increases if they meet organisational goals and targets. This may take the form of bonuses or share options or other incentives.

In order for any form of performance related pay to be successful in motivating managers to meet budgetary targets, the following elements must be in place:

- managers must know the strategic goals of the business and must be able to see how their budgets work towards this strategic goal

- the managers' budgets must be achievable although challenging

- the managers must have control over the costs that are being compared to the budget and must feel that they have the ability and freedom to meet the budgetary targets; a manager must not feel that their performance is dependent upon that of others

- the rewards being offered by the business must be great enough to have an effect.

Performance related pay can in some circumstances be a successful method of motivating managers to meet their budgetary targets. However care must be taken. Performance related bonuses tend only to work when there is a short time-scale between the target being met and the reward. This can however lead to a concentration by managers on meeting short-term goals rather than looking at the long-term aims of the business. As with all efforts at motivation, the success of performance related pay will depend largely on the individual's attitude to work in general and to the bonus system in particular.

## Task 6

An accountancy firm operates a bonus scheme for its managers. Individual managers and departments are set fee targets in the budget at the start of the year. The terms of the bonus scheme are such that Sally, a tax manager, will receive her bonus if she meets her individual targets and if the tax department meets its targets.

Describe the benefits and problems of using these budget targets to determine the bonus scheme.

## TIME PERIODS WITHIN A BUDGET

It is usual for an organisation to complete a budget which covers a full year. However, depending on the needs of the organisation, the budget will also be broken down into smaller time periods such as quarters, months, weeks or even days.

Returning to the reasons for budgets discussed at the start of this chapter, such a break-down is required because the comparison of the budgeted figures and the actual performance achieved by a business is used by management to monitor and control. What they find out from this evaluation may lead them to take decisions which may alter their initial plans. Suitable time intervals for making such decisions may correspond to the pattern by which a business generates income and incurs costs.

## HOW IT WORKS

A manufacturing business may have a budget split into weekly targets. If the monitoring of performance shows that there was idle time above that budgeted (that is, the available time of labour that week exceeded the actual hours required), the production department may take the decision to increase production and store any product not yet required, or redeploy workers to other areas of the business.

Other decisions may surround price. If the sales volume of a product is lower than budgeted, a decision may be taken to discount the price of the product to boost sales and shift inventory. Such monitoring and the resulting actions need to be taken on a timely basis. If the manager responsible were to wait until the end of the year to look at such issues, it would be too late to take the appropriate action to counter it.

The time periods of a budget, and how often it is compared to actual results, are therefore determined by how frequently such decisions need to be made, which may fit with the time periods for payments and receipts. In many businesses this may be on a monthly basis, but the time period could depend on the frequency or volume of transactions.

## HOW IT WORKS

A solicitor's firm may have an annual budget broken down into months. It will pay its staff salaries on a monthly basis and may also bill clients monthly. This means the actual results of the business are determined on a monthly basis and so it is appropriate that the budget reflects the same time periods, for meaningful comparison.

A pub company may have a budget broken into weekly periods. This is because levels of activity in the pub may vary significantly from week to week if, for example, during some weeks important football matches are played which attract people to the pubs, and so increased sales figures are forecast then.

A major chain of department stores may have a daily budget for sales generated during a sale period, to make decisions regarding further price changes which may be required on a daily basis.

## Task 7

A community social club holds a quarterly family fun day to raise funds for its activities throughout that quarter. For what time periods should the club prepare its budgets?

## RELEVANCE OF FORECASTS

So far we have discussed the purpose of budgets and given an overview of the budget-setting process. We considered an organisation's strategic plan and how a budget can be used as a plan to achieve this.

To an extent therefore, an organisation decides what it wants a budget to reflect, in terms of sales, and the costs that it is prepared to incur in achieving this. This is the planning aspect of budgeting.

However, not all aspects of an organisation's performance can be controlled or planned for. External factors including economic and political conditions, the actions of competitors, technological advances and more, all affect revenue and costs. The implications of these external forces on revenue and costs must be forecast, and these assumptions must be incorporated into the budget figures.

It is important to bear in mind there that one or all of the assumptions on which forecasts and related budgets are based may turn out to be incorrect. For example, due to economic or political conditions (including changes in taxation), materials and labour costs may rise more quickly than was assumed when the forecast and budget were constructed. Therefore, assumptions and sources of information used when creating forecasts and budgets should always be documented so that anyone using them is aware of the risks and uncertainties involved.

Forecasts and budgets should be updated when necessary to take account of new relevant information, such as changes in inflation or increases/decreases in predicted sales demand. Regular re-forecasting and re-budgeting can help to mitigate the inherent risks relating to the assumptions made when budgeting.

## FORECASTS AND PLANS

Although the words are often used interchangeably, there is a distinction in budgeting between a FORECAST and a PLAN. A FORECAST is no more than an expectation or estimate of what might happen in the future based on historical data and analysis using various assumptions, whereas a PLAN is a deliberate commitment or intent. A budget is a plan but it takes into account forecasts of factors over which the organisation does not have control.

When preparing budgets, it is important to distinguish which factors are under the control of the organisation and which are outside its control so have to be managed.

The data required to prepare forecasts and forecasting techniques will be considered in the next chapter.

---

### Task 8

What is the difference between a forecast and a plan?

---

## CHAPTER OVERVIEW

- Budgets can help management in their planning and control functions, in authorising and co-ordinating departments and functions and in motivating employees

- The first stage of the planning process is to determine the strategic plan of the business and identify and choose strategies that will meet that strategic aim

- Once the strategic plan is in place the operational plans or shorter term budgets can be set with the aim of meeting those strategic aims

- The budget manual and budget committee are usually essential elements of control of the budgeting process

- Budgets can be set using a variety of different methods including incremental budgeting, zero based budgeting, programme based budgeting and activity based budgeting

- There are various ways of implementing a budgetary control system, each of which is likely to have behavioural effects on management. These include Top down and Bottom up budgeting

- If managers are to be motivated to meet the budget then it can be argued that they need to be involved in the process of setting the budget and the budget must be an attainable although challenging target

- If the managers of the business are personally motivated to work towards the same goals as the business then there is said to be goal congruence – one method of achieving goal congruence is through a system of performance related pay

- Budgets are broken down into smaller time periods to enable monitoring of performance and subsequent actions to take place on a timely basis. The intervals of the budget may correspond to the income and expenditure pattern of the organisation

- Not all factors impacting an organisation's performance are within its control. A budget is an organisation's plan which reflects forecasts of the impact of external factors on revenue and costs

## Keywords

**Budget** – a formalised, numerical, often financial, plan of action

**Goal congruence** – the aims of the individual functions or departments are consistent with the aims of the organisation overall

**Strategic plan** – sets out the overall strategy of a business for the next few years, including its medium- to long-term aims

**Operational plan** – the shorter-term plans or budgets to achieve the long-term aims

**Budget manual** – set of detailed instructions as to how the budgets should be prepared

**Budget committee** – committee of senior executives from all areas of the business who oversee the preparation of the budgets

**Budget officer** – an accountant who helps the budget committee in preparation of the budgets

**Budget holder** – the manager responsible for preparing a resource budget

**Master budget** – budgeted income statement, budgeted statement of financial position and cash budget

**Rolling budget** – a budget that is constantly updated to cover the next 12 month period

**Incremental budgeting** – a method of budgeting that takes last year's budgeted figure and adjusts for any change in activity level and inflation

**Zero based budgeting** – a method of budgeting in which all items of expenditure must be fully justified before being included in the budget

**Programme based budgeting** – a method of budgeting that allocates funds to programmes rather than cost centres

**Activity based budgeting** – setting a budget based upon Activity Based Costing principles

**Top down budgeting** – a budgeting system in which the budget is set and imposed by senior management

**Bottom up budgeting** – a budgeting system in which operational managers have a degree of input into the budget

**Budgetary slack** – an extra amount of cost built into a budget by managers in order to make targets easier to meet

**Performance related pay** – method of remuneration which rewards managers or employees for reaching set targets

**Forecast** – an expectation of what might happen in the future

**Plan** – a deliberate commitment or intent

## TEST YOUR LEARNING

1 Explain what is meant by a budget and how budgets can be useful.

2 How does a business go about determining the strategies that it is to follow?

3 The strategy of a business is to increase its market share over the next three years. Suggest two ways in which this strategy might be reflected in next year's budget.

4 In a bottom up budgeting system, with a full budget committee, explain how the budget for the next 12 months would be set.

5 Select the appropriate person to contact in each of the following situations:

The draft budget is ready for review: [ ▼ ]

The managing director needs help in interpreting the draft budget:

**Picklist:**

The budget holder

The budget committee

The budget officer

6 A business has an incremental system of budgeting. The transport costs for delivery of goods was budgeted as £240,000 last year. It is estimated that inflation is at the rate of 3% and that sales this year are likely to be 10% lower than last year. What would be the budgeted amount for transport costs this year?

£ [          ]

7 Explain how far performance related pay may help in ensuring goal congruence between managers and the organisation.

# chapter 3:
# FORECASTING

─── **chapter coverage** 📖 ───

In this chapter we will look at the information and techniques used to prepare forecasts.

The topics that are to be covered are:

✍ Types of budget to be prepared eg income and expenditure, production, labour, materials etc, and their content and purpose

✍ The use of forecasts in budgeting

✍ Internal and external sources of data required to prepare forecasts

✍ Forecasting of future income including the techniques of sampling and time series analysis (moving averages and seasonal variations) and indexing

✍ The relevance of life cycle and the external environment to forecasting

✍ Forecasting of expenditure including the technique of linear regression

✍ The uncertainties inherent in forecasts

# TYPES OF BUDGET

The financial plans of the business are set out in the form of budgets. In Chapter 1 we explained that there should be budgets for almost all aspects of a business's activities. Here we will consider the main ones, in terms of their content and also the information that is required to construct them.

A budget may include items of income (such as sales revenue) or expenditure (costs as discussed in Chapter 1) or both.

## Sales budget

The SALES BUDGET will normally be in two parts. There will be a forecast for the number of units that it is anticipated will be sold and also there will also be a **sales revenue budget** calculated by multiplying the estimated unit sales by the expected selling price per unit.

The sales budget will be fairly short-term and is usually for the forthcoming year. We will be considering methods of determining future sales forecasts later in this chapter.

## Resource budgets

RESOURCE BUDGETS (or COST BUDGETS) are those that deal with all aspects of the short-term operations of the business. There will be a budget set for each resource and activity of the business – production, production facilities, human resources, selling overheads, administration etc.

The resource budgets will usually be for the next year and will include:

**Production budget** (units of finished goods) – this is a budget for the number of units that it is planned to produce during the forthcoming period, taking account of any planned changes in finished goods held in inventory.

**Materials usage budget** (units of materials) – this is based upon the production budget and is a budget for the estimated quantity of materials that is to be used in the forthcoming period.

**Materials purchases budget** (units and £) – this is the amount of raw materials that must be purchased each period to satisfy the production and inventory demands and will be expressed in both units and monetary amounts.

**Labour usage budget** (hours) – this is based upon the production budget and is an estimate of the labour hours required during the period to meet the production figures.

**Labour cost budget** (£) – this is based upon the labour usage budget and is the monetary cost of the labour hours for the period including any overtime.

**Machine hours budget** (hours) – this is based upon the production plans and shows the number of hours that the machinery must be working in order to produce the required level of production.

**Variable overheads budget** (£) – this will be based upon the production budget as the variable overheads will vary with the amount of production.

**Fixed overheads budget** (£) – this is independent of the level of production which should not affect the amount of fixed overheads.

There may also be sundry other resource budgets such as the selling and distribution costs budget, advertising budget or the administration budget. The details of how to prepare these budgets, specifically how their construction depends on each other, will be covered in Chapter 4.

## HOW IT WORKS

A Rugby Club might set the following budgets:
- ticket sales budget (units + £)
- shop sales budget (units + £)
- inventory purchases budget (units + £)
- player costs budget (£)
- advertising budget (£)
- administration budget (£)

---

### Task 1

State whether each of the following quantities would be used in the materials usage budget.

| | |
|---|---|
| Opening and closing materials inventories | ▼ |
| Production budget | ▼ |
| Material quantity (kg) per unit | ▼ |
| Material cost per kg | ▼ |

**Picklist:**
Yes
No

---

## Capital budgets

So far the costs we have considered such as materials, labour, and overhead costs such as salaries of administrative employees, marketing costs etc have been items of REVENUE EXPENDITURE. These are costs that do not have an enduring benefit for the company, but relate to the day-to-day running of the business and may be used in the production of units either directly or indirectly. Such items will be charged against the income of business to determine its profit.

In contrast to revenue expenditure, CAPITAL EXPENDITURE is the purchase of non-current assets for long-term use in the business. This may include purchases of buildings, machinery, fixtures and fittings, cars and other motor vehicles.

Capital expenditure for a business will be one of its largest outgoings and one of the most important purchases. It is important that the purchase of non-current assets is correctly timed for two reasons:

- non-current assets should be replaced at a time when the costs for the business are minimised – for example, machinery should be replaced before the maintenance costs become so great that they outweigh the benefits of the machinery

- often a large amount of money will have to be found in order to purchase non-current assets required, so the precise timing of the purchase must be known in order to ensure that the finance is available.

The CAPITAL BUDGET will be a long-term budget, probably covering a number of years ahead, showing the details of the organisation's planned capital expenditure. In many businesses the capital budget is also the authorisation for incurring the budgeted capital expenditure.

# HOW IT WORKS

In Smythes Ltd, a manufacturing business, the capital budget will cover the purchase of new machinery or building a new unit or factory. The cost of an extension to an existing building would also be considered capital expenditure, as it represents an improvement or enhancement over what existed before.

In contrast to this if machinery is repaired, or parts or components of a larger piece of equipment are replaced, then such expenditure would be revenue in nature.

## Task 2

State and explain whether each of the following is an item of capital or revenue expenditure.

Paper for laser printers

Service of fire alarm system

Purchase of factory unit

New motor for existing machine replacing broken one

# FORECASTS

We now know the types of budget we must construct, and their content. As discussed in Chapter 2, this content must be forecast and then a budget constructed from these forecasts, reflecting both the plans or intentions of the business, and the impact of external factors.

This chapter will consider where to get the information to create these forecasts, and then the specific techniques required for forecasting.

# INFORMATION REQUIRED FOR FORECASTING

Now that we understand the content of these separate budgets, we need to consider where to obtain the information needed to construct them. For example in a sales budget, how does the sales director estimate the number of units that will be sold, and the sales price per unit that can be achieved? Similarly, in terms of a resource budget such as a materials budget, how does an organisation estimate the material cost for the coming year, and how much each unit will require?

Such budget data is gathered from a wide variety of sources, which may be internal to the organisation itself, or external. The manager preparing his or her budget must be able to select the most appropriate and reliable source for the information he or she requires. A good budget will state the sources that have been used in its preparation.

Note that the terms data and information are used interchangeably here, although technically data is unprocessed facts and figures, and information has been processed into a useable form.

Information for forecasting comes from both internal and external sources.

## INTERNAL INFORMATION

Some data can be collected from internal documents and sources, often called in-house data. Other data might need to be collected from external sources, if it is about the environment the business operates in, other organisations within the industry or about suppliers or customers.

Much of the information required for forecasting can be found within the organisation itself. The financial accounting records and related files will contain a wealth of historical information that can be used as a starting point.

| | |
|---|---|
| **Purchase invoices** | these contain details of the quantity and cost of materials purchased, details of terms such as discounts |
| **Wages information** | the information held by the wages department will include the current wage rates for different grades of labour, summaries of hours worked, details of absenteeism, lateness, sickness etc |
| **Sales information** | this will include analysis of customer demand and repeat orders, sales orders outstanding, aged receivables (debtors) analysis, details of customer complaints |
| **Inventory records** | these will include details of inventory levels, orders outstanding, goods received notes, goods returned notes, purchase orders |

These are just some examples of information that can be obtained from the internal records, not just the financial records of the business itself.

---

## Task 3

What information might be found from the personnel department of a large firm of solicitors which might be useful when constructing forecasts?

---

## EXTERNAL INFORMATION

External information takes a variety of different forms. The ability to access information is almost endless, particularly through the internet.

### Government statistics

One of the main published government statistics that is regularly used is the RETAIL PRICE INDEX published by the Office for National Statistics. This is an index that is published monthly, based upon the price of a particular 'shopping basket' of products compared with the price in the base month.

The Retail Price Index gives an indication of the general level of prices in the UK economy. This can then be used by businesses in forecasting, particularly in relation to costs (or achievable prices). We look at this in more detail later.

Although the Retail Price Index is one of the most commonly used government statistics, the management of a business will also require information about the economy as a whole and social trends of the UK in order to make informed predictions or forecasts.

## National statistics

The government appreciates the importance of statistics regarding the state of the nation, both for their own purposes and for those of businesses and the public. Statistics on a variety of themes (listed below) are provided by the Office for National Statistics.

## Themes

The statistics available are divided into 11 separate themes covering distinct areas of national life. The themes are:

- Agriculture and environment
- Business and energy
- Children, education and skills
- Crime and justice
- Economy
- Government
- Health and social care
- Labour market
- People and places
- Population
- Transport and travel

Statistics on each of these themes can be accessed via the internet (www.statistics.gov.uk) or by registering with the Office for National Statistics.

No business can operate in a vacuum and on many occasions it is likely that information about the economy, the population, social trends etc will be required. All of this information can now easily be accessed from these national statistics.

National statistics can be invaluable for businesses that need this sort of information. However, there are limitations to their use, for example:

- they can rapidly become outdated, especially in relation to fast-changing areas, such as consumer needs

- they may not be directly relevant to the needs of the business that is trying to apply them.

## Trade information

Most industries have trade journals which can provide useful information about all sorts of aspects of business life in that industry. Examples of such publications include *Campaign* for the advertising and marketing industry and *Accountancy Age* for the accountancy profession.

For example, such trade information may be used by an organisation to forecast possible sales prices it might expect to achieve in the forthcoming period, by comparison with the trade average.

## Financial newspapers

There is a wide variety of informed newspapers which provide intelligent information about all elements of business life, probably the best known being the *Financial Times*. Information from the financial press can be useful to management in general terms but can be particularly useful if there is information about competitors' performances. It is often very difficult for a business to find out anything about its competitors and therefore any reports in the press will be useful. Such information can be used in forecasting sales volume for different products, as an organisation becomes more aware of its competitors' plans in that market.

The financial press may also give information that enables an organisation to judge what might happen in terms of costs in the future – either raw material costs or the cost of finance etc. The newspapers cannot predict these costs but may highlight trends.

A further area of reporting that can be useful to a business is reporting of matters such as financial problems of a long term supplier. This may be the first that has been heard of such problems and it may help the purchasing team in forecasting expenditure, as they are likely to have to find alternative suppliers if the financial problems are severe.

## Internet

As you will know from personal experience the internet can be used to find information about virtually any topic imaginable. This wealth of information can and should be harnessed by businesses, although controls should be put in place to ensure that only reliable sources are used.

An organisation may seek information by asking its market directly. This is considered in more detail as a forecasting technique below.

## Task 4

You are constructing a budget and require the following pieces of information. Select which source you could use to find the appropriate information.

| Information required | Source | |
| --- | --- | --- |
| Population figures for areas in the UK | | ▼ |
| VAT rates | | ▼ |
| Possible sales prices achievable in the market place | | ▼ |

**Picklist:**

HM Revenue & Customs

The Daily Mail newspaper

Office for National Statistics

Trade journal

Purchasing manager

## TECHNIQUES FOR FORECASTING INCOME

In order to prepare budgets any business will need to produce forecasts of its sales, production costs and other costs. A FORECAST is an estimate of what may happen in the future based upon historical data and various assumptions. In particular a business will need to make the following important forecasts:

- once the key budget factor has been determined (see below), it will be necessary to forecast the activity level that the business will be operating at due to this factor

- other items of income or cost may also require forecasts in order to determine what the income or cost is for budget purposes.

## Key budget factor

The KEY BUDGET FACTOR is the element or resource of the business that is likely to be the one that places limitations on the activities of the business. It is also known as the limiting factor.

In most businesses the key budget factor will be sales. Most businesses will find that there is a limit to the amount of sales that they can make due to demand for their products and their own market share. However it is also possible that the key budget factor may be the availability of materials, the availability of labour or machine capacity. Resource as a limiting factor is discussed further in Chapter 6.

Once the key budget factor has been identified then the budget for this factor must be set first. If sales are the key budget factor then the sales quantity forecast will be initially made. This can then be used to determine the amount of the product that must be produced each period in the production budget and from this the other resource budgets can follow.

Alternatively if the key budget factor is machine capacity then the machine hours usage budget must be set first which will then determine the maximum production for each period on which the other resource budgets can be based.

The forecasting of the activity level which is set by the key budget factor is a vital element of the budgeting process, as the figures that are determined in this forecast will affect all of the other resource budgets. Therefore it is important to ensure that this forecast is as reliable as possible.

Assuming sales volume is the key budget factor, we therefore consider how to forecast future sales. Then, we will consider methods of dealing with activity levels that are determined by other key budget factors.

## SALES FORECASTS

There are a number of methods that can be used for this, alone or (more likely) in combination:

- Knowledge of sales experts
- Market research and sampling
- Time series analysis – moving averages, trends and seasonal variations
- Product life cycle analysis and market knowledge
- Indexing
- Linear regression

Many of these techniques (particularly time series analysis, indexing and linear regression) can also be used to forecast expenditure. We consider most of them in terms of forecasting income or sales here. However, linear regression is most commonly used to forecast semi-variable costs so that technique is considered in the section on forecasting expenditure at the end of this chapter, along with other methods of forecasting costs.

You may have seen these techniques in your earlier studies. In this assessment, detailed explanations of the techniques are not required but you will need to be able recognise when they should be used and why, and the limitations to their use.

## SALES EXPERTS

A good starting point when trying to forecast future sales is to consult with the sales experts within the business. The sales department staff will have a feel for how current sales are progressing and whether any market trends are likely to continue. They will also be able to provide details of any promotional activity in relation to a particular product and the anticipated impact on future demand.

It might also be possible in some businesses to discover from major customers their likely demand for the coming period although, as this is not a promise of orders to be placed, the eventual sales figures may differ substantially from any figures determined in this manner.

## MARKET RESEARCH AND SAMPLING

Market research as a method of estimating demand for a product is particularly appropriate before the launch of a new product or substantially modified product. Market research will normally involve finding out the opinions of potential customers regarding the product and will always involve taking a sample of customers. Sampling is a technique that you have learned in previous studies, so is only briefly mentioned here.

SAMPLING involves collecting data about a small number of items from the whole population, which is then used to estimate data regarding the whole POPULATION. There are several methods of sampling.

### Random sampling

RANDOM SAMPLING can be used when the entire population being considered is known.  Random numbers are used to select a sample from the population.

When the sampling is completed and the results considered then the sample results can be used to infer results for the whole population.

However, in the case of market research, the entire population is not always known and cannot be quantified. Say the business creating the forecasts wishes to determine market opinion about a new product they are about to launch, and so estimate possible sales volumes of the product for the forthcoming period. The population would be potential purchasers of the product but this cannot be known or quantified. Therefore, instead a non-random sampling method called quota sampling can be used.

## Quota sampling

QUOTA SAMPLING is used in situations where a number of different groups of the population can be identified. The number of samples required from each group is then determined and the data is taken from that required number in a non-random manner.

For example if a business has commissioned a market research survey about a potential major new product it may decide that it wants public views of this product from the following relevant consumers:

- Males aged 18 to 30                    200 samples
- Males aged 31 to 40                    100 samples
- Females aged 18 to 30                  300 samples
- Females aged 31 to 40                  250 samples

The market researchers would then collect the information from individuals until each quota was satisfied on a totally non-random basis. This is the type of sampling that will often be used by researchers standing in the street, who question people who walk by.

## Limitations of market research and sampling

Care must be taken in the market research to ensure that the sampling is unbiased as possible, so that the results are representative of the sample as a whole.

A further problem with market research is that it can be expensive. Therefore the cost and benefits of the research must be considered to determine if it should be carried out.

## Task 5

Market research is to be conducted into the potential sales of a new product by questioning shoppers in a shopping centre. What would be the most appropriate sampling method to use?

# TIME SERIES ANALYSIS

If we have collected cost or income data over a number of periods, such as sales revenue or production costs, this is known as a TIME SERIES. Such historic data may be used as a basis for forecasting future values. One of the key elements of information that management might require from a time series is an indication of the TREND. The trend is a feel for how the figure in question is changing over time – is it increasing rapidly, is it decreasing slightly?

The technique for determining the trend and other underlying components of a time series of figures is known as TIME SERIES ANALYSIS.

Time series analysis can be used to determine forecasts of sales figures. We can analyse an historic time series into a trend and the seasonal variations (the regular short-term pattern of increases or decreases in figures). We can then use the trend information to determine future deseasonalised sales and then, by adjusting for the seasonal variations, forecast the actual sales for the period.

So first, we need to analyse an historic time series into a trend and the seasonal variations.

## Determining trend and seasonal variations

The technique is to take the actual figures from the time series and determine the trend from these using moving averages. If these averages change over time then there is evidence of a trend in the series.

Once the trend has been identified, it can be compared to the actual figure to ascertain the seasonal variation:

Actual figure – trend = seasonal variation

Therefore by deducting the relevant trend figure from the actual figure the seasonal variation can be calculated.

We will consider first the calculation of the trend using moving averages.

## Moving averages

The technique of calculating a MOVING AVERAGE is a key tool in time series analysis and is a method of finding averages for a number of consecutive periods. The number of periods' data to be included in the average is chosen such that a whole cycle of seasonal variations is included. Averaging these will thus smooth out seasonal variations. As each successive group of data is averaged, the underlying trend is highlighted.

Note that it is unlikely that you would be asked to complete a lengthy moving averages calculation, but you do need to understand how a trend can be derived in this way, and also the use of time series analysis as a forecasting technique.

67

## HOW IT WORKS

Suppose that the sales figures for a business for the first six months of the year are as follows:

|  | £ |
|---|---|
| January | 35,500 |
| February | 37,500 |
| March | 34,500 |
| April | 40,000 |
| May | 42,000 |
| June | 39,000 |

It is felt that the sales cycle is on a quarterly basis – ie the seasonal variations repeat themselves every three months. What is required, therefore, is a three month moving average. This is done by first totalling the figures for January, February and March and then finding the average:

$$\frac{35,500 + 37,500 + 34,500}{3} = £35,833$$

Then we move on one month, and the average for February, March and April sales is calculated:

$$\frac{37,500 + 34,500 + 40,000}{3} = £37,333$$

Then the average for March, April and May:

$$\frac{34,500 + 40,000 + 42,000}{3} = £38,833$$

Then finally the average for April, May and June:

$$\frac{40,000 + 42,000 + 39,000}{3} = £40,333$$

Now we can show these moving averages together with the original figures – the convention is to show the moving average next to the middle month of those used in the average.

|  | Actual data | Moving average |
|---|---|---|
|  | £ | £ |
| January | 35,500 | |
| February | 37,500 | 35,833 |
| March | 34,500 | 37,333 |
| April | 40,000 | 38,833 |
| May | 42,000 | 40,333 |
| June | 39,000 | |

## Centred moving averages

The trend for a time series is essentially the moving average for the time series. However, if the number of periods used in the moving average is an even number, such as the four quarters of the year, then there is a further calculation to make – the CENTRED MOVING AVERAGE. The reason for this is that if the moving average is based upon an even number of periods then there is no central period to place the moving average against – a further average, the centred average, is required in order to find the trend.

## Calculating seasonal variations

We will now deal with identifying the seasonal variations. Remember the relationship between the actual figures, the trend and the seasonal variation in our simplified model:

Actual figure – trend = seasonal variation

We now include a final column on our table to show the seasonal variation for each quarter that can be directly compared to the trend. For example, if the moving average (the trend) for January-March is 35,833 and the actual observation for the same period is 37,500, the difference, which is due to seasonal variation, is +1,667 (37,500-35,833).

# HOW IT WORKS

Therefore, from our previous example, another column is added to give the seasonal variation.

| | Actual data £ | Moving average = Trend £ | Seasonal variation £ |
|---|---|---|---|
| January | 35,500 | | |
| February | 37,500 | 35,833 | +1,667 |
| March | 34,500 | 37,333 | -2,833 |
| April | 40,000 | 38,833 | +1,167 |
| May | 42,000 | 40,333 | +1,667 |
| June | 39,000 | | |

Once the trend and seasonal variations have been determined for an historical time series, we can use these to forecast future sales.

## HOW IT WORKS

From analysis of its historical sales data Fenton Products has estimated that the trend of its sales figures in units over the last three years has been a 2% increase in each quarter. The trend sales in Quarter 4 of 20X8 were 68,000 units. The time series analysis has also indicated the following seasonal variations:

| | |
|---|---|
| Quarter 1 | −12,000 units |
| Quarter 2 | −5,000 units |
| Quarter 3 | +7,000 units |
| Quarter 4 | +10,000 units |

Forecast the sales for each quarter of 20X9.

| | | | | |
|---|---|---|---|---|
| Quarter 1 | Trend | 68,000 × 1.02 | = | 69,360 units |
| | Forecast | 69,360 − 12,000 | = | 57,360 units |
| Quarter 2 | Trend | 69,360 × 1.02 | = | 70,747 units |
| | Forecast | 70,747 − 5,000 | = | 65,747 units |
| Quarter 3 | Trend | 70,747 × 1.02 | = | 72,162 units |
| | Forecast | 72,162 + 7,000 | = | 79,162 units |
| Quarter 4 | Trend | 72,162 × 1.02 | = | 73,605 units |
| | Forecast | 73,605 + 10,000 | = | 83,605 units |

### Additive model and multiplicative model

The seasonal variations in time series analysis can be expressed as additions to or subtractions from the trend – the additive model – as shown in the example above. They can also be shown as percentages of the trend in the multiplicative model.

# HOW IT WORKS

The trend figures for sales in units for Earthware Design for the four quarters of 20X0 are given below:

| | |
|---|---|
| Quarter 1 | 158,400 |
| Quarter 2 | 159,900 |
| Quarter 3 | 161,500 |
| Quarter 4 | 163,100 |

The seasonal variations are expressed as follows:

| | |
|---|---|
| Quarter 1 | +8% |
| Quarter 2 | −5% |
| Quarter 3 | −17% |
| Quarter 4 | +14% |

What are the forecast sales for each of the quarters of 20X0?

| | | | |
|---|---|---|---|
| Quarter 1 | 158,400 × 1.08 | = | 171,072 |
| Quarter 2 | 159,900 × 0.95 | = | 151,905 |
| Quarter 3 | 161,500 × 0.83 | = | 134,045 |
| Quarter 4 | 163,100 × 1.14 | = | 185,934 |

## Problems with time series analysis

Time series analysis can be a useful tool in the determination of sales forecast figures. However if using time series analysis you do need to be aware of some of the assumptions behind it and its limitations:

- unless the figures are considered for many years, it is impossible to isolate the cyclical changes due to general changes in the economy

- the forecast seasonal variations are an average of the seasonal variations for each period and again unless this is based on a large amount of historical data the figure could be misleading

- any random variations are ignored

- the trend and the seasonal variations are assumed to continue in the future in the same manner as in the past

- if the time series analysis is based upon value the figures will include past inflation which may not be an indication of the future amounts

However provided these assumptions and limitations are realised then time series analysis can be useful, particularly if used in conjunction with other information such as data from the sales force.

## Task 6

The trend sales volume for quarter 4 of last year was 248,000 units and it is estimated that the trend of sales has been a 3% increase in volume in each quarter. The seasonal variations are expressed as:

Quarter 1        −35%
Quarter 2        −15%
Quarter 3        +30%
Quarter 4        +20%

What are the sales volume forecast figures for the four quarters of the forthcoming year?

| Quarter | £ |
| --- | --- |
| Quarter 1 | |
| Quarter 2 | |
| Quarter 3 | |
| Quarter 4 | |

# PRODUCT LIFE CYCLE AND MARKET KNOWLEDGE

In the previous paragraphs we have seen how time series analysis makes the assumption that the sales figures will continue to change in line with the trend. Such statistical projections are helpful in forecasts but a manager should not ignore knowledge of the market or product itself.

The trend will not continue unchanged in practice as most products have a limited PRODUCT LIFE CYCLE which will show different sales and profitability patterns at different stages of the life cycle.

The product life cycle is generally thought to split naturally into five separate stages:

- development
- launch
- growth
- maturity
- decline

### Development and launch stages

During this period of the product's life there are large outgoings in terms of development expenditure, purchase of non-current assets necessary for production, the building up of inventory levels and advertising and promotion

expenses. It is likely that even after the launch sales will be quite low and the product will be making a loss at this stage.

## Growth stage

If the launch of the product is successful then during the growth stage there will be fairly rapid increases in sales and a move to profitability as the costs of the earlier stages are covered. These sales increases however are not likely to continue indefinitely.

## Maturity stage

In the maturity stage of the product life cycle, the growth in demand for the product will probably start to slow down and sales volumes will become more constant. In many cases this is the stage where the product is modified or improved, in order to sustain demand, and this may then result in a small surge in sales.

## Decline stage

At some point in a product's life, unless it is a consumable item such as chocolate bars, the product will reach the end of its sale life. The market will have bought enough of the product and sales will decline. This is the point where the business should consider no longer producing the product.

## Product life cycle and time series analysis

If the future demand for a product is to be forecast using time series analysis it is obviously important that the stage in the product life cycle that has been reached is taken into account. For example, if the trend is based upon the growth stage whereas in fact the product is moving into the maturity stage, then the trend would show an overly optimistic forecast for sales.

## Market considerations

In addition to considering where a business's individual products are in their life cycle when producing sales forecasts it is also important to consider the overall market for a particular product. Is it a new, emerging market for a new product, an established market for a long-standing product or a declining market for a product which is no longer of great interest to consumers?

For example, no matter how technologically advanced a VHS video recorder is, DVD players mean that demand for video recorders is in terminal decline.

## Market analysis

So a business has to consider not only its products' sales trends but also the stage of the life cycle of each product and the state of the market for that product.

However, the analysis could go even further, into the general state of the environment in which the business operates. This can often be efficiently done by carrying out a PEST analysis. This examines the following factors:

> **P**olitical
> **E**conomic
> **S**ocial
> **T**echnological

## Political factors

Political factors may affect a forecast of future sales. This might particularly be the case if the business is an exporter, as the political development of other countries can either help or hinder the export drive. In the UK legislation such as health and safety and minimum wage requirements might have an effect on the cost of producing products.

## Economic factors

The general economic climate will have a huge effect on the sales of a business, and indeed on its costs. All economies have stages, similar to the product life cycle. The four main stages are:

| | | |
|---|---|---|
| Recession | – | employment, consumer confidence and consumer spending start to fall |
| Depression | – | heavy unemployment and low consumer demand are typical in this phase, though very often economies go straight from recession to recovery without experiencing depression |
| Recovery | – | investment and employment start to regenerate and consumer spending rises |
| Boom | – | consumer spending is rising fast |

Clearly, these factors will affect the future forecast sales of a business. For example, if the trend of sales has been taken from historical data collected in a recovery period followed by a boom period, and a period of recession is about to follow, then the projected trend figure will be completely misleading.

## Social factors

The way in which society operates and changes can have a fundamental affect on the sales of a business. Factors such as family sizes, lifestyle expectations, divorce rates and average life span can all affect, in the medium to long term, the prospects for sales of a particular product. Other factors such as fashion and health concerns can also impact upon the future sales of a business's product.

## Technological factors

Technological factors are probably one of the most important factors in the current high-tech consumer market place. Once a product is outdated and replaced by superior technology then this will have a huge impact on sales levels. For example, the launch of Playstation 2 virtually ended the sales of the original Playstation; PS3 had the same effect on its predecessor.

# INDEXING

We have seen how we can get a feel for how a time series is changing over time by calculating the trend using moving averages. From this future sales can be forecast. indexing is another simple and convenient method of examining the trend of an expense or revenue item over time. The actual figures are converted into a series of INDEX NUMBERS.

Index numbers measure the change in value of a figure over time, by reference to its value at a fixed point.

This is done by determining first a BASE PERIOD, which is the period for which the actual figure is equated to an index of 100. Each subsequent period's figure is converted to the equivalent index using the following formula:

$$\text{Index} = \frac{\text{Current period's figure}}{\text{Base period figure}} \times 100$$

# HOW IT WORKS

The monthly sales figures for a business for the first six months of the year are as follows:

|  | £ |
| --- | --- |
| January | 136,000 |
| February | 148,000 |
| March | 140,000 |
| April | 130,000 |
| May | 138,000 |
| June | 145,000 |

We will set the January figure as the base period with an index of 100.

This means that the index for February is calculated as:

$$\frac{\text{Current period's figure}}{\text{Base period figure}} \times 100 = \frac{148{,}000}{136{,}000} \times 100 = 109$$

The index for March is:

$$\frac{140{,}000}{136{,}000} \times 100 = 103$$

The index for April is:

$$\frac{130{,}000}{136{,}000} \times 100 = 96$$

The index for May is:

$$\frac{138{,}000}{136{,}000} \times 100 = 101$$

The index for June is:

$$\frac{145{,}000}{136{,}000} \times 100 = 107$$

## Interpreting an index

If the index for a period is greater than 100 this means that the current period figure is larger than the base period figure. If it is less than 100 the figure is lower than the base period figure. If the index is generally rising then the figures are increasing over the base period but if the index is decreasing the figures are decreasing compared to the base period.

Remember when interpreting an index that it represents the current period figure compared to the base period, not compared to the previous period.

## HOW IT WORKS

We can show the actual sales together with the index for the previous example.

|  | £ | Index |
| --- | --- | --- |
| January | 136,000 | 100 |
| February | 148,000 | 109 |
| March | 140,000 | 103 |
| April | 130,000 | 96 |
| May | 138,000 | 101 |
| June | 145,000 | 107 |

The index shows that although sales start to increase in February they then fall again with April being lower than January. However by June the sales are again increasing almost to the February level.

## Retail Price Index

As mentioned earlier in this chapter, the Retail Price Index (RPI) is a measure of general price changes which is published each month by the government.

A business can use the RPI as a form of indexing, to determine the extent to which its income and its costs have changed in line with general inflation.

## HOW IT WORKS

A business has had the following sales for the last eight years:

|        | £       |
|--------|---------|
| 20X1   | 513,600 |
| 20X2   | 516,300 |
| 20X3   | 518,400 |
| 20X4   | 522,400 |
| 20X5   | 530,400 |
| 20X6   | 535,200 |
| 20X7   | 549,800 |
| 20X8   | 558,700 |

If we use 20X1 as the base year and then index these sales figures on that basis the index will be as follows:

|        |                               | Index |
|--------|-------------------------------|-------|
| 20X1   | 100.0                         |       |
| 20X2   | 516,300/513,600 × 100         | 100.5 |
| 20X3   | 518,400/513,600 × 100         | 100.9 |
| 20X4   | 522,400/513,600 × 100         | 101.7 |
| 20X5   | 530,400/513,600 × 100         | 103.3 |
| 20X6   | 535,200/513,600 × 100         | 104.2 |
| 20X7   | 549,800/513,600 × 100         | 107.0 |
| 20X8   | 558,700/513,600 × 100         | 108.8 |

This index shows a small but steady increase in sales revenue over the years. But is this due to an increase in sales volume, or simply the effects of inflation increasing the selling price?

We can consider the general increases in prices over these years by looking at the average Retail Price Index (RPI) for each of the years:

|        | RPI   |
|--------|-------|
| 20X1   | 140.7 |
| 20X2   | 144.1 |
| 20X3   | 149.1 |
| 20X4   | 152.7 |
| 20X5   | 157.5 |
| 20X6   | 162.9 |
| 20X7   | 165.4 |
| 20X8   | 170.2 |

We apply the RPI to the annual sales figures in order to show the RPI adjusted figures. This is done by using the following formula:

$$\text{Sales for current year} \times \frac{\text{RPI for year 1}}{\text{RPI for current year}}$$

| 20X1 | Adjusted sales figure | = | 513,600 × 140.7/140.7 | = | £513,600 |
| 20X2 | Adjusted sales figure | = | 516,300 × 140.7/144.1 | = | £504,118 |
| 20X3 | Adjusted sales figure | = | 518,400 × 140.7/149.1 | = | £489,194 |

and so on:

|  | Sales | Adjusted sales |
|---|---|---|
|  | £ | £ |
| 20X1 | 513,600 | 513,600 |
| 20X2 | 516,300 | 504,118 |
| 20X3 | 518,400 | 489,194 |
| 20X4 | 522,400 | 481,347 |
| 20X5 | 530,400 | 473,824 |
| 20X6 | 535,200 | 462,263 |
| 20X7 | 549,800 | 467,696 |
| 20X8 | 558,700 | 461,863 |

In 'real' terms, ie without inflationary effects, sales have fallen. This could be due to:

- falling sales volumes
- selling prices failing to keep up with general inflation

or a combination of these.

What has been done here is to turn each period's sales into 20X1 price terms to illustrate that, in terms of the prices then prevailing, the sales over time have decreased.

We can now calculate an index based upon these adjusted sales figure which shows a very different picture from the earlier index:

|  | Sales | Adjusted sales | Index |
|---|---|---|---|
|  | £ | £ |  |
| 20X1 | 513,600 | 513,600 | 100.0 |
| 20X2 | 516,300 | 504,118 | 98.2 |
| 20X3 | 518,400 | 489,194 | 95.2 |
| 20X4 | 522,400 | 481,347 | 93.7 |
| 20X5 | 530,400 | 473,824 | 92.3 |
| 20X6 | 535,200 | 462,263 | 90.0 |
| 20X7 | 549,800 | 467,696 | 91.1 |
| 20X8 | 558,700 | 461,863 | 89.9 |

This shows that the sales for the last eight years have in fact dramatically failed to keep up with the general rise in prices as shown by the RPI adjusted sales index.

Like time series analysis, indexing is another technique for analysing figures for income (or cost) collected over a period of time. From this, management have a greater awareness of the trend of this income, and by extrapolating this trend, sales forecasts can be produced.

As with time series analysis, however, the trend will not continue indefinitely into the future, and external factors regarding the product's market and also its life cycle, as discussed above, should also be taken into account.

## FORECASTING EXPENDITURE

We have considered how to forecast sales above. In this section we will consider the forecasting of the actual costs of production given the production level that has been set according to the key budget factor. There is some overlap in terms of techniques that can be applied but additionally in the case of expenditure, we also need to consider cost behaviours.

There are three types of cost or expense that we must consider:

- variable costs
- fixed costs
- semi-variable costs

These cost behaviours were considered in Chapter 1 and in this chapter we will consider the problems involved in forecasting these costs for future periods.

### Variable costs

Variable costs, by definition, are dependent upon the activity level. Therefore variable production costs will be based upon the level of production and variable sales costs will be based upon the level of sales.

## HOW IT WORKS

The production and sales levels for Yewtree Ltd for the next six months are as follows:

|  | July | Aug | Sept | Oct | Nov | Dec |
|---|---|---|---|---|---|---|
| Production – units | 7,500 | 7,000 | 7,000 | 7,200 | 7,500 | 7,800 |
| Sales – units | 7,300 | 6,800 | 7,200 | 7,100 | 7,400 | 8,000 |

The variable production costs are £6 per unit and the variable selling costs are £2 per unit.

What are the forecast figures for variable production and selling costs?

The variable production costs are based upon the number of units produced each month and the variable selling costs are based upon the number of units sold in each month.

|  | July £ | Aug £ | Sept £ | Oct £ | Nov £ | Dec £ |
|---|---|---|---|---|---|---|
| Variable production costs | 45,000 | 42,000 | 42,000 | 43,200 | 45,000 | 46,800 |
| Variable selling costs | 14,600 | 13,600 | 14,400 | 14,200 | 14,800 | 16,000 |

## Price level changes

A further problem in forecasting costs and expenses is that the current price of the materials/labour/expenses will be known but these may be expected to increase in the forthcoming period. Therefore as well as forecasting the amount of the variable cost it may also be necessary to forecast any changes in price levels during the period.

This can often be done using price indices – specific price indices for a particular cost, or the Retail Price Index as a measure of general inflation. The use of indices was considered above and here we will apply them to the specific problem of forecasting costs.

## HOW IT WORKS

The variable production costs of making XTC's products are currently £10 per unit for direct materials and £8 per unit for direct labour. The production levels that are anticipated for the next six months are:

|  | Oct | Nov | Dec | Jan | Feb | Mar |
|---|---|---|---|---|---|---|
| Production – units | 10,000 | 10,200 | 10,500 | 9,800 | 9,500 | 9,900 |

A specific price index is available for the direct materials and it is currently 115.0. The price index for the following six months is anticipated to be:

|  | Oct | Nov | Dec | Jan | Feb | Mar |
|---|---|---|---|---|---|---|
| Specific materials price index | 115.8 | 116.2 | 116.5 | 117.0 | 118.3 | 119.0 |

The direct labour wages are always reset on 1 January to reflect any increase in the Retail Price Index over the past year. The current direct labour cost is based

upon the RPI of 176.5 on the previous 1 January. The RPI is expected to have risen to 189.5 by the forthcoming 1 January.

You are to prepare forecasts of the direct materials and direct labour costs for each of the next six months.

## Direct materials cost

First we forecast the cost based upon the current price of £10 per unit and the anticipated production level:

|  | Oct | Nov | Dec | Jan | Feb | Mar |
|---|---|---|---|---|---|---|
| Production – units | 10,000 | 10,200 | 10,500 | 9,800 | 9,500 | 9,900 |
| Direct materials cost – £ | 100,000 | 102,000 | 105,000 | 98,000 | 95,000 | 99,000 |

Now we adjust these forecast figures to include the anticipated price rises over the forthcoming months. This will be done by the following adjustment to the forecast figures above:

$$\text{Price adjusted forecast} = \text{Forecast figure} \times \frac{\text{Future index level}}{\text{Current index level}}$$

Therefore the calculations will be:

$$\text{October} \quad = \quad £100,000 \times \frac{115.8}{115.0}$$

$$= \quad £100,696$$

$$\text{November} \quad = \quad £102,000 \times \frac{116.2}{115.0}$$

$$= \quad £103,064$$

and so on .........

The final forecast for the direct materials cost will be:

|  | Oct | Nov | Dec | Jan | Feb | Mar |
|---|---|---|---|---|---|---|
| Production – units | 10,000 | 10,200 | 10,500 | 9,800 | 9,500 | 9,900 |
| Direct materials cost – £ | 100,000 | 102,000 | 105,000 | 98,000 | 95,000 | 99,000 |
| Specific materials price index | 115.8 | 116.2 | 116.5 | 117.0 | 118.3 | 119.0 |
| Price adjusted forecast – £ | 100,696 | 103,064 | 106,370 | 99,704 | 97,726 | 102,443 |

### Direct labour cost

The current direct labour cost is £8 per unit. This will not change until January when it becomes:

$$\text{New labour cost} \quad = \quad \text{Current labour cost} \times \frac{\text{Future RPI}}{\text{Current RPI}}$$

$$= \quad £8 \times \frac{189.5}{176.5}$$

$$= \quad £8.59 \text{ per unit}$$

The direct labour cost can now be forecast:

|  | Oct | Nov | Dec | Jan | Feb | Mar |
|---|---|---|---|---|---|---|
| Production – units | 10,000 | 10,200 | 10,500 | 9,800 | 9,500 | 9,900 |
| Cost per unit | £8.00 | £8.00 | £8.00 | £8.59 | £8.59 | £8.59 |
| Direct labour forecast – £ | 80,000 | 81,600 | 84,000 | 84,182 | 81,605 | 85,041 |

---

## Task 7

The direct materials cost for Quarter 1 and Quarter 2 of the following year have been estimated in terms of current prices at £346,700 and £394,500 respectively. The current price index for these materials is 164.7 and the price index is estimated as 177.9 for Quarter 1 of next year and 191.3 for Quarter 2.

What are the forecast direct materials costs for Quarters 1 and 2 of next year?

| Quarter | £ |
|---|---|
| Quarter 1 |  |
| Quarter 2 |  |

---

### Fixed costs

As fixed costs are not related to the level of production then the forecasting process becomes simpler. The forecasting of fixed costs will often be based upon last year's fixed costs with an estimated increase for any specific or general price increases.

Alternatively forecast fixed costs may be calculated based upon information about future activities within the business.

## HOW IT WORKS

A computer software company rents its premises annually from 1 January to 31 December. The rent for the year ending 31 December 20X8 was £24,000. The company is now trying to forecast its costs for the year ending 31 December 20X9. It is believed that the rental increase will be based upon the increase in the RPI in the period between 1 January 20X8 and 1 January 20X9. The RPI on 1 January 20X8 was 176.5 and it is believed that it will be 189.5 on 1 January 20X9.

The personnel manager of the company has planned that there will be 600 hours of training courses for employees in the year ending 31 December 20X9 and the hourly cost of each training course is estimated at £25.

What are the forecast costs for rent and for training for the year ending 31 December 20X9?

**Rent**

$$\text{Forecast cost} \quad = \quad £24,000 \times \frac{189.5}{176.5}$$

$$= \quad £25,768$$

**Training**

$$\text{Forecast cost} \quad = \quad 600 \text{ hours} \times £25 \text{ per hour}$$

$$= \quad £15,000$$

### Semi-variable costs

Forecasts for semi-variable costs are more complex as these costs have a fixed element which is not related to the level of activity, and a variable element which is related to the level of activity. In order to determine the forecast for semi-variable costs, at any given level of activity, both the fixed element amount and the variable element rate must be known.

### Hi lo method of cost estimation

One method of estimating the fixed and variable elements of a semi-variable cost is to use the HI LO METHOD. Under this method historical data regarding the amount of the semi-variable cost at various activity levels is collected. A comparison is then made between the costs at the highest level of activity and at the lowest level of activity, in order to isolate the variable rate of increase in the cost and then to find the fixed element of the cost. This method assumes that there is a linear relationship between the cost and output at the highest and lowest activity levels.

# HOW IT WORKS

The costs of the factory maintenance department for Kilman Ltd appear to be partially dependent upon the number of machine hours operated each month. The machine hours and the maintenance department costs for the last six months are given below:

|  | Machine hours | Maintenance cost £ |
| --- | --- | --- |
| June | 4,000 | 104,000 |
| July | 4,800 | 127,000 |
| August | 4,200 | 111,000 |
| September | 4,500 | 119,000 |
| October | 3,800 | 107,000 |
| November | 4,100 | 107,000 |

## Step 1

Find the highest and lowest levels of activity (note that this is the activity level and is not necessarily the highest and lowest cost).

In this case the highest level is 4,800 hours and the lowest level is 3,800 hours.

## Step 2

Compare the activity level and costs for each of these:

|  | Machine hours | Cost £ |
| --- | --- | --- |
| Highest | 4,800 | 127,000 |
| Lowest | 3,800 | 107,000 |
| Increase | 1,000 | 20,000 |

This shows that for an increase in 1,000 machine hours there has been an increase of £20,000 of costs. Therefore the variable cost per machine hour can be estimated as:

| Variable rate of increase | = | £20,000/1,000 hours |
| --- | --- | --- |
|  | = | £20 per machine hour |

## Step 3

We can now find the fixed element of the cost by substituting the variable rate into either the highest or lowest activity level with the fixed element appearing as the balancing figure. This will provide you with the same answer whether you use the highest or lowest level of activity.

## Highest level

|  | £ |
|---|---|
| Variable element 4,800 hours × £20 | 96,000 |
| Fixed element (balancing figure) | 31,000 |
| Total cost | 127,000 |

## Lowest level

|  | £ |
|---|---|
| Variable element 3,800 hours × £20 | 76,000 |
| Fixed element (balancing figure) | 31,000 |
| Total cost | 107,000 |

Therefore the fixed element of the maintenance department costs is £31,000 and the variable rate is £20 per machine hour.

### Step 4

We can now use this analysis of the semi-variable cost to forecast figures for the maintenance department. The anticipated machine hours for the next three month period are as follows:

|  | Dec | Jan | Feb |
|---|---|---|---|
| Machine hours | 4,000 | 4,500 | 5,000 |

The forecast maintenance department costs for these three months can be calculated:

|  | Forecast maintenance department costs |
|---|---|
|  | £ |
| Dec (4,000 × £20) + £31,000 | 111,000 |
| Jan (4,500 × £20) + £31,000 | 121,000 |
| Feb (5,000 × £20) + £31,000 | 131,000 |

## Interpolation and extrapolation

In the previous example we used our calculated figures about the cost movement in order to estimate the future costs of the maintenance department. In order to find the variable and fixed elements of the cost we looked at an activity range of 3,800 hours to 4,800 hours and estimated how the costs moved within that range.

For December and January the anticipated machine hour levels fall within this range therefore it is likely that our estimates of cost will be fairly accurate (although they do not coincide with the historical costs associated with those levels – our model is not totally accurate as it is based on the assumption of a linear relationship which is unlikely to apply perfectly in practice). When the

levels being forecast are within the range considered this is known as INTERPOLATION.

However for February the machine hours are estimated to be 5,000. This is outside the range that we considered and therefore our estimate of future cost is known as EXTRAPOLATION. Extrapolation may not be as accurate as interpolation as the activity level is outside our historical data range and therefore we do not know how the costs will behave outside of the range.

---

## Task 8

The production costs at various levels of production for a business are given below:

| Production level | Production costs |
| --- | --- |
| units | £ |
| 24,000 | 169,000 |
| 20,000 | 143,000 |
| 28,000 | 191,000 |

Calculate the variable rate element and the fixed cost element of these production costs.

Variable cost per unit =

| £ | |
| --- | --- |

Total fixed cost =

| £ | |
| --- | --- |

---

## LINEAR REGRESSION

There is a further technique that can be used in forecasting semi-variable costs and also, in assessments, is sometimes used for forecasting sales volumes. This technique is known as LINEAR REGRESSION. Regression analysis involves the prediction of one variable eg cost, based on another variable eg volume of output, on the assumption that there is a linear relationship between the two variables.

## The equation of a straight line

Given below is a straight line drawn onto a graph

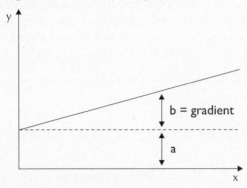

Any such straight line will have a defining equation in the following form:

$$y = a + bx$$

Both a and b are constants and represent specific figures:

- a is the point on the graph where the line intersects the y axis
- b represents the gradient of the line

## Using the equation of a straight line

We can use the equation for a straight line, or LINEAR REGRESSION EQUATION, in two possible ways in forecasting:

- to forecast the amount of a semi-variable cost at a given production level

- to forecast future sales volumes using the linear regression equation as the equation for the trend of sales.

In assessments you will not be required to derive the linear regression equation for a straight line – you will always be given this equation. However some care must be taken with what the variables x and y represent.

## Dependent and independent variables

Given the equation of a straight line: $y = a + bx$:

- y is always the DEPENDENT VARIABLE

  (plotted on the vertical axis)

- x is always the INDEPENDENT VARIABLE

  (plotted on the horizontal axis).

The dependent variable y can be calculated using the linear regression equation provided that a value is known for the independent variable x.

## HOW IT WORKS

(a) A linear regression equation expresses the relationship between the costs of producing a product and the quantity of production.

Which is the dependent variable and which the independent variable?

The cost of production is the dependent variable as this will depend upon the quantity. Therefore x represents the quantity of production and y represents the cost of production.

(b) A linear regression equation expresses the trend line for a time series of sales volumes.

Which is the dependent variable and which the independent variable?

The volume of sales depends upon the time period in which the sales were made so volume is represented by y and time is represented on the x axis (note, time is ALWAYS an independent variable!).

## Task 9

A linear regression equation expresses the relationship between advertising costs and sales volume. Which is the dependent variable and which is the independent variable?

|  | Dependent | Independent |
| --- | --- | --- |
| Sales volume |  |  |
| Advertising costs |  |  |

### Forecasting semi-variable costs

If we are given the linear regression equation for a semi-variable cost then provided that we know our forecast level of activity, x, we will be able to calculate the forecast level of cost, y.

## HOW IT WORKS

The linear regression equation for the canteen costs (y) of a business for a month is as follows:

$$y = 20{,}000 + 45x$$

The variable x represents the number of employees using the canteen – the independent variable.

It is anticipated that the number of employees using the canteen in the next three months is as follows:

|  | Number of employees (x) |
|---|---|
| January | 840 |
| February | 900 |
| March | 875 |

What are the forecast canteen costs for each period?

|  |  | £ |
|---|---|---|
| January | 20,000 + (45 × 840) | 57,800 |
| February | 20,000 + (45 × 900) | 60,500 |
| March | 20,000 + (45 × 875) | 59,375 |

## Task 10

The linear regression equation for production costs (y) for a business is:

$$y = 63,000 + 3.20x$$

If production (x) is expected to be 44,000 units in the next quarter, what are the anticipated production costs?

Production costs:

£ _____

### Forecasting sales

If we are given a linear regression equation which represents the trend for sales, then we can use this to estimate sales for future periods. The x variable is the time period and therefore this is normally given a sequential number starting with 1 for the first period of the time series. Given the trend equation we can then calculate the trend for sales for any future period. Note that this will only give meaningful results if the trend is observed to be approximately linear, ie a straight line, from its graph.

## HOW IT WORKS

The trend for sales volume for one of Trinket Ltd's products is given:

$$y = 16.5 + 0.78x$$

where y is the volume of sales in thousands in any given time period and x is the time period.

The time series is based upon quarterly sales volumes starting in Quarter 1 of 20X6.

The seasonal variations for each quarter are:

| | |
|---|---|
| Quarter 1 | −10% |
| Quarter 2 | +16% |
| Quarter 3 | +8% |
| Quarter 4 | −14% |

Estimate the sales volume for each quarter of 20X9.

## Step 1

Find the values of x for the four quarters in 20X9 by counting from the first quarter of 20X6.

| | | |
|---|---|---|
| Q1 | 20X6 | x = 1 |
| Q2 | 20X6 | x = 2 |
| Q3 | 20X6 | x = 3 |
| Q4 | 20X6 | x = 4 |
| Q1 | 20X7 | x = 5 |

... and so on until

| | | |
|---|---|---|
| Q1 | 20X9 | x = 13 |

## Step 2

Calculate the trend for each quarter before seasonal adjustments using the linear regression equation.

| 20X9 | x value | y = 16.5 + 0.78x |
|---|---|---|
| Q1 | 13 | 26.64 |
| Q2 | 14 | 27.42 |
| Q3 | 15 | 28.20 |
| Q4 | 16 | 28.98 |

Step 3

Adjust the trend figures for the seasonal variations to find the seasonally adjusted sales volume.

| Quarter | Trend ('000 units) | Seasonal adjustment volume | Seasonally adjusted sales (units) |
|---------|--------------------|----------------------------|-----------------------------------|
| Q1 | 26.64 | −10% | 23,976 |
| Q2 | 27.42 | +16% | 31,807 |
| Q3 | 28.20 | +8% | 30,456 |
| Q4 | 28.98 | −14% | 24,923 |

## Interpolation and extrapolation

Again we have to consider that interpolation, an estimation within the historical range, is more reliable than extrapolation, an estimation beyond the historical range.

When using linear regression analysis to estimate future sales from a trend line this is always extrapolation and this means that there is an underlying assumption that the current trend will continue into the future.

## Task 11

The linear regression equation for the trend of sales in thousands of units based upon time series analysis of the monthly figures for the last two years is:

$$y = 4.8 + 1.2x$$

What is the estimated sales trend for each of the first three months of next year?

| Month | Estimated sales units (000's) |
|-------|-------------------------------|
| 1 | |
| 2 | |
| 3 | |

## UNCERTAINTIES INHERENT IN FORECASTING

Any attempt to look into the future in order to try to determine what is going to happen will obviously not result in a perfectly accurate picture. Forecasting is not a exact science.

However by using a variety of techniques and being aware of the assumptions behind these forecasting techniques, the forecast can still be of use to a business and often reasonably accurate. All forecasts are likely to include errors but be aware of some of the following general limitations in the use of forecasting:

- the more data that is used the better the results of the forecast will be, so a forecast based on limited data will inevitably be of limited use

- the further into the future that the forecast considers, the more unreliable it will become

- forecast figures will often be based upon the assumption that current conditions will continue in the future, eg extrapolation of a trend based upon historical data, which may not be a valid assumption

- if the forecast is based upon a trend, there are always random elements or variations which cause the trend to change

- the forecast produced from the historical data may be quite accurate but the actual future results may be very different from the forecast figures due to changes in the political, economic or technological environment within which the business operates.

In assessments the limitations of any income or expenditure forecasts will depend upon each scenario and the task set. Therefore try to use the information given and consider these general limitations within that context.

## CHAPTER OVERVIEW

- The financial plans of the business are set out in the form of budgets and may include budgets for sales, resources or costs (revenue expenditure) and capital (capital expenditure budget)

- The creation of budgets requires information or data

- Both internal and external sources of data must be used in forecasting and budgeting

- Internal information can be found from the historical financial accounting records, files of documents such as invoices, payroll details and inventory records, and many other sources in an organisation

- External information can be found from the Office for National Statistics, trade associations, financial press and the internet

- To prepare budgets, forecasts must be constructed

- Forecasts of activity will be required, in particular for the key budget factor, but also for other elements of income and expense

- The key budget factor may not necessarily be sales demand but may instead be related to a shortage of materials, a shortage of suitable labour or a lack of production capacity

- Forecasting is not an exact science and you need to understand the limitations of, and assumptions behind, forecasts and be able to use the details in a scenario to discuss this area

- The natural starting point for a sales forecast would be information from the sales experts within the business

- Market research might be an appropriate method of forecasting sales for a new or substantially improved product

- Time series analysis can be used to estimate the trend for future periods and then apply seasonal variations to find the forecast sales figures

- The position of the product within its life cycle will be an important factor when determining the validity of any trend figures from time series analysis

- When considering the sales forecasts consideration should also be given to market conditions – political, economic, social and technological factors

- Indexing can also be used to look at trends over time. Index numbers measure the change in value of a figure over time, by reference to its value at a fixed point

CHAPTER OVERVIEW (continued)

- Any forecast for variable production costs will depend upon production levels for each period; any forecast for variable selling costs will depend upon the level of sales for each period

- If there are any anticipated price changes in the future period these can be included in the forecasts for expenses using indices

- Fixed overhead forecasts will often require the use of indices to reflect price changes and may also be based upon budgeted activity of other parts of the business

- When forecasting semi-variable costs both the fixed element of the cost must be known and the variable rate element – one method of calculating these two elements is to use the hi lo method

- Linear regression analysis can be used in order to estimate either semi-variable costs at a particular activity level or future sales based on a linear trend

- The linear regression line, $y = a + bx$, will always be given to you in an assessment, you will not need to derive it. Care should be taken with the variables $x$ and $y$ – $x$ is always the independent variable and $y$ is the dependent variable

- When using either the hi lo method or linear regression to estimate costs or income remember that interpolation will generally produce a more accurate forecast than extrapolation

## Keywords

**Sales budget** – short-term forecast for income (derived from expected number of sales × expected selling price)

**Resource budget** – budget set for each resource and activity of the business eg production, labour usage, materials usage and so on

**Revenue expenditure** – costs that are incurred in the day-to-day running of the business but which do not have an enduring benefit

**Capital expenditure** – the purchase of non-current assets for long term use in the business

**Capital budget** – a long-term budget showing the organisation's planned capital expenditure

**Retail Price Index** – a measure of the increase or decrease in general prices in the UK

**Forecast** – an estimate of what may happen in the future based upon historical data and knowledge of future changes

**Key budget factor** – the element or resource of the business that places limitations on the activities of the business

**Sampling** – a method of finding information about a population by only testing a sample of the items in the population

**Population** – all of the items of data we are interested in for a particular data collecting purpose

**Random sampling** – all items in the population are known and are picked using random numbers

**Quota sampling** – the number of items required from each group is determined and then a non-random sample is taken to provide the required numbers

**Time series** – a series of income or expense figures recorded for a number of consecutive periods

**Trend** – the underlying movements of the time series over the period

**Time series analysis** – a method of calculating the trend and other relevant figures from a time series

**Seasonal variations** – the regular short-term pattern of increases or decreases in figures in a time series

**Moving average** – the calculation of an average figure for the results of consecutive periods of time

**Centred moving average** – the average of two consecutive moving averages when the period for the moving average is an even number

**Product life cycle** – the various stages of sales growth and profitability that most products will go through in their lives (development, launch, growth, maturity and decline)

**Index number** – conversion of actual figures compared to a base year where the base year index is expressed as 100

**Base period** – the period for which the index is expressed as 100 and against which all other period figures are compared

**Hi lo method** – a method of estimating the fixed and variable elements of a semi-variable cost using historic data

**Interpolation** – estimation of a forecast figure within the range of activity levels considered

**Extrapolation** – estimation of a forecast figure outside the range of activity levels considered

**Linear regression** – a technique for forecasting semi-variable costs or future sales using the equation for a straight line

**Linear regression equation** – $y = a + bx$

**Dependent variable** – $y$ is always the dependent variable

**Independent variable** – $x$ is always the independent variable

## TEST YOUR LEARNING

1   You are constructing a budget and wish to obtain the following information. Whom would you contact to find the information?

| Information required | Source |
|---|---|
| Budgeted units of production per product | ▼ |
| Price of materials | ▼ |
| Sales brochure costs | ▼ |
| Mortgage interest on factory | ▼ |

**Picklist:**

Buyer

Marketing Director

Production planning manager

Finance Director

2   Given below are the production cost figures for a business for the last year.

|  | £ |
|---|---|
| July | 397,500 |
| August | 403,800 |
| September | 399,600 |
| October | 405,300 |
| November | 406,100 |
| December | 408,500 |
| January | 407,900 |
| February | 410,400 |
| March | 416,000 |
| April | 413,100 |
| May | 417,500 |
| June | 421,800 |

If constructing a budget for the forthcoming year, using this data, suggest a technique which might be used to forecast production costs.

Explain the limitations of this technique.

3   Describe three sources for collecting information for the production of sales forecasts and their limitations.

4   The sales data for the last three years have been subject to a time series analysis and the trend has been estimated as an increase of 1.5% per quarter in unit sales. The unit sales for Quarter 4 of 20X1 were 175,000 units.

The time series analysis also shows the following seasonal variations:

Quarter 1     +15%
Quarter 2     −10%
Quarter 3     −30%
Quarter 4     +25%

The forecast sales units for each of the four quarters of 20X2 are:

| Quarter 1 | |
| --- | --- |
| Quarter 2 | |
| Quarter 3 | |
| Quarter 4 | |

5   The trend figures for sales in units for a business for the four quarters of 20X0 and the seasonal variations are estimated as follows:

| | Trend unit sales | Seasonal variations |
| --- | --- | --- |
| Quarter 1 | 210,000 units | −16% |
| Quarter 2 | 212,600 units | −25% |
| Quarter 3 | 215,400 units | +18% |
| Quarter 4 | 217,200 units | +23% |

The forecast sales units for each of the quarters of 20X0 are:

| Quarter 1 | |
| --- | --- |
| Quarter 2 | |
| Quarter 3 | |
| Quarter 4 | |

6   State the five stages of a product life cycle.

7   What factors would be considered in a PEST analysis?

8   The production and sales levels for the next six months for a business are estimated as follows:

| | Jan | Feb | Mar | Apr | May | Jun |
| --- | --- | --- | --- | --- | --- | --- |
| Production – units | 1,200 | 1,320 | 1,480 | 1,280 | 1,300 | 1,340 |
| Sales – units | 1,250 | 1,300 | 1,320 | 1,320 | 1,400 | 1,400 |

Variable production costs are currently £14.00 per unit and variable selling costs are £6.00 per unit. The price indices for the production costs and selling costs are currently 142.3 and 121.0 respectively.

The anticipated price indices for production and selling costs for the next six months are given below:

|  | Jan | Feb | Mar | Apr | May | Jun |
|---|---|---|---|---|---|---|
| Production costs index | 144.3 | 145.0 | 145.6 | 148.6 | 149.2 | 150.0 |
| Selling costs index | 121.5 | 122.0 | 122.7 | 123.4 | 124.1 | 125.0 |

Complete the following:

|  | Jan | Feb | Mar | Apr | May | Jun |
|---|---|---|---|---|---|---|
| Forecast variable production costs £ |  |  |  |  |  |  |
| Forecast variable selling costs £ |  |  |  |  |  |  |

9   Given below are the activity levels and production costs for the last six months for a factory:

|  | Activity level units | Production cost £ |
|---|---|---|
| July | 103,000 | 469,000 |
| August | 110,000 | 502,000 |
| September | 126,000 | 547,000 |
| October | 113,000 | 517,000 |
| November | 101,000 | 472,000 |
| December | 118,000 | 533,000 |

Complete the following:

The fixed element of production cost is estimated as £ ☐

The variable element of production cost is estimated as £ ☐ per unit.

The production cost for January which has a budgeted activity of 120,000 units is forecast as £ ☐

The production cost for February which has a budgeted activity of 150,000 units is forecast as £ ☐

The forecast production cost for ☐ ▼ is the more accurate.

**Picklist:**
January
February

Explain why you think the forecast production cost for the period you have chosen is more accurate.

10  The linear regression equation for costs of the stores department of a business is given as follows:

$$y = 13,000 + 0.8x$$

where x is the number of units produced in a period.

The anticipated production levels for the next six months are:

|  | Jan | Feb | Mar | Apr | May | June |
|---|---|---|---|---|---|---|
| Production – units | 5,400 | 5,600 | 5,700 | 6,000 | 5,500 | 6,100 |

Complete the following

|  | Jan | Feb | Mar | Apr | May | Jun |
|---|---|---|---|---|---|---|
| Forecast store department costs (£) |  |  |  |  |  |  |

11  A time series analysis of sales volumes each quarter for the last three years, 20X6 to 20X8, has revealed that the trend can be estimated by the equation:

$$y = 2,200 + 45x$$

where y is the sales volume and x is the time period.

The seasonal variations for each quarter have been calculated as follows:

Quarter 1        −200
Quarter 2        +500
Quarter 3        +350
Quarter 4        −650

Complete the following for 20X9:

The sales volumes are estimated as:

| | |
|---|---|
| Quarter 1 | |
| Quarter 2 | |
| Quarter 3 | |
| Quarter 4 | |

# chapter 4:
# BUDGET PREPARATION

## chapter coverage 📖

In this chapter we will look at how to prepare budgets.

The topics that are to be covered are:

✍ Standard costs and their use in budgeting

✍ Budget preparation:

 – Sales budget and production resource budgets

 – Capital budget

✍ Integrity of budgets

## RESPONSIBILITY FOR BUDGET PREPARATION

In Chapter 1 we looked at the responsibility centres (cost centres, profit centres and investment centres) which must be appropriately defined in order to construct a budget. Then, in Chapter 3, we looked in closer detail at the content of these specific budgets and forecasting techniques used in their construction. Now, we will consider how the managers or heads of those centres will prepare these specific budgets relating to their responsibility centres. In particular, this involves preparation of the physical plans (materials, labour, production requirements etc) upon which budgets are calculated.

## STANDARD COSTING

Before we look at the preparation of specific budgets, we return to a subject you will have seen in earlier studies, standard costing. A STANDARD COSTING SYSTEM is one in which the expected cost of each unit of production is set out in a standard cost card. As such, standard costing complements budgeting, since budgets are constructed using standard costs per unit, such as material, labour and other production costs, combined with forecasts of sales volumes etc.

As we shall see in later chapters, a budget can be compared with actual performance to monitor and control a business. Broken down, on a line by line basis, this effectively compares standard costs with actual costs, which comparison leads to the calculation of differences (variances). These are investigated by management, and actions taken to rectify any performance issues. The action may lead to the setting of new standards, and so there is a cycle of continuous improvement.

The purposes of a budget in planning and control are therefore facilitated by standard costing.

Variances are discussed in Chapter 7, but here we look at how standard costs are set, which will in turn enable a budget to be constructed.

## HOW STANDARD COSTS ARE SET

A standard cost is the planned unit cost of a product or service.

### Direct materials standard cost

The standard cost for the direct materials in a product is made up of two elements:

- ·the amount of the material expected to be used in one unit
- the price of the material per kg, litre etc

The amount of material required for each unit of a product can be found from the original product specification – the amount originally considered necessary for each unit.

This figure may however be amended over time as the actual amount used in production is monitored.

The basic price of the material can be found from suppliers' quotations or invoices. However when setting the standard the following should also be taken into account:

- general inflation rates

- any foreseen increases in the price of this particular material

- any seasonality in the price

- any discounts available for bulk purchases

- any anticipated scarcity of the material which may mean paying a higher price

- the effect of exchange rates if the material is purchased from a supplier in another country

Therefore the forecasting techniques described in the last chapter may be required here.

## Direct labour standard cost

The standard cost of the direct labour for a product will be made up of:

- the amount of time being spent on each unit of the product
- the hourly wage rate for the employees working on the product

The information for the amount of labour time for each unit may come from time sheets, clock cards and computerised recording systems on the machines being used, or from formal observations of operations known as a work study or more commonly a 'time and motion' study. Factors that should be taken into account when setting the standard for the amount of labour time include:

- the level of skill or training of the labour used on the product
- any anticipated changes in the grade of labour used on the product
- any anticipated changes in work methods or productivity levels
- the effect on productivity of any bonus scheme to be introduced

The hourly rate for the direct labour used on the product can be found from the payroll records. However consideration should be given to:

- anticipated pay rises

- any anticipated changes of the grade of labour to be used

- the effect of any bonus scheme on the labour rate
- whether any overtime is anticipated and whether the premium should be built into the hourly standard cost rate

## Fixed overhead standard cost

The costs of materials per unit and the costs of labour per unit are usually direct costs. There may also be other direct costs of production, which vary per unit produced. However, you will remember from Chapter 1 that overheads (indirect costs) can also be absorbed into the cost per unit.

The fixed overhead standard cost will be based on the total of the budgeted costs for each element of fixed overhead.

## Marginal costing

Under marginal costing, the cost of cost units is made up of their variable costs only and so there is no further calculation to be done. The fixed overheads are treated as period costs and are written off to the income statement as an expense of the period rather than being included in the cost of the cost units.

## Absorption costing

As previously discussed in Chapter 1, under a system of absorption costing the fixed overheads of the business are absorbed into the cost units on the basis of a pre-determined overhead absorption rate. This means that the standard cost of the unit of production is a 'full' cost including its share of **production** overheads.

Therefore, under absorption costing the total budgeted fixed overhead must be used to calculate the standard overhead absorption rate. This is found by dividing the total budgeted fixed overhead by the budgeted activity level, which may be measured in terms of:

- number of units produced
- direct labour hours
- machine hours

The information for determining the total budgeted fixed overhead will come from bills or invoices for past periods plus any anticipated price changes, either based upon specific indices or a general measure of inflation such as the Retail Price Index.

# TYPES OF STANDARD

As you will have seen above when we looked at how standards are set, there are various bases that can be used, for example are expected price rises included in the standard, are the effects of changes in work practices included in the standard etc?

There are therefore a number of different approaches that can be used when determining the standard cost.

## Ideal standards

IDEAL STANDARDS are standard costs which are set on the basis that ideal working conditions apply. Therefore there is no allowance for wastage, inefficiencies or idle time when setting the materials and labour cost standards.

There are two main problems with using ideal standards in budgeting:

**Planning** – if ideal standards are used for planning purposes it is likely that the results will be inaccurate, as the standard does not reflect the reality of working conditions. Therefore if a labour cost standard is set with no allowance for any inefficiency or idle time in operations, the reality is that the operations will take longer or will require more employees than planned for.

**Control** – if ideal standards are compared to actual costs then this will always result in adverse variances as the reality is that there will be some inefficiencies and wastage. This can de-motivate managers and employees who will feel that in reality these standards can never be met and therefore they may stop trying to meet them. A further problem with these adverse variances is that they will be viewed as the norm and be ignored, meaning that any corrective action that might be required is not taken.

## Attainable standards

ATTAINABLE STANDARDS are ones which better reflect the reality of the workplace and which allow for small amounts of normal wastage and inefficiency. An attainable standard is one that is achievable; however, it will only be met if operations are carried out efficiently and cost-effectively.

If attainable standards are well set, then the variances that result will tend to be a mixture of favourable and adverse variances, as sometimes the standard will be exceeded and sometimes it will not quite be met. Attainable standards are often viewed as motivational to managers and employees as they are not out of reach in the way that ideal standards are, but they can be met if all goes to plan.

BPP
LEARNING MEDIA

## Basic standards

BASIC STANDARDS are the historical standard costs, probably the ones set when the product was first produced. As such, they are likely to be out of date, as they will not have taken account of inflation or any changes in working practices.

If basic standards are used to compare to actual costs, then this will tend to result in large variances, both adverse and favourable, depending upon how out of date the basic standard is. These variances will therefore be little more than meaningless. For this reason basic standards are rarely used for variance analysis but may still be kept as historical information alongside other, more up-to-date standards.

---

## Task 1

A production manager is preparing a budget using a materials standard cost which makes no allowance for materials wastage in the production process. The manager says that this encourages workers to be careful with their use of material. The most experienced workers produce wastage of around 2% of the material they use.

Explain the problem with the use of this materials standard cost and suggest how the production manager should set the standard.

---

## PREPARING SALES AND RESOURCE BUDGETS

Chapter 3 detailed the different types of budget which need to be prepared, including the sales budget and all the resource budgets such as production budget, materials usage and purchases budgets, labour usage and cost budgets etc.

The process involves:

- Determining the key budget factor, as discussed in Chapter 3. For the purposes of this chapter it is assumed that the key budget factor is sales, and this determines the sales forecast from which the resource budgets flow. Chapter 6 considers the existence of resources as the limiting or key budget factor.

- Preparing the 'physical' plans in the case of each production resource which fit with sales forecasts eg determining quantities of material required, labour hours or machine hours necessary, taking account of inventory levels, wastage, available labour and production facility hours.

- Taking these physical plans and creating financial plans ie converting the physical quantities into costs, consistent with the organisation's costing system and reflecting standard costs; this gives specific resource budgets.

- Combining all resource budgets, and sales (income) budgets, along with capital and cash budgets to create a master budget for the organisation.

## SALES BUDGET

The quantity of sales in a period is often the limiting factor, in which case the sales forecast is prepared first. Forecasting of the quantity of sales for future periods was considered Chapter 3. Once the expected quantity of sales has been determined, then the anticipated price to be charged for the products or services can be applied to this forecast. This gives the budgeted income, usually referred to as the **sales revenue budget** (in £). From the sales budget, the resource budgets for production can also be prepared.

## HOW IT WORKS

Oliver Engineering produces a single product, the Stephenson. For budgeting purposes the year is divided into 13 four week periods, with five working days each week and therefore 20 working days per period. The forecast sales quantities for the first five periods of 20X0 are as follows:

| | | Units | | |
|---|---|---|---|---|
| Period 1 | Period 2 | Period 3 | Period 4 | Period 5 |
| 10,000 | 12,000 | 15,000 | 13,000 | 11,000 |

The current selling price of the Stephenson is £40 although it is anticipated that there will be a 10% price increase in Period 4.

The sales revenue budget can now be prepared.

| | Forecast revenue £ |
|---|---|
| Period 1 (10,000 × £40) | 400,000 |
| Period 2 (12,000 × £40) | 480,000 |
| Period 3 (15,000 × £40) | 600,000 |
| Period 4 (13,000 × £44) | 572,000 |
| Period 5 (11,000 × £44) | 484,000 |
| | 2,536,000 |

# PRODUCTION BUDGET

Once the sales budget has been prepared the next stage is to prepare the PRODUCTION BUDGET in finished goods units. There are two factors that will affect the amount of production that is required:

- any changes in inventory levels of finished goods that are anticipated
- the level of defective finished goods that are forecast.

## Changes in finished goods inventory levels

If all of the output from the production process is made up of good products that can be sold and there is to be no change in the levels of finished goods held in inventory, then the amount that must be produced is the same as the quantity of forecast sales. However if the level of finished goods held in inventory is to change then this will affect the quantity that is to be produced.

Once the sales quantity has been determined then the production quantity will be calculated as:

| | |
|---|---:|
| Sales quantity | X |
| Less: opening inventories of finished goods | (X) |
| Add: closing inventories of finished goods required | X |
| Production quantity | X |

The opening inventories of finished goods are deducted from the sales quantity as we already have these in inventory and therefore do not need to make them. However we do need to make the goods that are to be held as closing inventory of finished goods, therefore this must be added in to determine the production quantity.

---

## Task 2

A business has budgeted sales for the following period of 3,500 units of its product. The inventories at the start of the period are 800 units and these are to be reduced to 600 units at the end of the period. What is the production quantity for the period?

[        ] units

---

## Defective output

In many production processes it will be accepted that there will be a certain level of NORMAL LOSS or faulty production. This normal loss is the percentage of finished goods that it is anticipated will not be saleable, due to some defect from the production process. This percentage will normally have been determined by quality control procedures and sampling.

If there is an anticipated level of defective production, then the production quantity must be increased to ensure that there are enough units of the product available for sale, after the defective products have been deducted. Therefore the production quantity must be adjusted as follows:

| | |
|---|---:|
| Sales quantity | X |
| Less: opening inventories of finished goods | (X) |
| Add: closing inventories of finished goods required | X |
| Quantity required to meet sales demand | X |
| Add: anticipated defective units | X |
| Production quantity | X |

# HOW IT WORKS

Continuing with Oliver Engineering's budgets for the next five periods we know the forecast sales quantities are as follows:

*Units*

| *Period 1* | *Period 2* | *Period 3* | *Period 4* | *Period 5* |
|:---:|:---:|:---:|:---:|:---:|
| 10,000 | 12,000 | 15,000 | 13,000 | 11,000 |

Remember that each period is made up of four weeks with five working days in each week. Closing inventories of finished goods are to be enough to cover five days of sales demand for the next period. Past experience has also shown that 2% of production is defective and has to be scrapped with no scrap value. The inventory of finished goods at the start of Period 1 is expected to be 3,000 units.

We will firstly determine the levels of finished goods inventories required at the end of each period. The finished goods inventory levels are determined by finding five days of sales demand for the next period:

| Period 1 | 12,000 units × 5 days/20 days | = | 3,000 units |
| Period 2 | 15,000 units × 5 days/20 days | = | 3,750 units |
| Period 3 | 13,000 units × 5 days/20 days | = | 3,250 units |
| Period 4 | 11,000 units × 5 days/20 days | = | 2,750 units |

We can now start to forecast the production quantities that are required for the first four periods of next year. Remember that the closing inventory of finished goods at the end of each period will be the opening inventory of finished goods at the start of the following period:

## Production budget – units

| | Period 1 | Period 2 | Period 3 | Period 4 |
|---|---|---|---|---|
| Sales quantity | 10,000 | 12,000 | 15,000 | 13,000 |
| Less: opening inventories | (3,000) | (3,000) | (3,750) | (3,250) |
| Add: closing inventories | 3,000 | 3,750 | 3,250 | 2,750 |
| Good production quantity | 10,000 | 12,750 | 14,500 | 12,500 |

Note that when there is no change in inventory levels (Period 1), the quantity of good production is the same as that for sales demand. However when inventory levels are increasing (Period 2), the good production quantity must be larger than the sales quantity, and when inventory levels are decreasing (Periods 3 and 4), the good production quantity is less than the sales quantity.

We must now, however, recognise that not all of the production is good production and that it is anticipated that 2% of the production will be defective. Therefore, for Period 1, we need 10,000 units after defectives as good production, so we must produce more than this – there must be 10,000 good units left once the defective products have been scrapped. The 10,000 good units therefore represent 98% of total production and defectives 2% of total production.

The calculation required to determine the additional amount of production necessary in Period 1 is therefore:

10,000 units × 2/98 = 205 units

Therefore in order to have 10,000 good units at the end of the production run it will be necessary to produce 10,205 units.

We can now produce the final production budget for the next four periods:

## Production budget – units

|  | Period 1 | Period 2 | Period 3 | Period 4 |
|---|---|---|---|---|
| Sales quantity | 10,000 | 12,000 | 15,000 | 13,000 |
| Less: opening inventories | (3,000) | (3,000) | (3,750) | (3,250) |
| Add: closing inventories | 3,000 | 3,750 | 3,250 | 2,750 |
| Good production quantity (98%) | 10,000 | 12,750 | 14,500 | 12,500 |
| Defective production (2%) (2/98 × 10,000 etc)) | 205 | 261 | 296 | 256 |
| Total production quantity (100%) | 10,205 | 13,011 | 14,796 | 12,756 |

---

## Task 3

A production process has normal losses of 5% of all completed output. If production of 4,200 good units is required, how many units must be produced in total?

[          ]   units

---

## MATERIALS USAGE BUDGET AND MATERIALS PURCHASING BUDGET

The next stage in the process is to determine the amount of materials required for the level of production for the period in the MATERIALS USAGE BUDGET, expressed in materials units. This must be determined using a two stage calculation.

First, the materials to be used in the production during each period must be determined. The amount of material required for each unit of the product must be determined and this will normally come from the standard cost card. This quantity per unit will then be applied to the number of units to be produced, in order to determine the amount of material required to be used in production in each period.

## Materials wastage

In many production processes there will be a degree of wastage or normal loss as materials input into the process are lost. This may be in the form of shavings, off-cuttings or, in some processes, evaporation.

This wastage must be taken into account when determining the amount of materials that are required in order to produce the quantity of products set out in the production budget.

# HOW IT WORKS

Continuing the Oliver Engineering example, we know that the production quantities required for each of the first four periods of the year are as follows:

**Production budget – units**

| Period 1 | Period 2 | Period 3 | Period 4 |
|----------|----------|----------|----------|
| 10,205 | 13,011 | 14,796 | 12,756 |

From the standard cost card it is determined that each unit of production requires 2 kg of material X. However we also know that the production process has a normal loss of 20% of the materials input into the process.

This means that although each unit of product requires 2 kg of material X, this represents only 80% of the actual amount required. 20% more than 2 kg per unit must be input into the process. The amount of material X required for each unit is therefore:

2 kg x 100/80 = 2.5 kg

The amount of normal loss can be calculated separately as:

$$2 \text{ kg} \times \frac{20}{80} = 0.5 \text{ kg}$$

The materials usage budget can now be prepared:

**Materials usage budget**

| | Period 1 | Period 2 | Period 3 | Period 4 |
|---|----------|----------|----------|----------|
| Quantity of production | 10,205 | 13,011 | 14,796 | 12,756 |
| Materials usage (Quantity × 2.5 kg) | 25,513 kg | 32,528 kg | 36,990 kg | 31,890 kg |

## Task 4

A business requires 15,400 units of production in a period and each unit uses 5 kg of materials. The production process has a normal loss of 10% during the production process. What is the total amount of the material required for the period (to the nearest kg)?

| | kg

### Materials purchasing budget

Once the materials usage budget has been set, then this can be translated into the MATERIALS PURCHASING BUDGET in units of materials and £. The amount of materials that must be purchased will be based upon the materials usage budget but will be affected by any required changes in the levels of inventory of the material.

Just as with the production budget, the opening and closing levels of materials inventories must be taken into account, in order to determine how many materials must be purchased during each period. The quantity of purchases will be determined as follows:

| | |
|---|---|
| Materials usage | X |
| Less: opening inventory of materials | (X) |
| Add: closing inventory of materials | X |
| Quantity to be purchased | X |

The materials that must be purchased each period are those that are required for production in the period, taken from the materials usage budget, less the opening inventories of material which are already on hand, plus the materials that are required at the end of the period as closing materials inventories).

Finally once the quantity to be purchased is known, then the anticipated purchase price can be applied to this to determine the materials purchasing budget in terms of value.

## HOW IT WORKS

We know the materials usage budget for Oliver Engineering is as follows:

**Materials usage budget**

|  | Period 1 | Period 2 | Period 3 | Period 4 |
|---|---|---|---|---|
| Materials usage | 25,513 kg | 32,528 kg | 36,990 kg | 31,890 kg |

It is the policy of the company to hold enough materials to cover 10 days of the following period's production. The inventory level at the start of Period 1 is 12,000 kg of material and the materials usage in Period 5 is calculated as 28,000 kg.

First, we must determine the inventory levels of materials required at the end of each period. This has to be enough to cover 10 days out of the 20 days of production for the next period. The closing inventories of materials are as follows:

| Period 1 | 32,528 kg × 10 days/20 days | = | 16,264 kg |
|---|---|---|---|
| Period 2 | 36,990 kg × 10 days/20 days | = | 18,495 kg |
| Period 3 | 31,890 kg × 10 days/20 days | = | 15,945 kg |
| Period 4 | 28,000 kg × 10 days/20 days | = | 14,000 kg |

Now the materials purchasing budget can be prepared, first in units.

**Materials purchasing budget – kg**

|  | Period 1 | Period 2 | Period 3 | Period 4 |
|---|---|---|---|---|
| Materials usage | 25,513 | 32,528 | 36,990 | 31,890 |
| Less: opening inventories of materials | (12,000) | (16,264) | (18,495) | (15,945) |
| Add: closing inventories of materials | 16,264 | 18,495 | 15,945 | 14,000 |
| Materials to be purchased | 29,777 | 34,759 | 34,440 | 29,945 |

The cost of each kg of material X has been and will continue to be £5, therefore the materials purchasing budget in value can also be set by taking the quantity to be purchased for each period and applying the unit price. For example, for Period 1 the 29,777 kg must be purchased at a cost of £5 per kg – £148,885.

**Materials purchasing budget – £**

| Period 1 | Period 2 | Period 3 | Period 4 |
|----------|----------|----------|----------|
| £ | £ | £ | £ |
| 148,885 | 173,795 | 172,200 | 149,725 |

---

## Task 5

A business requires 124,000 litres of a material for its next month's production. The material costs £2.60 per litre and current inventories are 14,000 litres. The business aims to increase its inventory levels by 15% by the end of the month. What is the budgeted cost of materials for the month?

£ [ ]

---

# LABOUR USAGE BUDGET AND LABOUR COST BUDGET

Once the production budget has been set, then it is necessary to determine the number of hours of labour which are required for the production level in the LABOUR USAGE BUDGET in hours. This can be determined by referring to the standard cost card which will state the number of hours of labour required for each unit of product.

### Idle time

There is however a further problem that you may have to deal with. Although there is a standard time that each unit of the product requires, there may also be non-productive or IDLE TIME. Idle time is made up of hours for which employees are at work and for which they must be paid but these hours are not spent in producing the products of the business. For example, health and safety legislation lays down certain rules regarding break times that machine operators must take.

Therefore, if there is to be idle time built into the budget a greater number of hours will need to be paid than the standard time, in order to produce the required number of units.

## HOW IT WORKS

The standard cost card for the Stephenson, produced by Oliver Engineering, shows that the standard time for production of one unit is 1 grade A labour hour. However due to necessary break times only 80% of the time paid is productive, so there is 20% idle time.

To calculate the number of hours of labour required, again the starting point will be the production budget showing the number of units to be produced in each period. However the number of hours that must be paid in total in order to produce one unit is:

1 hour × 100/80 = 1.25 hours

The idle time per product can be calculated as 1 hour $\times \dfrac{20}{80}$ = 0.25 hours.

**Production budget – units**

|                         | Period 1 | Period 2 | Period 3 | Period 4 |
|-------------------------|----------|----------|----------|----------|
| Quantity of production  | 10,205   | 13,011   | 14,796   | 12,756   |

**Labour usage budget – hours**

|               | Period 1    | Period 2    | Period 3    | Period 4    |
|---------------|-------------|-------------|-------------|-------------|
| Labour hours  | 12,756 hrs  | 16,264 hrs  | 18,495 hrs  | 15,945 hrs  |

## Task 6

A product requires 10 labour hours for each unit. However 10% of working hours are idle time. How long must an employee be paid for in order to produce 20 units (to the nearest hour)?

☐ hours

### Labour cost budget

Once we know the number of hours to be worked in each period, then the LABOUR COST BUDGET in £ can be set by applying the wage rate to the number of hours. However care must be taken with any overtime hours that are to be worked.

## HOW IT WORKS

The labour usage budget for Oliver Engineering is as follows:

### Labour usage budget – hours

|  | Period 1 | Period 2 | Period 3 | Period 4 |
|---|---|---|---|---|
| Labour hours | 12,756 hrs | 16,264 hrs | 18,495 hrs | 15,945 hrs |

The grade A labour are paid at a rate of £9 per hour but only 16,000 hours can be worked within the normal working hours. Any hours above 16,000 are overtime hours that are paid at time and a third.

We will now produce the figures for the **labour cost budget**:

| Period 1 | 12,756 hours × £9 | £114,804 |
|---|---|---|
| Period 2 | (16,000 hours × £9) + (264 hours × £12) | £147,168 |
| Period 3 | (16,000 hours × £9) + (2,495 hours × £12) | £173,940 |
| Period 4 | 15,945 hours × £9 | £143,505 |

The labour cost budget will look like this:

### Labour cost budget – £

| Period 1 | Period 2 | Period 3 | Period 4 |
|---|---|---|---|
| £114,804 | £147,168 | £173,940 | £143,505 |

### Labour efficiency

It is also possible for a situation to arise where the standard hours for labour are taken from the standard cost card but the work force is known now to work more efficiently than these standard hours. Therefore there will be fewer hours required for production than are indicated by the standard cost card.

## HOW IT WORKS

Let us suppose that a business is to produce 100,000 units of its product in a period and the standard cost card shows that each unit requires four labour hours. However it is known that due to their skill level the workforce is producing at 110% efficiency. Therefore the number of hours of labour required to produce the 100,000 units will be calculated as follows:

100,000 units × 4 hours × 100/110 = 363,636 hours

## Task 7

A business wishes to produce 12,000 units of its product with a standard labour time of six hours per unit. However the workforce are currently working at 120% efficiency. How long will it take to produce the units required?

| | hours

## OVERHEADS BUDGET

In a manufacturing context, the main budgeting effort will be spent determining the budgets for sales revenue, production, materials and labour. However budgets must also be set for the overheads and production facilities related costs, which can include, for example, factory rent and costs of running machinery. Overheads will also include depreciation charges.

As we have already seen in Chapter 1 overheads may be variable, semi-variable, fixed or stepped costs.

In order to set the budget for the overheads the nature of each expense and its cost behaviour must be fully understood.

**Variable costs** – these vary directly with the cost of production, therefore the total amount of the cost will be – unit variable cost × number of units

**Semi-variable costs** – the variable and fixed cost elements must be determined, usually using the hi lo method (as explained in Chapter 3)

**Fixed costs** – these will remain the same whatever the level of production provided it is within the relevant range

**Stepped costs** – these will be fixed for a certain range of production levels and will then increase in one step to a higher fixed amount – the correct fixed amount must be estimated for the anticipated production level.

## HOW IT WORKS

Oliver Engineering is now trying to produce estimates for its overheads for the first four periods of the year.

The cost of machine power is felt to be a true variable cost and it has been estimated that each Stephenson uses £2.40 of machine power.

The cost of the maintenance department has been estimated at £12,000 if 8,000 units are produced and £16,000 if 12,000 units are produced.

The factory rent is £104,000 for each year.

The cost of production supervisors depends upon the level of activity within the factory. For an activity level of up to 12,000 units the production supervisors' costs are £2,000 per period, up to 14,000 units this increases to £3,000 and for activity up to 16,000 units the cost rises to £4,000 per period.

Before we can prepare the overhead budget we must use the hi lo method to determine the variable and fixed elements of the maintenance department costs.

## Maintenance department costs

|  | Production level | Total cost |
|---|---|---|
|  | Units | £ |
| Level 1 | 8,000 | 12,000 |
| Level 2 | 12,000 | 16,000 |
| Increase | 4,000 | 4,000 |

Variable cost = £4,000/4,000 units = £1 per unit

At 8,000 units:

|  | £ |
|---|---|
| Variable cost 8,000 × £1 | 8,000 |
| Fixed element (bal fig) | 4,000 |
| Total cost | 12,000 |

We can produce the budgeted figures for each of these overheads based as usual on the production budget:

Machine power is a variable cost = units × £2.40

Maintenance department is a semi-variable cost = (units × £1) + £4,000

Rent is a fixed cost = £104,000 × 4/52 = £8,000 per period

Supervisors' costs are a stepped cost:

| | |
|---|---|
| ≤ 12,000 units | = £2,000 |
| ≤ 14,000 units | = £3,000 |
| ≤ 16,000 units | = £4,000 |

## Production budget – units

| | Period 1 | Period 2 | Period 3 | Period 4 |
|---|---|---|---|---|
| | 10,205 | 13,011 | 14,796 | 12,756 |

**Overhead budget – £**

| | Period 1 | Period 2 | Period 3 | Period 4 |
|---|---|---|---|---|
| Machine power @ £2.40/unit | 24,492 | 31,226 | 35,510 | 30,614 |
| Maintenance department @ £1/unit + £4,000 | 14,205 | 17,011 | 18,796 | 16,756 |
| Rent – £8,000 per period | 8,000 | 8,000 | 8,000 | 8,000 |
| Supervisors' costs | 2,000 | 3,000 | 4,000 | 3,000 |
| | 48,697 | 59,237 | 66,306 | 58,370 |

## PREPARING A BUDGETED OPERATING STATEMENT

Having prepared detailed budgets many organisations put them all together to produce a BUDGETED OPERATING STATEMENT (or budgeted income statement) for the period in question. This provides managers with an overview of their expected performance.

A MASTER BUDGET is completed by adding a budgeted statement of financial position and a CASH BUDGET.

The statement of financial position reflects the assets and liabilities of the business. The assessor has stated that a full statement of financial position is unlikely to be tested but elements such as non-current assets could be tested. We consider non-current assets when looking at capital budgets later in this chapter.

Cash budgets will be considered in the next chapter.

Here we concentrate on the budgeted operating statement.

## HOW IT WORKS

Oliver Engineering now wants to produce a budgeted operating statement at the end of each of Periods 1 to 4. We will look at Period 1 here.

When producing a budgeted operating statement we must be careful about opening and closing inventories. In the case of Oliver Engineering, opening and closing inventories of finished Stephensons are 3,000, so because there is no change in inventory levels, there is no need to include them in cost of sales. However, we know that there is a change in materials inventories from 12,000 at the start of Period 1 to 16,264 at the end of Period 1.

In the budgeted operating statement below, we have taken the materials used to produce the finished goods sold, at the cost of £5 per kg, as the cost of materials. This comes straight from the materials usage budget. When there are different prices for materials in inventory and purchased, a different approach is required. In such a case, we could have arrived at the figure as follows:

|  | £ |
|---|---|
| Materials at start of Period 1 (12,000 kg x £5) | 60,000 |
| Materials purchased (29,777 kg x £5) | 148,885 |
| Less: closing inventory of materials (16,264 kg x £5) | (81,320) |
| Cost of materials used | 127,565 |

**Oliver Engineering – budgeted operating statement for Period 1**

|  | £ | £ |
|---|---|---|
| Revenue (from sales budget) 10,000 units x £40 | | 400,000 |
| Less: cost of sales (10,205 units) | | |
| Materials (from materials usage budget) 25,513 kg x £5 | 127,565 | |
| Labour (from labour cost budget) | 114,804 | |
| Overheads (from overhead budget) | 48,697 | |
| | | 291,066 |
| Budgeted gross profit for Period 1 | | 108,934 |

In an assessment, be careful not to include irrelevant data such as profit on sale of non-current assets, or increase in administration overhead, in gross profit. These would alter the net profit, but feature after gross profit. The same principles apply regarding where to place various expenditure in a budgeted income statement as to an actual one.

## Using the budgeted operating statement

The overview provided by a budgeted operating statement allows the organisation's managers to assess whether the expected performance is acceptable in terms of the organisation's overall objectives. If this is not the case, then they can plan to make adjustments to various areas of activity in order to try to meet their objectives. The same techniques can be applied to operating statements or income statements prepared from actual figures. In particular various performance indicators can be applied to both. We will look at the use of performance indicators in greater detail in Chapter 8 of this Text.

# HOW IT WORKS

When they see the budgeted operating statement for Period 1, Oliver Engineering's managers realise that it fails to meet their objectives of a gross profit percentage (measured as gross profit / revenue × 100%) of 35%. The relevant operational managers work on various ideas to improve results, and come up with the following:

(a) Increase selling price by 5% (this is not expected to have any effect on sales volume)

(b) Using bulk discounts, reduce the unit cost per kg of material by 7%

(c) Improve training and efficiency of labour, so labour cost is reduced by 3%

(d) Cut £10,000 from overheads

You are to restate Oliver Engineering's budgeted operating statement for Period 1, and state whether the organisation's objective can be met using these measures.

**Oliver Engineering – restated budgeted operating statement for Period 1**

|  | Original | Change | Restated |
|---|---|---|---|
|  | £ |  | £ |
| Revenue | 400,000 | ×<br>1.05 | 420,000 |
| Cost of sales |  |  |  |
| Materials | 127,565 | × 0.93 | 118,635 |
| Labour | 114,804 | × 0.97 | 111,360 |
| Overheads | 48,697 | - £10,000 | 38,697 |
|  | 291,066 |  | 268,692 |
| Gross profit | 108,934 |  | 151,308 |
|  |  |  |  |
| Gross profit percentage % | 27% |  | 36% |

The measures suggested should achieve the desired improvement in gross profit percentage from 27% to 36%.

## CAPITAL BUDGETS

Capital budgets were mentioned in Chapter 3. A CAPITAL BUDGET is a budget for the cost of non-current assets, ie for the purchase of non-current assets. Some non-current assets are purchased by one payment of the total cost. However as non-current assets are major items of expenditure, the payment for them may often be spread over a number of instalments. Most capital budgets will show these payments in the relevant periods.

As mentioned earlier in this chapter, a master budget includes a budgeted statement of financial position, showing budgeted assets and liabilities at the end of the period of the budget. The statement will therefore include a figure, or figures, for budgeted non-current assets. The figure represents the expected carrying amount of non-current assets at the end of the period, and so will comprise existing assets, plus forecast purchases (as featured in the capital budget), less forecast disposals, less depreciation ie the usual principles of accounting for non-current assets will apply.

## HOW IT WORKS

The senior management of Oliver Engineering have authorised the purchase of a new computer for the sales office and some new machinery. The computer has a cost of £2,500 and is to be paid for by cheque in Period 3. The machinery costs £500,000 and is to be paid for in instalments of £250,000 each in Period 1 and Period 4. We will now produce the capital budget.

### Capital budget

|  | Period 1 £ | Period 2 £ | Period 3 £ | Period 4 £ |
|---|---|---|---|---|
| Computer |  |  | 2,500 |  |
| Machinery | 250,000 | ____ | ____ | 250,000 |
|  | 250,000 | – | 2,500 | 250,000 |

## INTEGRITY OF BUDGETS

As was the case for the setting of standard costs, a budget must be realistic and motivational. Managers must have confidence in the budget's integrity otherwise it will be ignored, as not achievable or not appropriate. In order to achieve budget integrity, the following steps should be taken.

- Draft budgets should be planned and then agreed with all parties. In Chapter 2 we considered the budget setting process, with budgets being re-worked perhaps a number of times. The final version should be agreed by both the senior management and the manager of the responsibility centre concerned.

- Review of budgets. The managers of the responsibility centres should check and reconcile figures in the budget to ensure their accuracy and consistency. This may require revisions to the budget throughout the period to which it refers. The revisions may be required if actual results highlight an unrealistic plan or if the underlying forecasts or planning assumptions have to change because of external factors. The budgets must then be recalculated.

# CHAPTER OVERVIEW

- A standard costing system allows the standard cost of production to be compared to the actual costs and variances calculated.

- The use of standard costs complements budgets, together forming a system of planning and control

- The direct materials standard cost is set by determining the estimated quantity to be used per unit and the estimated price per material unit

- The direct labour standard cost is set by determining the estimated labour time per unit and the estimated rate per hour

- The fixed overhead standard cost is determined by finding a realistic estimate of each of the elements of the fixed overhead. The standards that can be set include ideal standards, attainable standards and basic standards

- The sales budget will normally be the first budget to be prepared, if it is the key budget factor, showing the anticipated sales in both units and value

- From the sales budget, the production budget will be prepared taking into account planned changes in inventory levels for finished goods and the anticipated level of defective finished goods

- The production budget is then used to prepare the materials and labour budgets in terms of both units and value

- The materials usage budget is based upon the production for the period but must take account of materials wastage during the production process

- The materials purchasing budget is based upon the materials usage budget but with adjustment for planned changes in inventories of materials – once the quantities of purchases are known, then they can be valued by applying the anticipated purchase price per unit

- The labour usage budget is based upon the production budget and the standard hours for each unit – however any idle time or labour efficiency must also be built into the number of hours required to complete the planned production. Once the hours have been determined, the labour cost budget can be calculated using the hourly rates of labour, taking account of any overtime hours required

- Budgets will also be set for overheads – in order to try to estimate the expected overhead or expense, the behaviour of the cost must be taken into account: variable, semi-variable, fixed or stepped

CHAPTER OVERVIEW (Continued)

- Detailed budgets may be summarised into a budgeted operating statement (or budgeted income statement) for the period, in order to provide managers with an overview of their expected performance. If this is not acceptable, then they can plan to make adjustments to various areas of activity in order to try to meet their objectives.

- A master budget is completed by adding a budgeted statement of financial position and a cash budget to the budgeted operating statement.

- A capital budget will be prepared for planned expenditure on non-current assets

- The integrity of budgets is increased by planning and agreeing budgets with all parties concerned at the outset, and by reviewing budgets, and revising them if necessary, on an ongoing basis

## Keywords

**Standard costing system** – a system which assigns standard costs to each cost unit and allows a comparison of standard costs to actual costs and the calculation of variances

**Variances** – the difference between the standard costs and the actual costs for a period

**Ideal standards** – standards set on the basis of perfect working conditions

**Attainable standards** – standards into which elements of normal wastage and inefficiency are built

**Basic standards** – historical standards that are normally set when the product is initially produced

**Production budget** – (finished goods units) budget for the number of units of production

**Normal loss** – the expected lost production or material wastage through defective goods or the production process

**Materials usage budget** – (units of materials) the budget for the units of materials to be used in the production process

**Materials purchasing budget** – (units and £) the budget for the quantity and value of materials purchases required

**Labour usage budget** – (hours) the budget for the number of labour hours required for the planned level of production

**Idle time** – non-productive hours that are worked and paid for

**Efficiency** – the workforce is known to work more or less efficiently than the hours indicated by the standard cost card

**Labour cost budget** – the cost of the labour hours required for the planned production

**Overheads budget** – the budget for indirect expenses of the business

**Budgeted operating statement** – a summary of the detailed budgets for the period, which provides managers with an overview of expected performance.

**Master budget** – a summary budget comprising a budgeted operating statement, budgeted statement of financial position and a cash budget

**Capital budget** – the expenditure planned on non-current assets

## TEST YOUR LEARNING

1   Complete the following production budget for an organisation's product. Closing inventory is to be 30% of the next period's sales. Sales in Period 4 will be 4,200 units.

Units of product

|  | Period 1 | Period 2 | Period 3 |
|---|---|---|---|
| Opening inventory | 1,140 | | |
| Production | | | |
| Units required | | | |
| Sales | 3,800 | 4,000 | 4,500 |
| Closing inventory | | | |
| Units required | | | |

2   For the organisation in Test 1, quality control procedures have shown that 5% of the completed production are found to be defective and unsellable.

Complete the following:

Units of product

|  | Period 1 | Period 2 | Period 3 |
|---|---|---|---|
| Units required (from Test 1) | | | |
| Actual production | | | |

3   The production budget for Product B shows 12,000 units in Period 1 and 11,000 units in Period 2.

Each completed unit of the product requires 4 kg of material. However, the production process has a normal loss of 10% of materials input. Inventory levels of materials are held in order to be sufficient to cover 35% of actual usage for the following period. The materials held in inventory at the beginning of Period 1 are 18,600 kg.

The price of each kilogram of material is £4.80.

Complete the following for Period 1:

- the materials usage budget in units is ⬚
- the materials purchasing budget in units is ⬚
- the materials purchasing budget in £ is ⬚

**4** Budgeted sales of Product P for the next quarter are 42,000 units.

Finished goods in inventory at the start of the quarter are 7,000 units and closing inventory will be 8,334.

The standard cost card indicates that each unit should take 3.5 labour hours, however it is anticipated that, due to technical problems, during the quarter the workforce will only be working at 92% efficiency.

The production budget for the quarter is [          ] units.

The labour usage budget for the quarter is [          ] hours.

**5** The production budget is as follows:

| Quarter 2 | Quarter 3 |
|---|---|
| 16,020 units | 17,850 units |

The details of overheads are:

*Light and heat* – this is estimated at a rate of £4.80 per unit of production in each quarter.

*Maintenance department* – previous periods have shown that at a production level of 13,000 units the maintenance department costs totalled £68,500 and at a production level of 17,000 units the costs totalled £86,500.

*Leased machinery* – some of the machinery is leased, and for production levels up to 17,000 units the leasing cost is £15,600 per quarter. However if production exceeds this level, then a further machine must be leased at a quarterly cost of £4,800.

*Rent and rates* – the rent and rates are £84,000 per annum.

Complete the following:

Overhead budget

| Overhead cost £ | Quarter 2 | Quarter 3 |
|---|---|---|
| Light and heat | | |
| Maintenance | | |
| Leasing | | |
| Rent and rates | | |

6   Sales of a product in the next four week period are expected to be 280 units. At the beginning of the period 30 units is held in inventory, although the budgeted closing inventory is expected to be five units.

Each unit of the product requires two hours of grade O labour and three hours of grade R labour. Grade O labour is paid £15 per hour, whereas grade R labour (16 workers) receive a guaranteed weekly wage of £280.

A unit of the product requires 7 kg of material. The expected price per kg of the material is £50.

For the following four week period, what is the

(a)   Production budget? [        ] units

(b)   Materials usage budget? [        ] kg costing £ [        ]

(c)   Labour cost budget? £ [        ]

7   Two products, J and K, are produced from the same material. The data below relates to Period 1.

(a)   Budgeted production     J                          450 units

                               K                          710 units

(b)   Material requirements   J                          25 kgs
      per unit

                               K                          40 kgs

(c)   Opening inventory of    40,000 kgs
      material

(d)   Closing inventory of    27,359 kgs
      material

The purchases budget (in kgs) for Period 1 is [        ]

8   Two products, X and Y, are manufactured. Budgeted production levels in Period 7 are 420 units of X, 590 units of Y.

Each X requires five labour hours, each Y four labour hours.

There are 25 production workers, each of whom works a 35-hour week. There are five weeks in each period.

The rate of pay per hour for production employees is £10. Any overtime is paid at 125% of basic rate.

(a)   What are the budgeted labour hours to be worked during Period 7, including any overtime? [＿＿＿] hours

(b)   What is the cost of labour budget for Period 7? £ [＿＿＿]

9   Four different services are offered to clients. The budgeted figures for the coming year are as follows:

|  | Service 1 | Service 2 | Service 3 | Service 4 |
|---|---|---|---|---|
| Charge per hour to clients | £20 | £25 | £30 | £40 |
| Budgeted chargeable hours | 10,584 | 6,804 | 5,292 | 7,560 |
| Payment per hour to employee | £8 | £10 | £11 | £14 |

Staff are expected to work a 35 hour week for 48 weeks per year. 10% of their time is non-chargeable. It is company policy to employ part-time staff (who work 17.5 hours per week for 48 weeks per year) as well as full-time staff, but a maximum of one part-time member of staff per service stream.

Complete the following (part time employees count as 0.5).

|  | Service 1 | Service 2 | Service 3 | Service 4 |
|---|---|---|---|---|
| Revenue budget (£) | | | | |
| Number of employees | | | | |
| Direct wages budget (£) | | | | |

**10** A company has constructed the following budgets about the coming month.

| | | |
|---|---|---|
| Selling price | £6.50 per unit | |
| Direct materials | 2 kg per unit | £0.75 per kg |
| Direct labour | 6 minutes per unit | £12 per hour |
| Fixed production overheads | £16,000 | |
| Car purchase | £20,000 | |

Budgeted production is 25,000 units and all units are sold in the month of production. No inventories of material are held.

Complete the following budgeted operating statement and capital budget.

**Budgeted operating statement (total absorption basis)**

| | £ | £ |
|---|---|---|
| Revenue | | |
| Less cost of sales: | | |
| Direct materials | | |
| Direct labour | | |
| Production overheads | | |
| Cost of sales | | |
| Gross profit | | |

**Capital budget**

| | £ |
|---|---|
| Capital purchase | |
| Total | |

# chapter 5:
# PREPARING CASH BUDGETS

―――― **chapter coverage** 📖 ――――

In this chapter we will look at how to prepare cash budgets.

The topics that are to be covered are:

✍  Format of a cash budget

✍  Sales receipts

✍  Payment for purchases

✍  Other cash payments and receipts

✍  Overdraft interest

✍  Payments for materials and labour in a manufacturing business

In Chapter 4, we considered budget preparation in terms of a business's income and expenditure, that is in terms of profit.

As you will be aware from your earlier studies, cash is as important to the survival of a business as profit. It follows therefore that management also need to plan and control cash flows (in and out), not just income and expenditure. This is done by preparing a cash budget.

You need to be able to explain the construction of, and prepare, cash budgets/forecasts.

## What is a cash flow forecast?

A CASH FLOW FORECAST is a method of determining the expected net cash flow for a future period and the expected cash or overdraft balance at the end of that future period. Cash flow forecasts can be prepared daily, weekly, monthly, quarterly or even annually depending upon the amount of detail required by management and the amounts of cash involved. Cash flow forecasts are often also referred to as CASH BUDGETS.

Note that the terms cash budget, cash flow budget and cash flow forecast are often used interchangeably.

There are two main types of cash flow forecast:

- a RECEIPTS AND PAYMENTS CASH BUDGET

- a STATEMENT OF CASH FLOWS that reflects an organisation's income statement and financial position such as might be found in statutory financial statements.

Note that the first method, the cash receipts and payments method, of preparing a cash forecast or budget is more common than the second method, and we concentrate on this here. Towards the end of the chapter, we look at techniques which use the balances in the statement of financial position such as receivables and payables to determine cash flows.

## Receipts and payments cash budget

In this type of cash flow forecast, the expected receipts for a period are listed and totalled, as are the expected payments in the period. The NET CASH FLOW is determined by deducting the payments from the receipts and this net movement is applied to the opening cash balance in order to find the anticipated closing cash balance.

A typical cash budget of this type is shown below:

|  | March £ | April £ | May £ |
|---|---|---|---|
| *Receipts* |  |  |  |
| Cash sales | X | X | X |
| Receipts from credit customers | X | X | X |
| Proceeds from sale of non-current assets | — | X | — |
| *Total receipts (a)* | X | X | X |
| *Payments* |  |  |  |
| Cash purchases | X | X | X |
| Payments to credit suppliers | X | X | X |
| Wages | X | X | X |
| Operating expenses | X | X | X |
| Purchase of non-current assets | X |  |  |
| Dividend | — | — | X |
| *Total payments (b)* | X | X | X |
| *Net cash flow (a–b)* | X | X | X |
| *Opening cash balance* | X | X | X |
| *Closing cash balance* | X | X | X |

Note that the closing cash balance each month becomes the opening cash balance at the start of the following month. This means it is important to periodically revisit the cash forecast and update it so that:

- the opening balance used is always the actual balance at the end of the previous period

- any changes in assumptions or conditions (such as new credit terms for customers or decreases in anticipated sales demand) are incorporated.

The detailed lines making up the receipts and payments will differ from business to business, depending upon the nature of their business and transactions. For example, for a retail business the cash flows will involve the purchase of goods which are then resold either for cash or on credit. However in a manufacturing business the materials required for production will have to be purchased and processed and then the finished goods will be sold.

Whatever the nature of the business, you should realise that the items included in the cash budget above are linked to the other budgets and forecasts, even though there is often a time lag between the related transaction in one budget and the cash movement in the cash budget.

For example:

- receipts from credit customers are linked to the forecast sales

- payments for assets purchased are linked to the capital budget

- payments to credit suppliers are linked to both budgets for materials purchases and for other expenses.

The cash budget above shows the cash flows for three months; in your assessment you may be required to complete the budget for one period only eg the month of April. However, as we will see, this may require information about sales and purchases in the periods before and after April, depending on when cash is received for sales, and when cash is paid for purchases.

## SALES RECEIPTS

As we saw in previous chapters, in the sales budget the number of units expected to be sold, and the sales price, is forecast for a period but cash inflows from these sales do not necessarily occur in the same month.

Most businesses will have a mixture of cash sales and sales on credit. When preparing the cash budget, the starting point will be the total expected sales for the period, which will probably be provided by the sales department. Of these total sales a certain amount, either reported as an absolute amount or as a percentage of total sales, will be cash sales, which means that the cash inflow will take place at the same time as the sale.

Sales on credit means that the cash for the sale will be received at some point in time after the sale, which might be within the credit terms, typically 30 days or 60 days after the invoice date, or beyond this.

## HOW IT WORKS

The fuel division of SC Fuel and Glass is preparing its quarterly cash flow forecast for the three months of October, November and December.

The sales of the fuel division for these three months are expected to be as follows:

| | |
|---|---|
| October | £680,000 |
| November | £700,000 |
| December | £750,000 |

Of these sales, 20% are cash sales and the remainder are sales on credit. Experience has shown that on average the receivables for credit sales pay the money according to the following pattern:

| | |
|---|---|
| The month after sale | 20% |
| Two months after sale | 50% |
| Three months after sale | 30% |

Therefore the cash for October credit sales will be received in November, December and January. If we are preparing the cash flow forecast for the period from October to December then some of the cash inflows will be from credit sales in earlier months, therefore you also require information about the credit sales for these earlier months.

The total sales in July to September for the fuel division (again 20% of these were cash sales) are:

| | |
|---|---|
| July | £600,000 |
| August | £560,000 |
| September | £620,000 |

We can now start to piece together the information required to prepare the cash flow from sales for October to December:

## Cash budget – October to December

| | October | November | December |
|---|---|---|---|
| | £ | £ | £ |
| *Cash receipts:* | | | |
| Cash sales | | | |
| (20% of month sales) | 136,000 | 140,000 | 150,000 |

Now we need to deal with sales on credit, which are more complicated and will require a working:

## WORKING – Cash from credit sales

|  | October £ | November £ | December £ |
|---|---|---|---|
| July sales | | | |
| (80% x 600,000 x 30%) | 144,000 | | |
| August sales | | | |
| (80% x 560,000 x 50%) | 224,000 | | |
| (80% x 560,000 x 30%) | | 134,400 | |
| September sales | | | |
| (80% x 620,000 x 20%) | 99,200 | | |
| (80% x 620,000 x 50%) | | 248,000 | |
| (80% x 620,000 x 30%) | | | 148,800 |
| October sales | | | |
| (80% x 680,000 x 20%) | | 108,800 | |
| (80% x 680,000 x 50%) | | | 272,000 |
| November sales | | | |
| (80% x 700,000 x 20%) | | | 112,000 |
| Cash from credit sales | 467,200 | 491,200 | 532,800 |

## Cash budget – October to December

|  | October £ | November £ | December £ |
|---|---|---|---|
| Cash receipts: | | | |
| Cash sales | 136,000 | 140,000 | 150,000 |
| Cash from credit sales | 467,200 | 491,200 | 532,800 |

## Task 1

A company makes credit sales with a typical payment pattern of 40% of the cash being received in the month after sale, 35% two months after the sale and 25% three months after the sale. Credit sales in August, September and October were £320,000, £360,000 and £400,000 respectively.

What are the cash receipts from credit sales received in November?

£ [                    ]

## PAYMENTS FOR PURCHASES

For a retail business, the cash outflows will include the purchase of goods which are then resold, giving the sales receipts discussed above. For a manufacturing business, the materials required for production will have to be purchased and processed before the finished goods can be sold to give the sales receipts above.

We consider first a retail business.

### Retail business

In a similar way to sales, purchases of the goods that a business buys can be made for cash or on credit. If the purchases are for cash then the cash outflow is at the same time as the purchase. However if the purchase is made on credit then there will be a LAGGED PAYMENT, where the cash is paid some time after the purchase is made. As with sales, the business will have a typical payment pattern for its credit suppliers which can be used to find the cash outflow for each period.

### Settlement discounts

When transactions are made on credit, it is common practice for the seller to offer the buyer a SETTLEMENT DISCOUNT (or cash discount or prompt payment discount). This means that if the buyer takes advantage of the discount and pays within a certain time period, then a certain percentage is deducted from the amount which is owed.

For cash budget purposes, if a settlement discount is taken on purchases, then this means that the cash payment will be earlier than normal but will be for the invoice amount less the settlement discount.

## HOW IT WORKS

The purchasing manager for SC Fuel and Glass has provided you with the following information about the anticipated purchases of fuel for the fuel division for the period October to December.

| | |
|---|---|
| October | £408,000 |
| November | £420,000 |
| December | £450,000 |

The accounts department provides you with the following information about the payment pattern for these purchases, which are all made on credit terms.

- 25% of purchases are offered a 2% discount for payment in the month of the purchase and SC Fuels takes advantage of all such settlement discounts offered.

- 60% of purchases are paid in the month following the purchase.

- 15% are paid two months after the date of purchase.

This means that 25% of purchases are paid in the month of purchase with 2% deducted. The remaining 75% of purchases are paid for in the following two months, therefore we need information about the purchases in August and September in order to complete the cash flow forecast.

| | |
|---|---|
| August purchases | £340,000 |
| September purchases | £360,000 |

Again we will need a working in order to determine the payments to suppliers in each of the three months.

## WORKING - Payments to credit suppliers

| | October £ | November £ | December £ |
|---|---|---|---|
| August purchases | | | |
| (340,000 x 15%) | 51,000 | | |
| September purchases | | | |
| (360,000 x 60%) | 216,000 | | |
| (360,000 x 15%) | | 54,000 | |
| October purchases | | | |
| (408,000 x 25% x 98%) | 99,960 | | |
| (408,000 x 60%) | | 244,800 | |
| (408,000 x 15%) | | | 61,200 |
| November purchases | | | |
| (420,000 x 25% x 98%) | | 102,900 | |
| (420,000 x 60%) | | | 252,000 |
| December purchases | | | |
| (450,000 x 25% x 98%) | | | 110,250 |
| Payments to credit suppliers | 366,960 | 401,700 | 423,450 |

We can now start to add figures to the cash payments section of the cash budget.

## Cash flow forecast – October to December

| | October £ | November £ | December £ |
|---|---|---|---|
| Cash receipts: | | | |
| Cash sales | 136,000 | 140,000 | 150,000 |
| Cash from credit sales | 467,200 | 491,200 | 532,800 |
| Cash payments: | | | |
| Payments for credit purchases | 366,960 | 401,700 | 423,450 |

## Gross profit margins

In the example above, the amount of purchases each month in total was given to you by the purchasing director. It is however possible that you may be given the sales for a month and the gross profit percentage and be expected to work out the relevant figure for purchases. Note that gross profit margin may also be called 'gross profit percentage' and 'gross profit on sales' as it expresses gross profit as a percentage of sales

Alternatively, you may be given the mark-up, which expresses gross profit as a percentage of costs rather than sales.

# HOW IT WORKS

The fuel division of SC Fuel and Glass operates with a gross profit margin of 40%. This means that the purchases figure (providing that inventories remain constant) is 60% of the sales for the month. Therefore you might have simply been given the sales for October to December and be expected to work out the purchases for each month.

|  |  | Purchases |
|---|---|---|
| October | £680,000 x 60% | £408,000 |
| November | £700,000 x 60% | £420,000 |
| December | £750,000 x 60% | £450,000 |

Instead of being told the gross profit margin was 40%, you could have been told that the mark-up was 66.67%. You would then have found the purchase for October for example, by calculating £680,000 x 100/166.67 = £408,000 etc.

## Task 2

A business makes all of its purchases on credit and it makes a consistent gross profit on sales of 25%. It keeps no inventory. 60% of the purchases are paid for in the month after purchase, and the remainder two months after the purchase.

The business has the following anticipated sales:

| July | £200,000 |
|---|---|
| August | £240,000 |
| September | £260,000 |

What is the cash payment to suppliers in October?

£

## OTHER CASH PAYMENTS AND RECEIPTS

In most cash budget calculations, determining the amounts of cash receipts from sales and cash payments for purchases are the hardest elements to deal with. However there will be a number of other types of cash payments and cash receipts that will need to be considered and included in the cash budget.

### Wages and salaries

In almost all cases, net wages and salaries tend to be paid in the month in which they are incurred and therefore there is no difficulty with either calculation or timing of the cash flows. Amounts due to HM Revenue & Customs in respect of PAYE and NIC, and to the pension administrator for pension deductions, normally represent the difference between gross and net wages and salaries, and are paid in the following month.

### Overheads

Expenses or overheads will normally be paid in the month in which they are incurred however care should be taken in an assessment to read the information given, as some may be lagged payments.

Care should also be taken with depreciation which is not a cash cost. Often the budget figure for overheads will include an amount which represents depreciation for the period and this must be excluded in order to find the cash payment.

### Irregular or exceptional payments

Other types of payment that are not incurred on a regular basis may be included in the information regarding cash payments. These may include:

- payment details for the acquisition of non-current assets
- dividend payments
- loan repayments

In an assessment, details of the precise timing of these payments will be given to you.

### Irregular or exceptional receipts

Again detailed information about such receipts will be given in an assessment. The most common type of irregular receipt is cash received from the sale of non-current assets. These are sometimes lagged receipts if the sale is made on credit and the cash is therefore received some time after the sale.

Another possible type of irregular receipt might be the receipt of additional capital. For a sole trader or a partnership this will be additional money paid into the business by the owner or partners. For a company this will be the proceeds of an issue of additional share capital. For a sole trader, partnership or company there might also be a cash receipt from further loans being taken out.

## HOW IT WORKS

Having dealt with the cash receipts from sales and the cash payments for purchases for the fuel division of SC Fuel and Glass we will now complete the cash budget using the following additional information:

- wages and salaries are £113,000 each month, payable at the end of the month in which they are incurred

- 75% of general overheads are paid in the month in which they are incurred, with the remainder being paid in the following month. General overheads are £80,000 in each of September and October rising to £87,000 in each of November and December

- included in the general overheads figures is a monthly amount of £12,000 for depreciation of non-current assets

- in January the fuel division is having a new property constructed and in December a down-payment of £120,000 is required to be paid to the building company

- in October a quarterly rental payment of £45,000 is to be paid

- in October a non-current asset is to be sold for £18,000 but it has been agreed that the asset will be paid for in two equal instalments in November and December

- the cash balance at the end of September is an overdraft balance of £29,500.

You are now to complete the cash budget for the fuel division for the three months ended 31 December.

- Wages and salaries are a straightforward cash payment in the month incurred.

- For the general overheads, firstly the depreciation charge must be removed as this is a non-cash expense and then a working will be required to ensure that the correct amount of cash payment is shown in each month, as 25% of the overheads are paid in the month after they are incurred

## WORKING – General overheads

| | October £ | November £ | December £ |
|---|---|---|---|
| September overheads | | | |
| (25% x (80,000 – 12,000)) | 17,000 | | |
| October overheads | | | |
| (75% x (80,000 – 12,000)) | 51,000 | | |
| (25% x (80,000 – 12,000)) | | 17,000 | |
| November overheads | | | |
| (75% x (87,000 – 12,000)) | | 56,250 | |
| (25% x (87,000 – 12,000)) | | | 18,750 |
| December overheads | | | |
| (75% x (87,000 – 12,000)) | | | 56,250 |
| Total overhead payment | 68,000 | 73,250 | 75,000 |

- The construction down-payment is a straightforward December cash flow

- The rent is a cash payment in October

- The non-current asset sale cash receipt will be £9,000 in the months of November and December

- Using the opening cash balance at 1 October, the opening and closing balances each month can be calculated

## Cash budget October to December

| | October £ | November £ | December £ |
|---|---|---|---|
| Cash receipts: | | | |
| Cash sales | 136,000 | 140,000 | 150,000 |
| Cash from credit sales | 467,200 | 491,200 | 532,800 |
| Sale of non-current assets | | 9,000 | 9,000 |
| Total cash receipts | 603,200 | 640,200 | 691,800 |
| Cash payments: | | | |
| Payments for credit purchases | 366,960 | 401,700 | 423,450 |
| Wages and salaries | 113,000 | 113,000 | 113,000 |
| General overheads | 68,000 | 73,250 | 75,000 |
| Capital expenditure | | | 120,000 |
| Rent | 45,000 | | |
| Total cash payments | 592,960 | 587,950 | 731,450 |
| Net cash flow for the month | 10,240 | 52,250 | (39,650) |
| Opening cash balance | (29,500) | (19,260) | 32,990 |
| Closing cash balance | (19,260) | 32,990 | (6,660) |

# Task 3

A company is preparing its cash flow forecast for the month of November. The estimated cash sales in November are £64,000 and sales on credit in October and November are estimated to be £216,000 and £238,000. It is estimated that 40% of credit customers pay in the month of sale, after deducting a 2% discount, and the remainder pay one month after the date of sale.

Purchases are all on credit, payable in the month following the purchase. Purchases are estimated at £144,000 in October and £165,000 in November.

Wages and salaries of £80,000 a month are payable in the month in which they are incurred, as are general overheads of £65,000. The general overheads figure includes a depreciation charge of £15,000 each month.

A dividend of £20,000 is to be paid to the shareholders in November.

The balance on the cash account at the beginning of November is anticipated to be an overdraft balance of £10,200.

Prepare the cash budget for the month of November.

|  |  | £ |
|---|---|---|
| Cash receipts: |  |  |
| Cash sales |  |  |
| Credit sales | November |  |
|  | October |  |
| Total cash receipts |  |  |
| Cash payments: |  |  |
| Purchases on credit |  |  |
| Wages and salaries |  |  |
| Overheads |  |  |
| Dividend |  |  |
| Total cash payments |  |  |
| Net cash flow |  |  |
| Opening balance |  |  |
| Closing balance |  |  |

## OVERDRAFT INTEREST

One final adjustment might be required to a cash budget if it is anticipated that the cash balance during the period will be an overdraft balance. If there is an overdraft balance, then the bank will charge interest on the amount of the overdraft. This interest will be a cash outflow based upon the overdraft amount, which will normally be paid in the following month.

## HOW IT WORKS

We will return to the cash budget for the fuel division of SC Fuel and Glass.

The cash budget to date appears as follows:

**Cash budget October to December**

|  | October £ | November £ | December £ |
|---|---|---|---|
| *Cash receipts:* |  |  |  |
| Cash sales | 136,000 | 140,000 | 150,000 |
| Cash from credit sales | 467,200 | 491,200 | 532,800 |
| Sale of non-current assets |  | 9,000 | 9,000 |
| *Total cash receipts* | 603,200 | 640,200 | 691,800 |
| *Cash payments:* |  |  |  |
| Payments for credit purchases | 366,960 | 401,700 | 423,450 |
| Wages and salaries | 113,000 | 113,000 | 113,000 |
| General overheads | 68,000 | 73,250 | 75,000 |
| Capital expenditure |  |  | 120,000 |
| Rent | 45,000 |  |  |
| *Total cash payments* | 592,960 | 587,950 | 731,450 |
| Net cash flow for the month | 10,240 | 52,250 | (39,650) |
| Opening cash balance | (29,500) | (19,260) | 32,990 |
| Closing cash balance | (19,260) | 32,990 | (6,660) |

At the end of September there is an overdraft balance of £29,500 and at the end of October an overdraft balance of £19,260. Say that interest is charged at 1% per month on these month-end balances in the following month. Therefore a further cash outflow line must be included for overdraft interest, based upon the balance at the end of the previous month. This in turn will have an effect on the net cash flow for the month and the overdraft balance at the end of October.

The overdraft interest cash payment in October will be based upon the overdraft balance at the end of September:

$$1\% \times £29,500 = £295$$

This is entered as a cash outflow which in turn means that the overdraft balance at the end of October will increase to (19,260 + 295) = £19,555. Therefore the overdraft interest in November will be:

1% x £19,555 = £196

**Cash budget – October to December**

|  | October £ | November £ | December £ |
|---|---|---|---|
| *Cash receipts:* |  |  |  |
| Cash sales | 136,000 | 140,000 | 150,000 |
| Cash from credit sales | 467,200 | 491,200 | 532,800 |
| Sale of non-current assets |  | 9,000 | 9,000 |
| *Total cash receipts* | 603,200 | 640,200 | 691,800 |
| *Cash payments:* |  |  |  |
| Payments for credit purchases | 366,960 | 401,700 | 423,450 |
| Wages and salaries | 113,000 | 113,000 | 113,000 |
| General overheads | 68,000 | 73,250 | 75,000 |
| Capital expenditure |  |  | 120,000 |
| Rent | 45,000 |  |  |
| Overdraft interest | 295 | 196 |  |
| Total cash payments | 593,255 | 588,146 | 731,450 |
| Net cash flow for the month | 9,945 | 52,054 | (39,650) |
| Opening cash balance | (29,500) | (19,555) | 32,499 |
| Closing cash balance | (19,555) | 32,499 | (7,151) |

Note that the introduction of the overdraft interest has affected each of the month end balances.

# MANUFACTURING ORGANISATIONS

The cash budgets that have been prepared so far in this chapter have been based upon a retail-type organisation, whereby goods are purchased for cash or on credit and then sold to customers either for cash or on credit. However we also need to consider how to prepare a cash budget for a manufacturing organisation.

In a manufacturing organisation the major difference is in the calculations required to determine the payments relating to production, particularly material purchases and labour.

## Material purchases

As discussed in Chapter 4, the production budget and materials usage budgets give rise to a materials purchases budget, giving the cost of material purchases in each month.

The payment pattern for these purchases must be determined for the cash flows for payments for materials to be entered into the cash budget.

## HOW IT WORKS

We will now consider the glass division of SC Fuel and Glass. The cash flow forecast for this division is to be prepared for the three months of October, November and December.

The production budget can be used to derive the materials usage and hence the materials purchases budget.

Estimated production for the glass division, which requires £32 material per unit, is as follows:

|  | Units |
|---|---|
| October | 12,200 |
| November | 13,200 |
| December | 14,200 |
| January | 14,800 |

|  | October | November | December | January |
|---|---|---|---|---|
| Material usage (£) | 390,400 | 422,400 | 454,400 | 473,600 |

Production × £32

To calculate the cash flow for purchases of materials, the purchasing and payment pattern for these purchases must be determined.

SC Fuel and Glass have a policy of purchasing the materials required for production in the month before that production takes place. They pay 40% of their suppliers in the month of purchase (ie the month before production) and the remainder one month after the purchase ie in the month of production.

We can now think this through:

| October's usage | – | purchased in September |
|---|---|---|
| Paid for: | | 40% in September |
| | | 60% in October |

Hence from materials usage budget:

|  | September | October | November | December |
|---|---|---|---|---|
| Material purchases (£) | 390,400 | 422,400 | 454,400 | 473,600 |

A working is needed to determine the payments to be made for purchases on credit in each of the three months:

## WORKING – Payments to credit suppliers

|  | October £ | November £ | December £ |
|---|---|---|---|
| September purchases | | | |
| (390,400 x 60%) | 234,240 | | |
| October purchases | | | |
| (422,400 x 40%) | 168,960 | | |
| (422,400 x 60%) | | 253,440 | |
| November purchases | | | |
| (454,400 x 40%) | | 181,760 | |
| (454,400 x 60%) | | | 272,640 |
| December purchases | | | |
| (473,600 x 40%) | | | 189,440 |
| Payments to suppliers | 403,200 | 435,200 | 462,080 |

We can now complete the first line of cash payments in the cash budget for the glass division:

### Cash budget – October to December

|  | October £ | November £ | December £ |
|---|---|---|---|
| *Cash payments:* | | | |
| Payments to suppliers | 403,200 | 435,200 | 462,080 |

### Wages

In a manufacturing organisation the wages paid to the production workers will often be dependent upon the hours that they work. This in turn is dependent upon the production quantity in each period which will have been calculated in the production budget.

## HOW IT WORKS

Returning to SC Fuel and Glass and the glass division cash budget, £12 of labour is required for each unit produced. The production budget we used previously can be used to construct the labour usage/cost budget for each month. This is paid in the month it is incurred and so the figures can be placed straight into the cash budget.

|  | October | November | December |
|---|---|---|---|
| Production (units) | 12,200 | 13,200 | 14,200 |
| Labour usage (£) | 146,400 | 158,400 | 170,400 |
| Production x £12 | | | |

## Cash budget – October to December

|  | October £ | November £ | December £ |
|---|---|---|---|
| Cash payments: |  |  |  |
| Payments to suppliers | 403,200 | 435,200 | 462,080 |
| Wages | 146,400 | 158,400 | 170,400 |

## Cash receipts from sales

Now we have dealt with the area where a manufacturing organisation's cash flow forecast differs from that of a retail business, we can return to the areas which are no different from a retailer such as cash receipts from sales. However we will introduce here the concept of IRRECOVERABLE DEBTS.

## Irrecoverable debts

When sales are made on credit, there is always a possibility that some of the credit customers will never pay the amounts due from them. We will consider the effect this has on producing the cash flow forecast.

If it is considered that some invoices will never be actually paid by credit customers, then these should be excluded from the cash receipts in the cash flow forecast. From their experience most businesses will have an idea of the percentage of debts which tend to turn bad or irrecoverable, and as these are likely never to be received, they are not included as cash receipts.

## Task 4

A business makes the following sales on credit:

| | |
|---|---|
| August | £120,000 |
| September | £100,000 |
| October | £150,000 |

A settlement discount of 2.5% is offered for payment in the month of sale and this is taken up by 10% of customers. A further 50% of total customers pay one month after the sale and the remaining customers pay two months after the month of sale, although on average 3% of all debts remain uncollected.

What is the cash inflow from credit customers for the month of October?

£

# HOW IT WORKS

The glass division of SC Fuel and Glass sells each sealed double-glazed unit for £80. All sales are on credit and the payment pattern from receivables is estimated as follows:

- 30% pay in the month following the invoice

- the remainder pay two months after the invoice date but irrecoverable debts are generally about 5% of sales.

As irrecoverable debts will never turn into a cash inflow, the amount of cash received two months after the invoice date is 65% of the month's invoices rather than 70%.

Estimated sales for the glass division are:

|  | Units |
|---|---|
| August | 10,200 |
| September | 12,000 |
| October | 13,200 |
| November | 14,100 |
| December | 14,800 |

Cash receipts from receivables can then be calculated using a working.

### WORKING – Receipts from sales

|  | October £ | November £ | December £ |
|---|---|---|---|
| August sales | | | |
| (10,200 x £80 x 65%) | 530,400 | | |
| September sales | | | |
| (12,000 x £80 x 30%) | 288,000 | | |
| (12,000 x £80 x 65%) | | 624,000 | |
| October sales | | | |
| (13,200 x £80 x 30%) | | 316,800 | |
| (13,200 x £80 x 65%) | | | 686,400 |
| November sales | | | |
| (14,100 x £80 x 30%) | | | 338,400 |
| Total receipts from sales | 818,400 | 940,800 | 1,024,800 |

These figures can now be entered into the cash budget:

**Cash budget – October to December**

|  | October | November | December |
|---|---|---|---|
|  | £ | £ | £ |
| Cash receipts: |  |  |  |
| Cash from credit sales | 818,400 | 940,800 | 1,024,800 |
| Cash payments: |  |  |  |
| Payments to suppliers | 403,200 | 435,200 | 462,080 |
| Wages | 146,400 | 158,400 | 170,400 |

## Other receipts and payments

Finally to complete the cash budget the other cash receipts and payments for the period will be included in the same way as for the retail business.

## HOW IT WORKS

The remaining figures need to be dealt with in the cash budget for the glass division.

- Production expenses are estimated as 15% of the materials and wages payments in the month, and are paid in the month in which they are incurred. This figure includes £18,000 of depreciation charge each month

- Selling costs are estimated as 10% of the sales revenue for the period and 75% are payable in the month in which they are incurred and the remainder in the following month

- Additional machinery has been acquired under a lease and the lease payments are £15,000 each month

- In October the corporation tax payment of £290,000 must be paid

- The cash balance at 1 October was anticipated to be £45,000 in credit

- In this example we are ignoring the complication of overdraft interest charges

The cash budget can now be completed:

## Cash budget – October to December

|  | October £ | November £ | December £ |
|---|---|---|---|
| *Cash receipts:* |  |  |  |
| Cash from credit sales | 818,400 | 940,800 | 1,024,800 |
| *Cash payments:* |  |  |  |
| Payments to suppliers | 403,200 | 435,200 | 462,080 |
| Wages | 146,400 | 158,400 | 170,400 |
| Production expenses (W1) | 64,440 | 71,040 | 76,872 |
| Selling costs (W2) | 103,200 | 111,000 | 117,000 |
| Lease payments | 15,000 | 15,000 | 15,000 |
| Corporation tax | 290,000 |  |  |
| *Total payments* | 1,022,240 | 790,640 | 841,352 |
| Net cash flow for the month | (203,840) | 150,160 | 183,448 |
| Opening cash balance | 45,000 | (158,840) | (8,680) |
| Closing cash balance | (158,840) | (8,680) | 174,768 |

## WORKINGS

### Working 1 – Production expenses

|  | October £ | November £ | December £ |
|---|---|---|---|
| *October* |  |  |  |
| ((15% × (403,200 + 146,400)) – 18,000) | 64,440 |  |  |
| *November* |  |  |  |
| ((15% × (435,200 + 158,400)) – 18,000) |  | 71,040 |  |
| *December* |  |  |  |
| ((15% × (462,080 + 170,400)) – 18,000) |  |  | 76,872 |

## Working 2 – Selling costs

|  | October £ | November £ | December £ |
|---|---|---|---|
| *September costs* |  |  |  |
| (10% × (12,000 x £80) x 25%) | 24,000 |  |  |
| *October costs* |  |  |  |
| (10% × (13,200 × £80) × 75%) | 79,200 |  |  |
| (10% × (13,200 × £80) × 25%) |  | 26,400 |  |
| *November costs* |  |  |  |
| (10% × (14,100 × £80) × 75%) |  | 84,600 |  |
| (10% × (14,100 × £80) × 25%) |  |  | 28,200 |
| *December costs* |  |  |  |
| (10% × (14,800 × £80) × 75%) |  |  | 88,800 |
| Total selling costs | 103,200 | 111,000 | 117,000 |

## Task 5

A company anticipates sales of 45,000 units of its product in August. Finished goods in inventory at 1 August are expected to be 4,000 units and this is to be increased by 2,000 units by the end of the month.

Each unit of the finished product requires 5 kg of materials each of which cost £7.50 per kg. Materials inventories are expected to consist of 40,000 kg at1 August, decreasing by 10,000 kg by the end of the month.

Purchases are made in the month prior to production and paid for in the month following purchase.

What are the payments to be made in August in respect of purchases?

£

# CASH FLOWS AND ACCOUNTING BALANCES

In the cash budgets in this chapter, we have worked out the cash inflows from sales, and the cash outflows on materials purchases, wages etc, using information regarding the pattern of payments received and made.

An alternative means of working out cash inflows or outflows is by looking at the balances of receivables or payables at the beginning and end of the period in question.

BPP
LEARNING MEDIA

## Receivables and sales

As we have seen in this chapter, a business can make both cash and credit sales. The fact that sales may be made in a period, but not paid for before the end of the period, means that a business has receivables at the end of each period. There is a relationship between the receivables at the start and end of a period, the sales made during the period and the cash received from those sales.

## HOW IT WORKS

James Manufacturing Ltd makes both cash and credit sales.

The receivables balance at the end of January was £15,000. The company has budgeted for sales of £130,000 during the month of February, and plans a receivables balance of no more than £25,000 at the end of February (this may be referred to as the closing receivables balance).

What is the budgeted cash inflow from sales?

Closing receivables £25,000 =            Opening receivables £15,000

plus

Sales made £130,000

less

Cash inflow from sales £?

Rearranging this means:

Cash inflow from sales       =       Opening receivables £15,000

Plus

Sales made £130,000

less

Closing receivables £25,000

                     =      £120,000

The level of receivables has increased during the period, which means the amount of cash collected was less than the amount of sales made.

Instead of absolute figures for receivables at the start and end of the period, you may only be given the increase or decrease in these balances. For example, in the case of James Manufacturing Ltd above, you could have been told that budgeted sales for February were £130,000 and that receivables were budgeted to increase by £10,000.

Cash inflow from sales = sales made – increase in receivables

$$= £130,000 – £10,000 = £120,000$$

If receivables are expected to decrease over the period, more cash has to be collected than sales made, so

Cash inflow from sales = sales made + decrease in receivables

A further alternative is to be given the budgeted sales and budgeted cash receipts, along with the opening receivables balance. You would then have to find the closing receivables balance.

## Task 6

Leyland Ltd has the following extract from its budgeted statement of financial position for Quarter 2, shown alongside the actual results for Quarter 1.

**Statement of financial position**

| | End of Quarter 1 £ | End of Quarter 2 £ |
|---|---|---|
| Receivables | 18,000 | 24,000 |

The cash inflow from sales is budgeted to be £84,000 in Quarter 2. What are the budgeted sales for Quarter 2?

£

### Payables and materials purchases

Just as cash inflows from sales may not occur in the same period as the sales, and so give rise to receivables, the delay in paying for purchases of materials or goods for re-sale means a business will also have payables at the end of each period.

Again, the actual cash outflow on such purchases in a period can be found by looking at the changes in the level of payables at the start and end of the period, and the level of purchases. You need to ensure that the payables balances you are using relate to the purchases figure you are using. For example, if you know the budgeted materials purchases figure for a period, you should make sure that the payables balances relate to amounts owed to the supplier of that material, and do not include, say, overhead amounts which have not yet been paid.

## HOW IT WORKS

James Manufacturing Ltd has the following extracts from its budgeted statement of financial position and income statement for February, shown alongside the actual results for January.

## Statement of financial position

|  | As at 31 January £ | As at 28 February £ |
|---|---|---|
| Payables | 34,000 | 16,000 |

## Income statement

|  | January £ | February £ |
|---|---|---|
| Materials purchases | 80,000 | 93,000 |

The payables balances relate to the purchase of materials only.

What is the budgeted cash payment for purchases, in February?

Closing payables £16,000 =
Opening payables £34,000
Plus
Purchases made £93,000
Less
Cash paid for purchases £?

Rearranging this means:

Cash paid for purchases =
Opening payables £34,000
Plus
Purchases made £93,000
Less
Closing payables £16,000
= £111,000

Take care to select the correct amount from the income statement; you need purchases made during the month of February.

The level of payables has decreased during the period, so the cash paid was more than the purchases made.

As with the case for receivables and sales, you may only be told the movement in payables balances, rather than the absolute balances themselves, so you have to find the cash outflow.

Cash outflow on purchases = purchases made – increase in payables

Cash outflow on purchases = purchases made + decrease in payables

You may also have to find the closing payables balance if given budgeted purchases, budgeted cash payments and the opening payables balance.

## Non-current assets and cash receipts or payments

When making capital purchases, the cash outflow often matches the amount shown as an addition in the statement of financial position. Alternatively, the payment may be made in instalments. These are simple to deal with and have already been seen in this chapter.

However, on the sale of an asset, the profit (or loss) that is recorded in the income statement is not a cash amount. For the purposes of your cash budget, you may have to calculate the proceeds on sale. This can be done using the profit (or loss), provided you know the carrying amount of the asset in the books of the business (ie in the statement of financial position) at the date of sale.

Cash inflows on sale of non-current assets = proceeds

Proceeds =      Carrying amount
                plus
                profit on sale (or minus loss)

# CHAPTER OVERVIEW

- A cash budget or cash flow forecast allows an organisation to plan and control future cash flows in and out, and the expected cash or overdraft balance at the end of future periods

- Receipts from cash sales will take place at the same time as the sale but receipts from credit sales may be spread over a number of subsequent months

- Payments for purchases on credit will similarly be typically spread over a number of future months

- If a settlement discount is offered on credit sales, then the amount of anticipated cash inflow must be reduced, and if settlement discounts are taken on purchases, then the amount of the cash outflow must be reduced to reflect the smaller payment

- In some instances the amount of purchases for a period will need to be calculated by reference to anticipated sales in the period and the anticipated gross profit margin

- Care must be taken with the timing of other cash flows such as overheads, which may not necessarily be all paid in the month incurred – any non-cash flows such as depreciation charges must be excluded from the cash flow forecast

- If information is given about overdraft interest then this must be calculated each month, based upon the overdraft balance at the end of the previous month, and shown as a cash outflow

- In a manufacturing organisation, the amount of payments for purchases will be dependent upon the production budget and the purchases pattern and supplier payment pattern

- The production budget will be affected by changes in inventories of finished goods whereas the purchases budget is affected by changes in materials inventories

- In a manufacturing organisation the wages payment for the period may also be dependent upon the production quantity each period

- If irrecoverable debts are anticipated, then these are amounts that will not be received in cash and are therefore excluded from the cash budget

- The movement in receivables during a period can be used with the budgeted sales to find the budgeted cash inflow (receipts) from sales during the period.

CHAPTER OVERVIEW (continued)

■ The movement in payables during a period can be used with the budgeted purchases to find the budgeted cash outflow (payment) for purchases during the period.

■ The proceeds on the sale of non-current assets can be found by adding the profit on sale to (or by subtracting the loss on sale from) the carrying amount of the asset.

## Keywords

**Cash flow forecast** – (also called **cash budgets**) method of determining the expected net cash flow for a future period and the expected cash or overdraft balance at the end of that future period.

**Receipts and payments cash budget** – the expected receipts for a period are listed and totalled, as are the expected payments in the period.

**Net cash flow** – determined by deducting the payments from the receipts and this net movement is applied to the opening cash balance in order to find the anticipated closing balance.

**Lagged receipt/payment** – receipt/payment of cash which takes place some time after the related transaction

**Settlement discount** – discount offered by the seller to the buyer in return for early payment of the amount due

**Irrecoverable debts** – invoiced amounts that it is considered will never be received in cash

# TEST YOUR LEARNING

1    A business has estimates of the following sales figures:

|  | £ |
|---|---|
| October | 790,000 |
| November | 750,000 |
| December | 720,000 |
| January | 700,000 |
| February | 730,000 |
| March | 760,000 |

Of these total sales figures 10% are likely to be cash sales and the remainder are credit sales. The payment pattern from receivables in the past has been such that 40% of the total sales pay in the month after the sale and the remainder two months after the month of sale. However there are also normally 5% irrecoverable debts.

Complete the following

|  | January | February | March |
|---|---|---|---|
| Budgeted cash receipts from sales (£) |  |  |  |

2    A business has estimates of the following sales figures:

|  | £ |
|---|---|
| October | 790,000 |
| November | 750,000 |
| December | 720,000 |
| January | 700,000 |
| February | 730,000 |
| March | 760,000 |

The business operates at a standard gross profit margin of 25%. Purchases are all made in the same month as the sale and are all on credit. 20% of purchases are offered a 2% discount for payment in the month after purchase and the business takes all such discounts. A further 65% of the purchases are paid for two months after the month of purchase and the remaining 15% are paid for three months after the date of purchase.

Complete the following.

| | January | February | March |
|---|---|---|---|
| Budgeted cash payments for purchases (£) | | | |

3    A business is about to prepare a cash flow forecast for the quarter ending 31 December.

Gross wages are expected to be £42,000 each month and are paid in the month in which they are incurred. General overheads are anticipated to be £30,000 for each of September and October, increasing to £36,000 thereafter. 80% of the general overheads are paid for in the month in which they are incurred and the remainder in the following month. Included in the general overheads figure is a depreciation charge of £5,000 each month.

The business has planned to purchase new equipment for £40,000 in November and in the same month to dispose of old equipment with estimated sales proceeds of £4,000.

Complete the following extracts from the cash budget for the three months ending 31 December.

| | October | November | December |
|---|---|---|---|
| | £ | £ | £ |
| Cash receipts: | | | |
| Sales proceeds from equipment | | | |
| Cash payments: | | | |
| Wages | | | |
| General overheads | | | |
| New equipment | | | |

4    Make-it Ltd intends to sell an industrial unit, making a budgeted profit of £58,000. The carrying amount of the unit is £212,000. What are the budgeted cash inflows on the sale of the unit ie the proceeds?

Select from:

£58,000
£154,000
£212,000
£270,000

# chapter 6:
# BUDGET PREPARATION –
# LIMITING FACTORS

## chapter coverage 📖

In this chapter we will look at varying limiting factors which dictate budget construction.

The topics that are to be covered are:

✍ Resources as a limiting factor including material, labour and production capacity shortages

✍ Alternative strategies to maximising contribution in the light of limiting factors:

– Product mix

– 'Buying in'

# RESOURCES AS LIMITING FACTORS

In Chapter 3, we discussed the budgets that need to be created by individual departments or responsibility centres in order to create an overall budget.

In Chapter 4, we looked at the preparation of sales budgets, and how this leads to production budgets, material usage budgets, material purchasing budgets, labour usage and cost budgets etc.

However, in the budgets considered so far, it was the expected sales volumes that dictated the number of units which had to be produced and so the other budgets grew from this.

The number of units that could be sold was therefore the KEY BUDGET FACTOR. The key budget factor is the element or resource of the business that is likely to place limitations on the activities of the business.

In most businesses the key budget factor will be sales. Most businesses will find that there is a limit to the amount of sales that they can make, due to demand for their products and their own market share. However it is also possible that the key budget factor may be dictated by resources: the availability of materials, labour or machine capacity. We consider these cases in this chapter.

## Shortage of materials

In a manufacturing organisation the sales demand for the product may be virtually unlimited however there may be a shortage of materials availability which will be the factor that will limit the production volume.

# HOW IT WORKS

S S Productions makes a single product for which each unit requires 3.5 kg of material LP1. Unfortunately due to a shortage of suppliers of LP1, only 525,000 kg of LP1 will be available in the coming year, with supplies being available on a monthly basis spread evenly over the year.

How many units of the product can be produced in total and each month?

| | | |
|---|---|---|
| Total production | = | $\dfrac{525,000 \text{ kg}}{3.5 \text{ kg}}$ |
| | = | 150,000 units |
| Monthly production | = | $\dfrac{150,000}{12}$ |
| | = | 12,500 units |

## Solving the problem of shortage of materials

In many cases it will be possible to overcome this problem of shortage of materials or at least to lessen the extent of the problem. The shortage of supply may be a long-term problem or it may only be a short-term blip. Possible longer term solutions include the following:

- **seeking an alternative supplier** – this is an obvious solution but it may not always be possible to find another supplier who can supply the correct quality at an acceptable price

- **finding an alternative material** – in some instances a product can only be made from one particular material but it may be possible to adapt the design of the product and the manufacturing process in order to use a substitute material that is widely available

- **manufacturing an alternative product** – it may be possible to switch the production process to manufacture of an alternative product which uses a different material which is not in short supply

- **buying in finished goods for resale** – instead of producing the product, it could be purchased in finished form from another producer who is not having the same problems with supply of the materials required. However this would probably lead to an under-utilisation of production resources and a major change in the organisation's strategy.

If the shortage is only temporary then there are a number of short-term solutions which could alleviate the problem:

- **using materials held in inventory** – the inventories of materials could be run down in order to maintain production and sales

- **using finished goods held in inventory** – in order to maintain sales in the short term, finished goods inventories can be run down even though production levels are not as high as would be liked

- **rescheduling purchases** – if the amount of the material required is available in some periods but not in others, then the materials purchases could be rescheduled to ensure that the maximum use is made of the available materials.

## HOW IT WORKS

The materials requirements for production for Selby Electronics for the next six months are as follows:

|  | May | June | July | Aug | Sep | Oct |
|---|---|---|---|---|---|---|
| Materials requirements – kg | 4,500 | 5,000 | 5,200 | 4,800 | 5,400 | 6,000 |

Selby is only able to purchase 5,000 kg of the material in each month.

How can the purchases be scheduled in order to ensure the maximum production over the six month period?

In total over the six month period 30,900 kg of material are required, whereas only 30,000 kg are available, therefore there will be a shortage of 900 kg which will have to be dealt with by possibly finding another supplier.

If only the amount required for production is purchased each month and 5,000 kg is purchased in months where the requirements are higher than this, then only 29,300 kg will be purchased, meaning that there will be an overall shortage of 1,600 kg (30,900 – 29,300).

However instead of purchasing what is required for production each month, if all of the available 5,000 kg are purchased every month, then the shortage can be reduced to just 900 kg (30,900 – 30,000). This will mean holding higher inventory levels of the material, however, which will incur extra costs.

This can be illustrated in the schedule below – on this basis production can be completed in full in every month other than October.

|  | May | Jun | Jul | Aug | Sep | Oct |
|---|---|---|---|---|---|---|
| Materials requirements – kg | 4,500 | 5,000 | 5,200 | 4,800 | 5,400 | 6,000 |
| Materials purchased – kg | 5,000 | 5,000 | 5,000 | 5,000 | 5,000 | 5,000 |
| (Shortage)/excess | 500 | – | (200) | 200 | (400) | (1,000) |
| Rescheduled purchases | (500) |  | 200 | (200) | 400 | 100 |
| Shortage after rescheduling | – | – | – | – | – | 900 |

## Task 1

A production process requires 7.5 kg of material per unit of production. For the first three months of next year only 165,000 kg of material will be available each month. Assuming production is spread evenly over the three months, what will be the maximum monthly production level?

## Labour shortages

In some instances the key budget factor might be the availability of labour with the correct skills or training. In this case the number of hours available will determine the quantity of production.

## HOW IT WORKS

Poldark Engineering requires a particular grade of skilled labour for one of its products. Each product requires four hours of this grade of labour but the business currently only has 20 employees with the skills required. They normally work a 35 hour week although by paying an overtime rate of double time it has been possible to negotiate for each employee to work 10 hours of overtime a week.

What is the maximum level of production each week?

| Hours available | = | 20 x (35 + 10) |
| | = | 900 hours per week |
| Maximum production | = | $\dfrac{900 \text{ hours}}{4 \text{ hours}}$ |
| | = | 225 units per week |

## Solving the problem of a shortage of labour

Labour shortage problems are normally fairly short-term, as it should be possible to obtain more of the labour required either by paying higher rates of pay or by investing in training of employees. There are a number of short-term solutions however that could be used to alleviate the problem until it can be solved:

- increase the overtime worked – it may be possible to agree additional overtime with the employees in order to maintain production

- use sub-contractors – in some types of business it may be possible to use agency workers or to sub-contract the work in order to maintain production levels. Either of these options is likely to be fairly costly

- use up finished goods held in inventory – if production levels are reduced then for the short term sales can still be maintained by running down the finished goods inventory

- buying in finished goods inventory – this could be an expensive option leaving factory capacity under-utilised and may have quality implications as well

- improving labour efficiency – this is not something that can be done quickly but with training and over a period of time it may be possible.

## Task 2

In the first week of the next quarter the sales demand is expected to be 2,000 units of a product. Each unit requires 5.5 hours of direct labour time and the business employs 280 employees each working a 35 hour week. How much overtime (to the nearest 0.1 hours per week) would each employee need to work in order to meet demand with the current workforce?

☐ hours per week

### Lack of production capacity

It is also possible for a lack of production capacity in terms of machinery or floor space in the factory to be the key budget factor. This time the production level will be dependent upon the maximum capacity of the factory.

## HOW IT WORKS

Henley Engineering operates out of one factory and operates two eight hour shifts each day for six days a week, with the production line working at full capacity. The production line is capable of producing 100 units of product per hour.

What is the maximum production level each week?

| | | |
|---|---|---|
| Total hours | = | 2 × 8 × 6 |
| | = | 96 hours |
| Maximum production | = | 96 hours × 100 units |
| | = | 9,600 units |

## Solving capacity problems

Capacity problems mean that the current operations are not sufficient to meet demand for the product from customers. These problems may be short-term or long-term.

If the capacity problem is short-term, such as the problem of dealing with high seasonal demand, there are a number of possible short-term solutions:

- build up inventories in advance – if the high demand is known or expected in advance, then as this is a seasonal problem production could be higher in the months before the high demand is expected and finished goods inventories would grow ready to meet the greater demand. There will obviously be costs involved in holding higher levels of finished goods in inventory

- additional shift – it may be possible to work additional shifts in order to increase capacity, however this could cause substantial overtime costs

- buying in finished goods – in order to meet the additional demand in the short term it may be possible to buy in the finished goods rather than to produce them

- renting equipment or premises – it may be possible to rent temporary equipment or premises in order meet the short-term excess demand.

Long-term capacity shortages are usually resolved by investing in long-term non-current assets and increasing the shifts and/or number of workers.

# MAXIMISING CONTRIBUTION

We have looked at the impact of material, labour and production capacity constraints above, and possible practical solutions for overcoming these constraints.

If these constraints cannot be overcome, the organisation may take one of the following options in order to maximise its profit.

- If the organisation produces more than one product, the product mix should be changed.

- Alternatively, it may be more profitable for the business to 'buy-in' the product or component.

The decisions regarding these alternative strategies can be taken by considering contribution, and by acting to maximise it. You will have seen limiting factor decisions based on contribution in your previous studies and the Budgeting assessor has said that detailed testing of this is unlikely but the principle needs to be understood.

## PRODUCT MIX

As fixed costs in total are assumed to be constant, whatever combination of product is made, maximisation of profit will be achieved by maximising contribution. The contribution per unit is the sales price less the variable costs per unit (usually materials and labour).

If a business has more than one product, and one limiting factor, the technique to use in order to maximise contribution is to determine the contribution per unit of the scarce resource or limiting factor and concentrate first upon the production of the product with the highest contribution per limiting factor unit.

## HOW IT WORKS

Farnham Engineering makes three products A, B and C. The costs and selling prices of the three products are as follows:

|  | A | B | C |
|---|---|---|---|
|  | £ | £ | £ |
| Direct materials @ £4 per kg | 8 | 16 | 12 |
| Direct labour @ £7 per hour | 7 | 21 | 14 |
| Variable overheads | 3 | 9 | 6 |
| Marginal cost | 18 | 46 | 32 |
| Selling price | 22 | 54 | 39 |
| Contribution | 4 | 8 | 7 |

Sales demand for the coming period is expected to be as follows:

| Product A | 3,000 units |
|---|---|
| Product B | 7,000 units |
| Product C | 5,000 units |

The supply of materials is limited to 50,000 kg during the period and the labour hours available are 28,000.

Step 1

Determine if there is a limiting factor other than sales demand. Consider the materials usage for each product if the maximum sales demand is produced. (You are not given the actual usage of materials of each product but you can work it out – for example, the materials cost for A is £8 and as the materials are £4 per kg, product A must use 2 kg etc.)

|  | A | B | C | Total |
|---|---|---|---|---|
| Materials (Demand × 2/4/3/kg) | 6,000 kg | 28,000 kg | 15,000 kg | 49,000 kg |
| Labour (Demand × 1/3/2 hrs) | 3,000 hours | 21,000 hours | 10,000 hours | 34,000 hours |

As 50,000 kg of materials are available for the period and only 49,000 kg are required for the maximum production level, materials are not a limiting factor.

However, only 28,000 labour hours are available whereas in order to meet the maximum demand 34,000 hours are required. Therefore labour hours are the limiting factor.

## Step 2

Calculate the contribution per limiting factor unit – so in this case the contribution per labour hour – for each product. Then rank the products according to how high the contribution per labour hour is for each one.

|  | A | B | C |
|---|---|---|---|
| Contribution | £4 | £8 | £7 |
| Labour hours per unit | 1 hour | 3 hours | 2 hours |
| Contribution per labour hour |  |  |  |
| £4/1 | £4.00 |  |  |
| £8/3 |  | £2.67 |  |
| £7/2 |  |  | £3.50 |
| Ranking | 1 | 3 | 2 |

A makes the most contribution per unit of scarce resource (labour hours) so in order to maximise contribution we must concentrate first on production of A up to its maximum sales demand (3,000 units), then on C up to its maximum sales demand (5,000 units), and finally, if there are any remaining hours available, on B.

## Step 3

Construct the optimal production plan.

The optimal production plan in order to maximise contribution is:

|  | Units produced | Labour hours required |
|---|---|---|
| A | 3,000 | 3,000 |
| C | 5,000 | 10,000 |
| B (balance) | 5,000* | 15,000 |
|  |  | (balancing figure) |
|  |  | 28,000 |

\* **Working**: After making A and C there are 15,000 hours left. Each unit of B needs 3 hours so there is sufficient to make 15,000/3 = 5,000 units.

The contribution earned from this production plan is:

|  |  | £ |
|---|---|---|
| A | (3,000 × £4) | 12,000 |
| B | (5,000 × £8) | 40,000 |
| C | (5,000 × £7) | 35,000 |
| Total contribution |  | 87,000 |

## 'BUYING IN'

Another possible scenario is for the organisation to stop production of one product completely and instead 'buy it in' from a supplier or sub-contractor. This strategy may be cheaper, and it will also free up production capacity in-house for other products.

When faced with decisions such as this, we take a marginal costing approach, looking initially at the difference between the contribution per unit of producing in-house and sub-contracting, and then at the changes in fixed costs that could occur.

## HOW IT WORKS

Mammon Ltd currently produces Ards in-house at a variable cost of £20 per unit. They sell for £55 per unit, and £15,500 per month of fixed overheads are attributed to them. Each month, 1,000 Ards are produced and sold, but this quantity is expected to fall soon (without affecting cost estimates).

Mammon Ltd has been approached by a sub-contractor, who can produce Ards at a cost to Mammon Ltd of £25 per unit. The managing director of Mammon Ltd estimates that by sub-contracting, £3,000 of monthly fixed overheads will be saved.

What should Mammon Ltd do?

First of all we calculate the contribution per unit on each of the two scenarios.

|  | In-house production £ per unit | Sub-contract £ per unit |
|---|---|---|
| Revenue | 55.00 | 55.00 |
| Variable cost | 20.00 | 25.00 |
| Contribution per unit | 35.00 | 30.00 |

On this analysis, if production is sub-contracted, contribution falls by £5 per unit, or £5 × 1,000 = £5,000 per month. However, we are also told that £3,000 of

monthly overhead will be saved, so in total there would be a decrease of (£5,000 – £3,000) = £2,000 of gross profit per month, or (£2,000/1,000) = £2 per unit.

If production and sales were estimated to continue at current levels, the decision would be to continue to make Ards in-house *unless* the capacity can be used to produce items with higher profitability.

But production and sales are estimated to fall in the future, which would make it harder for Mammon to recover the fixed costs of in-house production. As a result although sub-contracting involves additional variable costs, it may become more attractive at lower levels of output because of the saving in fixed costs.

We need to identify the level of sales/production at which we would be indifferent between making the product in-house and sub-contracting.

This will be where the additional variable costs incurred by buying in equal the savings in fixed costs.

Cost estimates do not change at different levels of production, so the difference between our variable costs and the cost of buying in (£25 – £20) = £5 per unit. As the monthly savings on fixed costs by sub-contracting production are £3,000, if we produced and sold £3,000/£5 = 600 Ards we would be indifferent as to whether to make or buy. At more than 600 units, we would want to continue making Ards; at less than 600 we would want to sub-contract. This can be shown as follows:

|  |  | Produce in-house £ | Sub-contract £ |
|---|---|---|---|
| **650 units:** |  |  |  |
| Contribution | (650 × £35) | 22,750 |  |
|  | (650 × £30) |  | 19,500 |
| Fixed costs |  | (15,500) | (12,500) |
|  |  | 7,250 | 7,000 |
| **600 units:** |  |  |  |
| Contribution | (600 × £35) | 21,000 |  |
|  | (600 × £30) |  | 18,000 |
| Fixed costs |  | (15,500) | (12,500) |
|  |  | 5,500 | 5,500 |
| **550 units:** |  |  |  |
| Contribution | (550 × £35) | 19,250 |  |
|  | (550 × £30) |  | 16,500 |
| Fixed costs |  | (15,500) | (12,500) |
|  |  | 3,750 | 4,000 |

The decision rests with the managers of Mammon Ltd, and depends on what level of production and sales they estimate will be experienced.

## CHAPTER OVERVIEW

- Normally production of products is limited by sales demand, however in some instances a resource such as the availability of material, labour hours or machine hours is the limiting factor

- It may be possible to take actions to counter material, labour and production capacity shortages

- If this cannot be done, an alternative strategy where there is more than one product and a limiting factor, is to maximise overall profit by concentrating production on the products with the highest contribution per limiting factor unit

- Alternatively, a decision may be made to 'buy in' a product or component rather than manufacture in-house

- In a make or buy decision with no limiting factors, the relevant costs are the differential costs between the two options. Typically this includes any variable costs incurred/saved as a result of the decision and any savings in attributable fixed costs

## Keywords

**Key budget factor** – the element or resource of the business that is likely to place limitations on its activities

**Contribution** – sales revenue or selling price per unit less variable costs

**Limiting factor** – a factor of production or sales that limits the amount of a product that can be produced or sold

## TEST YOUR LEARNING

1   The materials requirements for production for the next six months for a business are as follows:

|  | Jan | Feb | Mar | Apr | May | Jun |
|---|---|---|---|---|---|---|
| Materials requirements – kg | 2,600 | 3,100 | 3,000 | 3,100 | 2,800 | 3,200 |

It is only possible to purchase 3,000 kg of the product each month.

How many kg of the material should be purchased each month in order to maximise production assuming the minimum levels of material held in inventory are maintained?

2   For the next few months a business foresees having a shortage of highly skilled labour for its production process. This is due to a recent increase in sales which is expected to continue.

What options does the business have to alleviate this problem?

3   Over the coming weeks, a business foresees having a shortage of the appropriate quality material for its production process. This is due to a short-term supply issue which is not expected to continue.

What options does the business have to alleviate this problem?

4   A product requires 0.5 kg of material per unit and 24 minutes labour per unit. The demand for the product is 15,000 units per month.

Available material = 9,000 kg per month

There are 30 workers available to work on this product, each working 180 hours a month.

The limiting factor is

**Picklist:**

Sales demand

Material

Labour hours

5   The following two products use the same material. The cost of the material is £2 per kg, and the cost of labour is £10 per hour.

| Per unit | Product A | Product B |
|---|---|---|
| Sales price £ | 13 | 8 |
| Direct materials kg | 2 | 1.5 |
| Direct labour hours | 0.5 | 0.25 |
| Variable overhead £ | 1 | 0.5 |

Labour hours are limited. Tick the product which should be manufactured if profit is to be maximised.

| Product | Manufactured to maximise profit |
|---|---|
| Product A | |
| Product B | |

# chapter 7:
# FLEXED BUDGETS AND VARIANCES

<hr>

## chapter coverage 📖

In this chapter we will look at using budgets to monitor performance of responsibility centres.

The topics that are to be covered are:

- ✍ Fixed and flexed budgets
- ✍ Flexing a budget
- ✍ Reporting under absorption costing and marginal costing
- ✍ Changes in inventory levels and effect on profit
- ✍ Reasons for variances
- ✍ Interdependence of variances
- ✍ Investigating variances

## FIXED AND FLEXIBLE BUDGETS

We have already seen that budgeting plays a part in the management functions of planning and control. However, budgets can be set in different ways and some are more suitable than others for each of these functions.

### Fixed budgets

A FIXED BUDGET is a budget that is set in advance of a period and its purpose is to provide a single achievable target for the entire organisation to work to. This target level of activity means that all areas of the business will be co-ordinated towards achieving this goal.

The purpose of the fixed budget is to aid in the planning processes of the business. The budget will set out the resources that are required in order to achieve that target. In Chapter 4 we saw how, once the sales budget has been set, the production budget required to provide the necessary products for sale is then produced. From this production budget, the materials and labour necessary to meet this target can be identified from the materials usage budget and labour usage budget.

The control element of the budgeting system is in the comparison of the actual results for a period to the budgeted figures. However if the actual activity levels turn out to be significantly different from the target set in the fixed budget, then comparison of the actual results to the fixed budget will be fairly meaningless, as we will not be comparing like with like.

## HOW IT WORKS

Martin Engineering prepares detailed budgets for each quarter of the year. The budget for Quarter 4 of 20X0 was set as follows:

|  | Quarter 4 budget £ |
|---|---|
| Sales 1,000 units | 40,000 |
| Material | (10,000) |
| Labour | (12,000) |
| Production overhead | (3,000) |
| Gross profit | 15,000 |
| General expenses | (8,000) |
| Operating profit | 7,000 |

This budget was set on the basis of both production and sales of 1,000 units and no opening or closing inventories.

It is now the first week in January in 20X1 and the actual results for Quarter 4 are being compared to the budget:

|  | Quarter 4 budget £ |  | Quarter 4 actual £ |
|---|---|---|---|
| Sales 1,000 units | 40,000 | 1,200 units | 45,600 |
| Material | (10,000) |  | (12,480) |
| Labour | (12,000) |  | (13,800) |
| Production overhead | (3,000) |  | (3,200) |
| Gross profit | 15,000 |  | 16,120 |
| General expenses | (8,000) |  | (9,080) |
| Operating profit | 7,000 |  | 7,040 |

As part of the process of control, the management accountant of Martin Engineering now prepares a report showing the differences, known as variances, between the budget and the actual results. If the actual performance is better than budgeted (higher revenue or lower costs), the variance is described as favourable; if the performance is worse than budgeted (lower revenue or higher costs), the variance is adverse.

**Variance report**

|  | Quarter 4 budget £ |  | Quarter 4 actual £ | Variance £ |
|---|---|---|---|---|
| Sales 1,000 units | 40,000 | 1,200 units | 45,600 | 5,600 Fav |
| Material | (10,000) |  | (12,480) | 2,480 Adv |
| Labour | (12,000) |  | (13,800) | 1,800 Adv |
| Production overhead | (3,000) |  | (3,200) | 200 Adv |
| Gross profit | 15,000 |  | 16,120 | 1,120 Fav |
| General expenses | (8,000) |  | (9,080) | 1,080 Adv |
| Operating profit | 7,000 |  | 7,040 | 40 Fav |

It would appear that there is a mixture of variances, with favourable variances for sales and profit but adverse variances for all of the costs.

The problem however is that the budget and the actual figures are not strictly comparable: the budget was based upon sales and production of 1,000 units whereas the actual activity level was that there were 1,200 units produced and sold.

## Flexed budget

A FLEXED BUDGET is a budget that is prepared at the actual activity level that was achieved in the period, in order to show what the standard costs should have been at that activity level. When these costs are then compared to the actual costs, meaningful variances can be calculated.

The comparison of the flexed budget to the actual figures is therefore part of the control process.

## Variable costs and fixed costs

When a budget is being flexed to the actual activity level, care must be taken with the distinction between fixed and variable costs. The variable costs or variable element of a cost will increase as the activity level increases, whereas the fixed element of any cost should remain the same whatever the activity level.

## HOW IT WORKS

Given below again is the Quarter 4 budget for Martin Engineering:

|  | Quarter 4 budget |
|---|---|
|  | £ |
| Sales 1,000 units | 40,000 |
| Material | (10,000) |
| Labour | (12,000) |
| Production overhead | (3,000) |
| Gross profit | 15,000 |
| General expenses | (8,000) |
| Operating profit | 7,000 |

The details of the cost behaviour of each of the costs is given below:

| | |
|---|---|
| **Materials** | the materials cost is totally variable |
| **Labour** | each employee can only produce 250 units each quarter – the cost of each employee is £3,000 each quarter |
| **Production overhead** | the production overhead is a totally fixed cost |
| **General expenses** | the general expenses are made up of a budgeted fixed cost of £5,000 and a variable element |

We will now flex the budget to the actual activity level of 1,200 units.

**Sales**

Budgeted selling price
= £40,000/1,000 units
= £40 per unit

Therefore the budgeted sales revenue for 1,200 units is:

Sales
= 1,200 x £40
= £48,000

**Materials** are totally variable

Budgeted materials per unit
= £10,000/1,000 units
= £10 per unit

Budgeted materials cost for 1,200 units
= 1,200 x £10
= £12,000

**Labour** is a stepped cost

One employee is required for each 250 units, therefore for 1,200 units five employees will be required.

Budgeted labour cost
= 5 x £3,000
= £15,000

**Production overheads** is a fixed cost so remains unchanged

Budgeted cost for 1,200 units
= £3,000

**General expenses** are a semi-variable cost

| | | £ |
|---|---|---|
| At 1,000 units | Fixed element | 5,000 |
| | Variable element | 3,000 |
| | Total | 8,000 |

Variable element = £3,000/1,000 units = £3 per unit

|  |  |  | £ |
|---|---|---|---|
| At 1,200 units | Fixed element | = | 5,000 |
|  | Variable element |  |  |
|  | 1,200 × £3 | = | 3,600 |
|  |  |  | 8,600 |

The flexed budget will appear as follows:

|  | Quarter 4 flexed budget |
|---|---|
|  | £ |
| Sales 1,200 units | 48,000 |
| Materials | (12,000) |
| Labour | (15,000) |
| Production overhead | (3,000) |
| Gross profit | 18,000 |
| General expenses | (8,600) |
| Operating profit | 9,400 |

The flexed budget can then be compared to the actual figures in the form of an operating statement and the true variances calculated.

**Martin Engineering: Quarter 4 Operating Statement**

|  | Budget | | Actual | Variance |
|---|---|---|---|---|
|  | £ |  | £ | £ |
| Sales 1,200 units | 48,000 | 1,200 units | 45,600 | 2,400 Adv |
| Material | (12,000) |  | (12,480) | 480 Adv |
| Labour | (15,000) |  | (13,800) | 1,200 Fav |
| Production overhead | (3,000) |  | (3,200) | 200 Adv |
| Gross profit | 18,000 |  | 16,120 | 1,880 Adv |
| General expenses | (8,600) |  | (9,080) | 480 Adv |
| Operating profit | 9,400 |  | 7,040 | 2,360 Adv |

We can now see that, instead of an overall favourable profit variance being reported, there is in fact a significant adverse profit variance with all the variances other than labour being adverse. This is quite a different picture to the variances calculated using the fixed budget.

## Task 1

The budget for production supervisors' costs for a period for a business at an activity level of 120,000 units is £12,000. One production supervisor is required for every 50,000 units of production. If actual production is 180,000 units, what figure would appear in the flexed budget for production supervisors' costs?

£ [                    ]

### Limitations of budget flexing

Although it is useful to flex budgets to eliminate volume related variances you must bear in mind that the flexed budget is still indirectly based on the assumptions applied when the original budget was drawn up.

These assumptions may not always hold true at flexed volumes and the budget assumptions may need to be re-visited when assessing performance against a flexed budget.

Budget flexing, therefore, is not a means of re-budgeting for a new strategy, since this means the underlying assumptions, other than volume, will change.

Problems with budget flexing include the following:

- Splitting mixed costs is not always straightforward.
- Fixed costs may behave in a step-line fashion as activity levels increase/decrease.
- Consideration must be given to the assumptions upon which the original fixed budget was based. Such assumptions might include the constraint posed by limiting factors, the rate of inflation, judgements about future uncertainty, or demand for the organisation's products.
- By flexing a budget, a manager is effectively saying 'If I knew then what I know now, this is the budget I would have set'. It is a useful concept but can lead to some concern as managers can become confused and frustrated if faced with continually moving targets.

## Variable or semi-variable cost?

In some instances in assessments you may not be specifically told whether costs are variable, semi-variable or fixed. Instead you may be given budgets at different levels of activity and from these you must determine whether the costs are variable or semi-variable.

# HOW IT WORKS

Given below is the manufacturing cost budget for Katt Ltd at two different activity levels.

|  | 10,000 units<br>£ | 15,000 units<br>£ |
|---|---|---|
| Materials cost | 12,000 | 18,000 |
| Labour cost | 13,000 | 15,750 |
| Production overhead | 4,000 | 4,000 |

You are to determine the cost behaviour of each individual cost and then to determine the cost budget at an activity level of 12,000 units.

**Materials**

| | | |
|---|---|---|
| Cost per unit @ 10,000 units | = | £12,000/10,000 |
| | = | £1.20 |
| Cost per unit @ 15,000 units | = | £18,000/15,000 |
| | = | £1.20 |

This is, therefore, a purely variable cost.

| | | |
|---|---|---|
| Materials cost @ 12,000 units | = | 12,000 × £1.20 |
| | = | £14,400 |

**Labour**

| | | |
|---|---|---|
| Cost per unit @ 10,000 units | = | £13,000/10,000 |
| | = | £1.30 |
| Cost per unit @ 15,000 units | = | £15,750/15,000 |
| | = | £1.05 |

Therefore, this is not a purely variable cost but it is also clearly not fixed. We will have to assume that it is a semi-variable cost and use the costs at the two activity levels to determine the fixed and variable element.

|  | Activity level | Cost<br>£ |
|---|---|---|
| Level 1 | 10,000 | 13,000 |
| Level 2 | 15,000 | 15,750 |
| Increase | 5,000 | 2,750 |

| Variable element | = | £2,750/5,000 units |
| | = | £0.55 per unit |

Fixed element:

| Cost @ 10,000 units | £ |
|---|---|
| Variable element 10,000 × £0.55 | 5,500 |
| Fixed element (bal fig) | 7,500 |
| Total cost | 13,000 |

The labour cost at an activity level of 12,000 units will therefore be:

| | £ |
|---|---|
| Variable element 12,000 units × £0.55 | 6,600 |
| Fixed element | 7,500 |
| Total cost | 14,100 |

**Production overhead**

As this is the same cost at 10,000 units and 15,000 units, the production overhead can be assumed to be a fixed cost.

**Manufacturing cost budget @ 12,000 units**

| | £ |
|---|---|
| Materials cost | 14,400 |
| Labour cost | 14,100 |
| Production overhead | 4,000 |

---

## Task 2

The budgeted production overhead for a business is £15,800 at an activity level of 2,000 units and £19,950 at an activity level of 3,000 units. If the actual activity level is 2,600 units what is the flexed budget figure for production overhead?

£ [          ]

---

## ABSORPTION COSTING AND MARGINAL COSTING

You will remember from earlier that there are two methods of dealing with variable and fixed costs – absorption costing and marginal costing.

### Absorption costing

Under ABSORPTION COSTING the fixed production overheads are absorbed into the cost of a product unit and therefore included as part of cost of sales and in the valuation of closing inventory. This means that any closing inventory which is carried forward to the next period, by being deducted from cost of sales, includes an element of fixed cost which is also being carried forward to the next period.

### Marginal costing

Under MARGINAL COSTING, all fixed costs are treated as period costs and are written off in the income statement in the period in which they are incurred. This means that all fixed costs are written off in the period and none are carried forward to subsequent periods.

The key to producing a marginal costing budget or income statement is being able to identify the fixed and variable elements of all of the costs of the business.

## HOW IT WORKS

Given below is the fixed budget for Harvey Products for Quarter 1 of 20X8. There were no opening inventories at the start of the quarter.

| | Units | Quarter 1 budget Absorption costing £ | £ |
|---|---|---|---|
| Sales 10,000 units | 10,000 | | 60,000 |
| Materials | | 18,000 | |
| Labour | | 15,000 | |
| Production overhead | | 11,000 | |
| Cost of production | 11,000 | 44,000 | |
| Less: closing inventory | (1,000) | 4,000 | |
| Cost of sales | 10,000 | | 40,000 |
| Gross profit | | | 20,000 |
| General expenses | | | 10,400 |
| Operating profit | | | 9,600 |

Production is 11,000 units and sales are 10,000 units; as there were no opening inventories there are therefore 1,000 units of closing inventories. The materials

and labour are variable costs while the production costs and general expenses are fixed costs.

The budget has been prepared on the basis of absorption costing therefore a proportion of the fixed production overhead has been included in the valuation of closing inventories.

Cost of producing 11,000 units        =      £44,000
Cost of closing inventories of 1,000 units    =      £44,000 × 1,000/11,000
                                   =      £4,000

We will now redo the budget under marginal costing principles:

|  | Units | Quarter 1 budget Marginal costing £ | £ |
|---|---|---|---|
| Sales | 10,000 |  | 60,000 |
| Materials |  | 18,000 |  |
| Labour |  | 15,000 |  |
| Cost of production | 11,000 | 33,000 |  |
| Less: closing inventory | (1,000) | 3,000 |  |
| Cost of sales | 10,000 |  | 30,000 |
| Gross profit |  |  | 30,000 |
| Fixed production overhead |  |  | (11,000) |
| General expenses |  |  | (10,400) |
| Operating profit |  |  | 8,600 |

Only the variable expenses, materials and labour, have been included in the cost of production and therefore the cost of the closing inventory. All of the fixed costs – the production overhead and the general expenses – are deducted in full as a period expense.

## Difference in profit

If an organisation is using absorption costing, any change in the way overheads are absorbed into cost units will affect profit. Such changes include moving from a rate per unit to a labour or machine hour rate. Alternatively, the organisation may choose to move to an Activity Based Costing system, so that overheads for a particular product may rise or fall dramatically.

In addition, differences in profit arise in relation to whether absorption or marginal costing is used.

As you can see in the previous example, the profit reported under absorption costing is different from that reported under marginal costing. The difference in profit is due to the fact that using absorption costing £1,000 of fixed production costs is included in the valuation of closing inventory and carried forward to the next accounting period rather than written off in this accounting period.

Therefore if inventory levels are rising, the profits reported under absorption costing will be higher than those under marginal costing (as fixed production costs are carried forward to subsequent accounting periods). If an absorption costing system is in use it is therefore possible for profits to be manipulated by managers producing more goods than are required for sale and therefore building up large and expensive inventory levels.

## HOW IT WORKS

In the previous example the profits under absorption costing and marginal costing were as follows:

| | | |
|---|---|---|
| Absorption costing | = | £9,600 |
| Marginal costing | = | £8,600 |

The difference of £1,000 is due to the difference in valuation of inventory.

| | £ |
|---|---|
| Absorption costing – increase in inventory | 4,000 |
| Marginal costing – increase in inventory | 3,000 |
| Difference | 1,000 |

Under absorption costing a proportion of the fixed production costs are included in the inventory valuation:

Production cost included in inventory valuation   =   £11,000 × 1,000/11,000

                                                  =   £1,000

Under absorption costing, this is carried forward to the next period; under marginal costing it is charged against this period's income statement.

Note: In this example there were no opening inventories, so the difference in profit is entirely due to the closing inventory valuation. Where there is both opening and closing inventory, the difference is due to the fixed overheads included in the inventory movement for the period:

Thus a reconciliation of the profit figures can be prepared:

| | £ |
|---|---|
| Absorption cost profit | X |
| (Increase)/Decrease in inventory units × fixed cost per unit | (X) |
| Marginal cost profit | X |

## Task 3

A business has opening finished goods inventory of 4,500 units and closing finished goods of 3,200 units in inventory. Is profit higher under absorption costing or marginal costing?

Profit is higher under [　　　　　▼] costing

**Picklist:**
Absorption
Marginal

## Comparing actual results to budgeted figures

It is important to ensure that you prepare any budget in an appropriate format. This may be according to absorption costing principles or marginal costing principles, depending upon the policy of your organisation.

What is equally important is that the actual results are reported in the same manner as the budget, in order to ensure that any variances are meaningful. Therefore if the budget is set under marginal costing principles, the actual results that are compared to the budget must also be recorded under marginal costing principles.

# FIXED OVERHEADS

When we were considering standard costing in earlier chapters we saw how there was a relationship between the budgeted activity level of the business and the budgeted overhead absorption rate. It is possible in assessments that when preparing a flexed budget, you might be required to use information about the budgeted fixed overhead absorption rate and the budgeted level of activity, in order to work out fixed overhead to be included in the budget. Remember that fixed overheads do not vary with the number of units produced, so the budgeted fixed overhead should be the same in the fixed and flexed budgets ie at any activity level.

## HOW IT WORKS

A business has the following figures for a period:

Budgeted fixed overhead absorption rate  £2 per unit

Budgeted output  35,000 units

Actual fixed overhead  £80,000

Actual output  38,000 units

What is the fixed overhead variance?

The budgeted output is lower than the actual output, but the fixed overhead should not depend on the level of activity, so the total fixed overhead is the same in the fixed and flexed budgets.

Budgeted fixed overhead = budgeted fixedoverhead absorption rate × budgeted output

Budgeted fixed overhead = £2 × 35,000 = £70,000

Variance = actual fixed overhead – budgeted fixed overhead

= £80,000 – £70,000 = £10,000.

This is adverse as the actual costs are higher than budgeted.

## REASONS FOR VARIANCES

So far, we have learnt how to construct a flexed budget and ensured that we are comparing like with like, by making sure that the flexed budget and the actual results are both constructed using marginal costing, or both constructed using absorption costing.

By comparing the flexed budget with the actual results, we can calculate variances. However, these variances must then be investigated and reasons for them found, so that we can determine whether actions must be taken to improve the business's performance. We look at the investigation of variances, and actions that must be taken after they have been investigated, later in the chapter, but first we consider possible reasons for variances.

it is crucial to remember that if we examine a variance calculated using a flexed budget (which will usually be the case), then the variance **cannot** be explained by the fact that the volume of production or sales was different to the budgeted volume. The fact that we have flexed the budget means that the activity levels that we are comparing are the same. If you had compared figures using a fixed budget, then volume factors are important, but for variances calculated using a flexed budget, make sure that you do not give this as a reason.

Let's look at the specific types of variance in turn, and consider some possible reasons. When asked to give possible reasons for variances in a task, do not just repeat the list given below. Instead, you should refer to information that you are given in the task, which will flag possible reasons to you.

## Materials variance

When examining reasons for a materials variance, you should remember that the total cost of material in a period depends on both

- – the price of the material per kg or per litre etc, and also
- – the usage of the material per unit.

It follows that a materials variance may be due to differences between the budget and actual in terms either of price, or of usage, or of both. It may even be the case that the same reason/action would cause one of these factors to affect the cost favourably and the other adversely, with the overall variance being the net result of these effects. A typical example is if a lower grade material is purchased: it might be cheaper (and so be expected to give a favourable variance) but may give rise to much more wastage, so the materials costs end up higher (adverse variance).

### Adverse materials variance – price factors

- an unexpected price increase from a supplier

- loss of a previous trade or bulk buying discount from a supplier

- purchase of a higher grade of materials

- a deterioration in the sterling exchange rate where goods are bought from another country

### Adverse materials variance – usage factors

- greater wastage due to a lower grade of material
- greater wastage due to use of a lower grade of labour
- problems with machinery

### Favourable materials variance – price factors

- negotiation of a better price from a supplier

- negotiation of a trade or bulk purchase discount from a supplier

- purchase of a lower grade of materials

- an improvement in the sterling exchange rate when goods are bought from another country

## Favourable materials variance – usage factors

- use of a higher grade of material which led to less wastage
- use of more skilled labour leading to less wastage than normal
- new machinery which provides greater efficiency

In other studies, you may have seen variances split further ie the materials variance can be split into a price variance and a usage variance. The assessor has stated that he does not intend to ask you to calculate such specific variances based on standard costing in this assessment. Variances will appear in tasks involving budgets, especially in flexed budgets which you have to construct. When asked to discuss the reasons for variances, you can and should make broad reference to the numbers given in the task which may relate to materials price or to usage, as in the example below.

## HOW IT WORKS

The following is an extract from the flexed budget and actual results for TVX Ltd for the last month. (In the assessment, you may be given or have to construct the full flexed budget.)

|  | Flexed budget (£) | Actual results (£) |
|---|---|---|
| Materials cost | 144,000 | 142,800 |

When you investigate the reasons for the materials variance, the purchasing manager says that while the price of material per kg was 5% more expensive than expected, the material purchased was of greater quality.

Explain the materials variance.

The materials variance is £144,000 - £142,800 = £1,200 favourable, because the actual costs are lower than budgeted.

The increase in materials price would have been expected to give an adverse variance of 5% (ie material costs would be expected as £144,000 x 1.05 = £151,200). However, the overall variance is favourable because the improved quality must have reduced the materials usage by more than the effect of the increased price.

## Labour variance

The total cost of labour in a period depends on both

- – the labour rate per hour
- – the labour hours per unit

Therefore, you should consider both when examining a labour variance.

### Adverse labour variance – rate factors

- unexpected increase in the rates of pay for employees
- use of a higher grade of labour than anticipated
- unexpectedly high levels of overtime

### Adverse labour variance – hours factors

- use of a less skilled grade of labour
- use of a lower grade of material which takes longer to work on
- more idle time than budgeted
- poor supervision of the workforce
- problems with machinery

### Favourable labour variance – rate factors

- use of a lower grade of labour than budgeted for
- less overtime than budgeted for

### Favourable labour variance – hours factors

- use of a more skilled grade of labour
- use of a higher grade of material which takes less time to work on
- less idle time than budgeted
- use of new more efficient machinery

## Task 4

A business has a favourable labour variance of £2,500. During the period, one of the permanent workers was off sick and an unskilled casual worker was employed instead.

Explain the labour variance.

## Overhead and other costs

### Overhead variance – adverse or favourable

- an unexpected increase or decrease in the cost of any element of overheads

In addition to changes in expected material and labour costs, any other cost in the budget could experience an increase or decrease, leading to an adverse or favourable variance respectively. Be sure to comment on the variances relating to fixed overheads as well as variable production costs.

For example, investment in a new machine which may lead to material and labour variances may also lead to increased power costs, and increased depreciation. Alternatively, the costs of materials maintenance may decrease.

Other common cost variances surround salaries of directors and office staff. For example, an adverse marketing overheads variance may be caused by the employment of a new sales and marketing director with a higher salary than expected. However, this may also have an impact on the sales of the business, if the director implemented a change in sales price ie an increase in price would lead to a favourable variance. Note that the influence of the sales and marketing director may be such that sales volume may increase, but remember that a favourable sales variance cannot be due to an increased volume of sales, as the flexed budget already reflects this increase.

---

## Task 5

A business decides it needs to run an additional advertising campaign to boost sales.

Explain the effect this might have on income and cost variances calculated by comparing a flexed budget with the actual results for the period.

---

## Interdependence of variances

You may have noticed from some of the possible causes of variances given above that many of these are likely to be inter-related. This is known as the INTERDEPENDENCE OF VARIANCES.

We have already mentioned the conflicting effect of a lower grade of material on the materials variance alone.

A further example might be the use of a lower grade of labour on a job than budgeted, leading to a favourable labour variance (as the labour rate is lower) but an adverse materials variance, as the less skilled labour may cause more materials wastage.

## Responsibility for variances

Investigating the causes of variances and determining any interdependence between the variances is an important aspect of management control, as in a system of responsibility accounting the managers responsible for various elements of the business will be held accountable for the relevant variances.

Take the example of the lower grade material and the conflicting effects on the materials variance. The initial reaction might be to praise the purchasing manager for reduced cost and to lay blame for poor usage on the production manager. However, the true picture may be that, in the absence of any further reasons for the variance, the responsibility lies solely with the purchasing manager.

## Responsibility accounting

In Chapter 1 we considered RESPONSIBILITY CENTRES. These are areas of the business for which costs or revenues are gathered and compared to budgets for control purposes. They can be cost, profit or investment centres, depending upon the type of cost and/or revenue that the centre deals with.

RESPONSIBILITY ACCOUNTING is a method of budgeting and comparing actual costs to budgets for each of the responsibility centres.

It follows that the manager responsible for a cost centre has authority regarding the costs incurred by his or her area of responsibility and should be held responsible for cost variances.

The manager of the profit centre has authority over both costs and income and is responsible for the profit and thereby variances for both costs and revenues.

The manager of an investment centre not only has authority over the costs and income of the centre but also over its assets and liabilities. The capital budget, and whether this has been adhered to, will therefore be the responsibility of that manager.

## Other reasons for variances – errors in planning

In assigning responsibility for variances, managers should only be held accountable for factors that are within their control. We look at the issue of control again later in the chapter when considering which variances to investigate.

However, when asked to comment on variances, it might help if you consider the reasons for variances as falling into two categories, control factors and planning factors:

- control factors – as the production period goes on, managers must make a great many control decisions, such as buying material of a lower grade than planned, or taking advantage of a discount offered, which had not been anticipated at the planning stage.

- planning factors – when setting standards and formulating budgets for how much will be produced, we are engaged in planning. A great deal of planning is actually (well-informed) guesswork, and it is useful to try to separate out a variance caused by a guess that turns out to be wrong (and therefore to an extent uncontrollable), from variances caused by other decisions

In terms of planning, one fundamental reason for a variance, particularly one that recurs each period, may be that the standard costs being used to construct the budget are out of date. If the standard does not reflect the reality of the cost or usage of materials or labour then this will be a significant cause of any variances.

Standards should be regularly reviewed, at least annually, and kept up-to-date in terms of the costs of materials, labour and fixed overheads and in terms of the usage of materials and labour hours required for each product.

Further causes of variances may be one-off events such as a power cut or the breakdown of machinery, which are neither under the control of the manager involved, nor have been planned for.

---

## Task 6

A business has had an adverse labour variance for the past two years, which was when the legal minimum wage increased.

What action should be taken with regard to this variance?

---

## Alteration of standard costs

Later in the chapter, we look in more detail at the actions that should be taken once variances have been investigated. However, in the light of an inappropriate standard, the advice may be to change this. The decision to alter a standard cost should be not be taken lightly and should only be done when there is a long-term or permanent change in the cost of the resource or the usage.

For example, suppose a material variance has been caused by a change of supplier due to the fact that the normal supplier was out of inventory. Purchases will continue to be made from the normal supplier in future. In this case the standard should not be changed. However if there is a general price increase for the material in question, no matter which supplier is used, then the standard materials cost should be revised.

# HOW IT WORKS

Given below is an extract from the operating statement for Lawson Ltd. The budget has already been flexed to reflect actual levels of production and sales.

**Operating statement – July**

|  | Budget £ | Actual £ | Variance £ |
|---|---|---|---|
| Materials | 48,800 | 47,600 | 1,200 |
| Labour | 55,800 | 58,400 | (2,600) |
| Fixed overheads | 62,000 | 57,000 | 5,000 |

Upon investigation of the variances, the following is discovered:

- the supplier of the materials has permanently increased its prices but has also significantly improved the quality of the material

- some of the workforce used in the period were of a lower grade than normal and they were not as familiar with the production process as the normal workforce

- during the period there was a machine breakdown which caused a significant amount of idle time when the workforce was not actually able to make the product

- due to the machine breakdown, the power costs for the period were lower than anticipated

- Lawson Ltd has recently reduced the amount of factory space that it rents but the standard rental cost has not been adjusted.

You are to write a report to the Operations Manager identifying possible causes of the variances and making any suggestions for action that should be taken.

---

# REPORT

To:             Operations Manager, Lawson Ltd
From:           An Accountant
Date:           August
Subject:        Variances

The materials, labour and fixed overhead variances for the period have been calculated.

The supplier of the materials has permanently increased its prices, which might be expected to give an adverse materials variance. However, the quality of the material has also been improved, meaning that the usage of the material has improved by more than the effect of the increased price, leading to the overall favourable materials variance.

We should consider other suppliers for the supply of our materials, but if their prices are the same as our supplier's, or the material quality is not as good, then the standard cost of the materials should be altered. If it can be shown that the higher quality material has caused the favourable variance through reduced usage then consideration should also be given to alteration of the standard materials usage per unit ie to budgeted material costs in future periods.

A favourable labour variance may have been expected due to the use of lower grade labour than normal for some of the period but the adverse labour variance suggests that the lower grade labour may be less efficient than the previous labour ie take longer to perform the same tasks. These inefficiencies have overridden any benefit of the lower labour rate. Labour inefficiencies (and so an adverse labour variance) may also have been caused by the machine breakdown during the period, which meant that labour hours were paid for when no productive work was achieved (idle time).

The machine breakdown is a one-off event which should not be built into the budgeted costs for subsequent periods. However, if it is anticipated that the lower grade of labour will now normally be used for production, then the standard labour rate and hours should be changed.

The fixed overhead variance was favourable due to lower power costs, due to the machine breakdown and also a reduction in factory rental. This is despite additional costs of repair which may have been incurred because of the breakdown (and which would have been expected to lead to an adverse variance). The reduction in rent is a permanent reduction and therefore the budgeted fixed overhead should be altered to reflect this in future periods.

---

# INVESTIGATING VARIANCES

We have seen how variances should be calculated by comparing the actual results to a flexed budget for the same level of activity. However, it is possible that every single cost and stream of income will give rise to a variance and we need to understand where efforts should be concentrated in investigating them.

Variances are calculated as part of the management control process. The calculation and reporting of the variances is therefore only the starting point of the process. Once the variances have been calculated and reported, management will have to decide whether to investigate the variances in order to determine the reasons for them. There are three main aspects of variances that should be taken into account when deciding whether or not to investigate them:

- their materiality or significance
- the trend
- their controllability

## Materiality of variances

Only variances that are material (that is, significant to the operations and results of the organisation) will need to be investigated. The materiality level will be set by each individual organisation but there are two main methods of determining whether a variance is material:

- an absolute amount may be set, such as £10,000, and all variances, both adverse and favourable, of more than this amount will be investigated

- a variance may be deemed to be material if it exceeds a set percentage of the standard cost – for example all variances of more than 10% of standard cost, again both adverse and favourable, might be investigated.

## Trend of variances

Sometimes a variance in a particular period may not appear to be material. However if the trend of the variance is the same in each period, either favourable or adverse, although each individual variance itself is not material, the trend indicates that there is an underlying reason for the variance rather than simply random factors. Therefore management may decide that the cause of the variance should in fact be investigated.

## Controllability of variances

A cost is a CONTROLLABLE COST for the manager of a responsibility centre if the manager has an influence over that cost. We saw the concept of controllability earlier in the chapter; operations managers can only be responsible in the short term for variances arising out of control decisions rather than out of inaccuracies in planning.

In a responsibility centre, the manager is responsible for the costs and/or revenues of the business. However, in some cases the actual cost and resulting variance may be outside the control of the manager. Examples might include:

- an adverse production overhead variance, as the rent for the factory was unexpectedly increased by the landlord – the factory manager cannot be held responsible for this price increase

- a general expenses variance for a division of a business caused by head office costs that are allocated to all divisions – the manager of the division has no control over the allocation of the head office costs and therefore cannot be responsible for them

- a production overhead variance in a factory caused by the machinery depreciation charges where the rates and methods of depreciation are set by the accounting function – the factory manager cannot be held responsible for the depreciation charge.

In some cases, a cost may not be totally under the control of the manager but as the manager has considerable influence on the cost it will be treated as a controllable cost. For example, the factory manager may schedule the labour grades that are required for a production run but the actual wage rates paid to the workers are determined by the personnel department. However, the labour cost would generally be deemed to be a controllable cost from the perspective of the factory manager.

## Motivation of managers

The importance of identifying controllable costs and revenues is that it can motivate or de-motivate managers. If costs, revenues and variances are reported as part of the responsibility of a manager but in fact he or she has no control, then this will have a de-motivational effect.

## Feedback and feedforward

The process of continual comparison of actual results to budgeted results is known as FEEDBACK.

The budget period is normally for the forthcoming year but the feedback process should take place on a much more frequent, regular basis. Calculation and reporting of variances should take place daily, weekly or monthly depending upon the organisation. Any resulting action that must be taken in order to eliminate variances or improve efficiency should then take place as soon as possible.

The information that is being received about the current performance of the business in terms of the current actual results can then also be used to influence the budget for future periods. This system of using information about the current performance for budgeting for the future is known as FEEDFORWARD.

The budgeting cycle therefore consists of setting organisational goals, planning, using budgets, obtaining feedback from comparison of actual to budgeted results and implementing feedforward from actual results to the budgeting process.

## CHAPTER OVERVIEW

- A fixed budget is set in advance of a budgeting period as a pre-determined plan of activity for all areas of a business

- A flexed budget can be prepared which adjusts the budget to reflect the actual activity level or volume for the period

- A flexed budget is used in the control aspect of the budgetary system as the actual results are compared to the flexed budget in order to determine any variances

- In order to flex a budget, a distinction must be drawn between variable costs and fixed costs and the variable or fixed elements of a semi-variable cost – the variable elements of cost will increase or decrease with changes in activity level, whereas the fixed elements of cost do not vary with changes in activity levels

- Budgets and actual results may be reported either using absorption or marginal costing techniques – under absorption costing the fixed production overheads are absorbed into the cost of a product unit and included in cost of sales and the closing inventory valuation – under marginal costing all fixed costs, including fixed production costs, are written off in total in the period in which they are incurred as period costs

- If there are changes in the levels of finished goods inventory in a period, then there will be a difference between the profit reported under absorption costing and the profit reported under marginal costing – because under absorption costing fixed production overheads are carried forward to future periods in finished goods closing inventory, whereas they are written off in the period under marginal costing

- Fixed overhead absorption rates and budgeted activity levels can be used to calculate budgeted fixed overheads for use in a flexed budget

- Each type of variance can have a variety of causes – often the variances are interdependent meaning that one factor which caused one variance is also the factor that caused other variances.

- Once the reasons for the variances have been discovered then responsibility for the variances, favourable as well as adverse, can be assigned to the relevant managers

- Responsibility accounting assigns the responsibility for variances to the appropriate cost, profit or investment centre

- Consideration must be given to whether or not variances should be investigated – the three main considerations are the materiality (significance) of the variance, the trend of variances and the controllability of costs

CHAPTER OVERVIEW (Continued)

The reporting of variances and allocation of responsibility for them can have an important effect on the motivation of managers

## Keywords

**Fixed budget** – a budget set in advance of a period in order to act as a plan of action for the whole organisation

**Flexed budget** – a budget prepared for the actual activity level for the period

**Absorption costing** – a method of costing where fixed production overheads are absorbed into the unit cost of a product and included in closing inventory valuations

**Marginal costing** – a method of costing where all fixed costs are written off in the period in which they are incurred

**Interdependence of variances** – this is where the factor which causes one variance can also be the cause of another variance

**Responsibility centres** – areas of a business for which costs or revenues can be gathered and made the responsibility of a particular manager

**Responsibility accounting** – a method of budgeting and comparing actual costs to budgets for each responsibility centre

**Controllable costs** – costs over which the manager of a responsibility centre has influence

**Feedback** – the process of continual comparison of actual results to budgeted results

**Feedforward** – the use of current actual results in the future budgeting process

## TEST YOUR LEARNING

1   Explain the difference between a fixed and a flexed budget and the purpose of each.

2   You are required to complete the following operating statement. Do this by flexing the budget (fill in the flexed budget numbers), calculating variances (fill in the variance numbers) and selecting whether each variance is favourable or adverse.

The budget for a production company for the month of December and the actual results for the month are given below:

| | Budget | Flexed Budget | Actual | Variance | Favourable/ Adverse |
|---|---|---|---|---|---|
| | 4,000 units | 3,600 units | 3,600 units | | |
| | £ | £ | £ | £ | Fav/Adv [Picklist] |
| Sales | 96,000 | | 90,000 | | ▼ |
| Materials | 18,000 | | 15,120 | | ▼ |
| Labour | 27,200 | | 25,200 | | ▼ |
| Production overhead | 5,700 | | 5,900 | | ▼ |
| Gross profit | 45,100 | | 43,780 | | ▼ |
| General expenses | 35,200 | | 32,880 | | ▼ |
| Operating profit | 9,900 | | 10,900 | | ▼ |

The materials and labour costs are variable costs, the production overhead is a fixed cost and the general expenses are a semi-variable cost with a fixed element of £11,200.

3    Given below for January are the original budget figures, the revised budget figures and the actual figures.

|  | Original budget 24,000 units | | Revised budget 28,000 units | | Actual 30,000 units | |
|---|---|---|---|---|---|---|
|  | £ | £ | £ | £ | £ | £ |
| Sales |  | 72,000 |  | 84,000 |  | 86,000 |
| Materials | 19,200 |  | 22,400 |  | 22,500 |  |
| Labour | 33,000 |  | 37,000 |  | 41,200 |  |
| Production expenses | 5,600 |  | 5,600 |  | 5,800 |  |
| Production cost |  | 57,800 |  | 65,000 |  | 69,500 |
| Gross profit |  | 14,200 |  | 19,000 |  | 16,500 |
| General expenses |  | 12,600 |  | 14,200 |  | 14,700 |
| Operating profit |  | 1,600 |  | 4,800 |  | 1,800 |

Complete the following operating statement showing a flexed budget to reflect the actual level of activity for the month, and variances from that flexed budget for each figure.

**Operating statement: January**

|  | Flexed budget 30,000 units | | Actual 30,000 units | | Variance |
|---|---|---|---|---|---|
|  | £ | £ | £ | £ | £ |
| Sales |  |  |  | 86,000 |  |
| Materials |  |  | 22,500 |  |  |
| Labour |  |  | 41,200 |  |  |
| Production expenses |  |  | 5,800 |  |  |
| Production cost |  |  |  | 69,500 |  |
| Gross profit |  |  |  | 16,500 |  |
| General expenses |  |  |  | 14,700 |  |
| Operating profit |  |  |  | 1,800 |  |

4   Given below is the fixed budget for a period prepared under absorption costing principles. There were no opening inventories.

|  | £ | £ |
|---|---|---|
| Sales 50,000 units | | 900,000 |
| Materials | 216,000 | |
| Labour | 324,000 | |
| Production overhead | 108,000 | |
| Cost of production 54,000 units | 648,000 | |
| Less: closing inventory 4,000 units | 48,000 | |
| Cost of sales | | (600,000) |
| Gross profit | | 300,000 |
| General expenses | | (198,000) |
| Net profit | | 102,000 |

The materials and labour costs are variable costs. The production overhead and general expenses are fixed costs.

Complete the following redraft of the budget using marginal costing principles.

**Marginal costing budget**

|  | £ | £ |
|---|---|---|
| Sales | | |
| Materials | | |
| Labour | | |
| Cost of production | | |
| Closing inventory | | |
| Cost of sales | | |
| Gross profit | | |
| Fixed production overhead | | |
| Fixed general expenses | | |
| Net profit | | |

Explain the difference in budgeted profit between the two budgets.

5    A business has the following budgeted and actual figures for a period:

Budgeted output                    240,000 units
Actual fixed overhead              £480,000
Fixed overhead absorption rate     £1.90 per unit

The fixed overhead variance comparing flexed and actual results is

£ [          ] [                 ▼]

**Picklist:**

Favourable

Adverse

6    What is a controllable cost? Why is it important that managerial performance is only judged on the basis of controllable variances?

7    The following report has been prepared, relating to one product for March. This has been sent to the appropriate product manager as part of the company's monitoring procedures.

*Variance report: 31 March*

|                              | *Actual* | *Budget* | *Variance* |
|------------------------------|---------|---------|-----------|
| Production volume (units)    | 9,905   | 10,000  | 95 A      |
| Direct material (kgs)        | 9,800   | 10,000  | 200 F     |
| Direct material (£)          | 9,600   | 10,000  | 400 F     |
| Direct labour (hours)        | 2,500   | 2,400   | 100 A     |
| Direct labour (£)            | 8,500   | 8,400   | 100 A     |
| Total variable costs         | 18,100  | 18,400  | 300 F     |

The product manager has complained that the report ignores the principle of flexible budgeting and is unfair.

Prepare a report addressed to the management team which comments critically on the monthly variance report. Include, as an appendix to your report, the layout of a revised monthly variance report which will be more useful to the product manager. Include row and column headings, but do not calculate the contents of the report.

**8** Given below are key variances for the month of November, calculated using the flexed budget.

**Key variances – November**

|  | Variances | |
| --- | --- | --- |
|  | *Adverse* | *Favourable* |
|  | £ | £ |
| Variances: | | |
| Materials | 23,700 | |
| Labour | | 2,200 |
| Fixed overhead | 7,200 | |

You also discover the following information:

- due to staff shortages a more junior grade of labour than normal from one of the other factories had to be used in the production process, giving rise to inefficiencies and additional wastage

- the materials price has been increased by all suppliers and it is doubtful that the materials can be purchased more cheaply than this in future

- due to its inventory-holding policy the factory has had to rent some additional space but this has not been recognised in the standard fixed overhead cost

- due to the inefficiencies of labour more hours had to be worked than normal in the month

Write a report to the Managing Director explaining the possible reasons for the variances for the month and making any suggestions about future actions that should be taken.

# chapter 8:
# PERFORMANCE INDICATORS

— **chapter coverage** 📖 —

In this chapter we look at the use of performance measures in monitoring budgets.

We look first at the various forms they take, and how such measures compare budgeted and actual performance.

We then consider possible measures in the areas of:

✍ Quality

✍ Wastage

✍ Efficiency and productivity

✍ Capacity

We also look at specific indicators for service organisations

# PERFORMANCE INDICATORS IN BUDGETING

We have seen that a purpose of budgeting is to control and evaluate performance and to motivate staff. This is done by comparing actual performance with budgeted figures, and acting on the information this gives. Earlier in this Text we looked, specifically using variances, at the differences between actual and budgeted performance, as a means of analysing performance and determining the actions needed to improve, and drive the business forward.

In this chapter, we look at an alternative means of monitoring performance using budgets, by the setting of targets or PERFORMANCE INDICATORS. The budgeted value of these performance measures will be consistent with the key planning assumptions of the organisation. They can then be compared against the actual values achieved by an organisation and so performance can be evaluated in this way.

This technique of monitoring performance can be used on a regular, even daily basis at an operational level by the production and departmental managers of a business so that they can quickly react to any deviations from budget.

You have studied performance indicators in other Texts, but in this assessment you will not be asked, for example, to calculate the return on capital employed or the operating profit margin. Instead you will be asked to suggest suitable performance measures in given scenarios, for the activities of a variety of businesses. You should explain your suggested measure and might have to calculate and compare the budget and actual values for this measure. You may have to give some clear advice to enable the budget to be achieved if the actual values fall short of the target.

## Form of performance indicators

The indicators that you will need to consider for use in this assessment are particularly concerned with the operations of a business. You should ask yourself - what do the operational or production managers need to know, in order to effectively manage the business on a day-to-day basis?

Some of the performance measures will be expressed as **absolute figures**. For example, when considering materials usage, a production manager may want to know how much material (in kg) has been wasted in a day. This is an absolute number. In relation to labour, he or she might want to know the total number of hours that were idle ie paid for, but not used in production. He or she will compare these actual results with the targets, or budgeted figures (which may be nil), for these measures, and take action accordingly.

Instead of expressing absolute figures, performance measures can also be expressed in percentage terms eg how much material is wasted as a percentage of the total material used in production that day.

Such absolute or percentage measures are often referred to as **physical**, or **non-financial**. They are numerical, but are not expressed in £ terms. By contrast, if the materials wastage in the day (in kg) is then multiplied by the cost per kg, this gives a **financial** measure as it is expressed in money terms ie it is the cost to the company of the material wastage in that day.

## Simple financial measures

You should be familiar with a range of financial measures from your previous studies and, as we will see, the relevance of any particular measure will depend on the nature of the organisation, the comparisons that can be made and the controllability of the components of each measure. Examples of some very simple financial measures that may be used when assessing performance include:

- Average selling price per unit – this could be compared against the retail price to give an idea of how much the price has been discounted to achieve actual volumes

- Profit as a percentage of sales revenue – this could be based on gross or net profit and could be compared with other businesses to see how the organisation's percentage returns on sales compare to that of competitors

- Materials cost per unit of purchase – when compared with the total unit cost this can help management understand how much of a unit cost for a product is made up of the raw materials

- Labour rate per hour – if this increases over the year by more than the average wage increases for the industry, management will probably want to know why

- Cost per unit of production – as we have seen, management often want to attribute costs to cost units and monitor the movements in that cost.

In addition, as we have already seen, sales and cost variances are used to monitor performance when actual performance is compared with budgeted performance.

For Level 4 Budgeting, an awareness of common financial measures such as these will not be enough on its own. You need to be able to apply knowledge of how and why performance indicators of various types are constructed so that, as stated earlier, you can look at a scenario and suggest suitable measures. As you progress through the chapter you will come across a number of examples of different measures, but it is not possible to cover every measure. However, if you understand how performance measurement works you should be able to identify relevant measures for any given scenario.

## Comparability

As the performance measures can be used in comparison with budgets or targets, then it is important that we are comparing like with like. For example, if the production manager finds out that the material wastage in a day is actually 20 kg, but the budgeted figure is 50 kg, he or she will be happy with the performance. However if the budgeted figure actually relates to the targeted wastage over a period of five days ie 10 kg wastage per day on average, the actual performance is shown to be poor.

## Areas of performance

Performance indicators can be calculated to cover different aspects of operational performance. We will look at examples of typical performance measures in the following areas.

- Quality – usually in relation to units of finished goods, but sometimes used when considering materials

- Wastage of materials

- Efficiency and productivity – relates to labour, but also machinery

- Capacity – can also relate to machinery or labour

However, it is important that you do not just learn the measures discussed in this chapter as a definitive list. In the assessment, you may be asked to identify suitable performance measures for a particular business or scenario which is not specifically covered here. Think carefully about the resources used by the business and this should help you identify useful measures.

Suitable performance indicators will vary depending on whether a business is in manufacturing, retail or service, and you should consider this when asked to identify appropriate measures.

# QUALITY

Suitable performance indicators for the QUALITY of physical goods could be a mixture of non-financial and financial performance indicators.

## Non-financial indicators

Performance measures to assess quality might consider defective units discovered before they have left the factory (and so which are rejected following production) or customer satisfaction with the products (lack of which may lead to return of the goods after being purchased).

Therefore possible measures or indicators of quality might be:

- number of goods returned

- percentage of number of goods returned to number of goods sold

- number of warranty claims as a percentage of total units sold

- number of customer complaints as a percentage of total number of sales

- percentage of defective materials compared to total materials

- number of anticipated defective units

- percentage of defective units to total of units produced

## Financial indicators

Other indicators may be financial, and could include:

- cost per customer of the customer service department
- cost per customer of after-sales service
- the percentage of the sales value of returned goods to total sales value
- unit cost of returned goods
- unit cost of repair of returned goods
- cost of reworking defective goods as a percentage of total production cost

## Measuring quality of services

Finding performance indicators for quality of manufactured goods is much more straightforward than finding performance indicators for the quality of services.

Measuring the quality of a service again involves measuring customer satisfaction, therefore the first stage is to ensure that the organisation knows what it is that the customer expects from the service.

Some of the performance indicators for quality of a service may be qualitative, such as surveys of customer opinion. A further method of assessing the quality of a service may be by inspection, either by an internal or an external body, such as government inspections of schools.

There can also be quantitative, although normally non-financial, performance indicators for a service, such as average waiting times for hospital operations or the percentage of train journeys that did not run on time.

## Task 1

What type of quality performance indicators might a taxi firm consider?

## WASTAGE OF MATERIALS

One concern of the production manager will be the amount of materials wastage in the production process. It will be preferable for this to be minimised but some wastage may be inevitable in a production process. A budget may set a target for the amount (or percentage) of wastage in an attempt to keep this to a low level.

## HOW IT WORKS

Lane Engineering has the following materials wastage figures for four days of production.

|       | Total materials used (kg) | Materials wastage (kg) |
|-------|---------------------------|------------------------|
| Day 1 | 3,500                     | 50                     |
| Day 2 | 4,200                     | 70                     |
| Day 3 | 4,800                     | 100                    |
| Day 4 | 5,000                     | 80                     |

The targets set for materials wastage in the budget were that wastage should exceed no more than 1.5% of the materials used each day, and also no more than 90 kg per day should be wasted in total.

The production manager can see immediately that the absolute target of 90 kg per day was exceeded on day 3 but he also calculates the percentage wastage.

|       |                      | Percentage wastage |
|-------|----------------------|--------------------|
| Day 1 | $\dfrac{50}{3,500}$  | 1.43%              |
| Day 2 | $\dfrac{70}{4,200}$  | 1.67%              |
| Day 3 | $\dfrac{100}{4,800}$ | 2.08%              |
| Day 4 | $\dfrac{80}{5,000}$  | 1.60%              |

The percentage target was exceeded not only on day 3 but also on days 2 and 4.

The reasons for the materials wastage should be investigated, as the target is not met on three out of four days. There may be a short-term reason why the materials wastage is excessive eg if a grade of labour with lower skills than usual is being used or if the material batch is of lower quality than usual. However, it may be that this is the best that can be achieved, and such wastage is likely to continue. If this is the case, then the target materials wastage measure is unrealistic and should be amended.

You can see that this is similar to the process of investigating and acting upon variances that we saw in Chapter 7. However, it is arguably easier for the production manager to see and assess these performance measures on a daily or weekly basis, and so make operational changes accordingly (eg redeploying more skilled labour to this activity).

When trying to identify possible performance measures in the assessment, you should bear in mind that the purpose of these measures is to monitor actual performance against budget but in a swift and easy fashion. Good measures are often the simplest.

The targets or measures which were used above were non-financial but could have been turned into financial measures by multiplying the materials wastage figures (in kg) by the cost of the material in £.

---

## Task 2

The assembly department of a toy manufacturing business carries out the activity of attaching wheels onto toy cars. Occasionally, the wheels break as they are attached, and have to be discarded.

Suggest two possible performance indicators relating to the usage of wheel components by the assembly department.

---

## EFFICIENCY, PRODUCTIVITY & CAPACITY

Efficiency, productivity and capacity are aspects of performance which in a manufacturing business often relate to labour. However, the efficiency and capacity of equipment or machinery can also be monitored if machine hours, rather than labour hours, are considered.

### Measuring labour performance

A simple performance measure for direct labour of a business is how many units workers manage to produce in a period, compared with the budgeted level.

There could be two reasons why labour managed to produce more units than expected in the budget:

- The employees worked harder ie they were more efficient or productive.

- There were more labour hours available than expected, either through overtime or an increased number of employees ie there was increased capacity.

Alternatively, an increase in activity may be due to a mixture of both these factors. A decrease in the activity could be due to employees working less hard (lower productivity), there being less labour hours available (lower capacity) but also if there was idle time (workers paid but without there being work to do).

Therefore, when considering performance measures to assess labour, both productivity/efficiency and capacity may be considered.

## Productivity and efficiency

The terms 'efficiency' and 'productivity' are strongly related, and may be used interchangeably.

PRODUCTIVITY is a measure of how hard the employees are working or how productive they are being in their hours at work and is often measured in terms of units of output.

Possible performance measures relating to productivity are therefore how many units of product or service are being produced either each hour or by each employee. These measures are shown below in an equation format to help your understanding. However, in an assessment just stating "productivity" when asked to give a performance measure will not answer the task. You need to say what you mean by this.

$$\text{Productivity per labour hour} = \frac{\text{Output in the period}}{\text{Hours worked in the period}}$$

$$\text{Productivity per employee} = \frac{\text{Output in the period}}{\text{No of employees working on output}}$$

## HOW IT WORKS

Harris Engineering has budgeted and actual results for the month of June as follows:

|  | Actual | Budget |
|---|---|---|
| Units produced | 285,000 | 250,000 |
| Number of production workers | 30 | 28 |
| Hours worked | 4,800 | 4,400 |

Two possible performance measures of productivity are:

1. The number of units produced per labour hour

$$\text{Actual productivity} = \frac{285,000 \text{ units}}{4,800 \text{ hours}}$$

$$= 59.4 \text{ units per hour}$$

$$\text{Budgeted productivity} = \frac{250,000 \text{ units}}{4,400 \text{ hours}}$$

$$= 56.8 \text{ units per labour hour}$$

2. Number of units produced per employee

|  | | *Actual* | *Budget* |
|---|---|---|---|
| Productivity per employee | = | $\dfrac{285,000}{30}$ | $\dfrac{250,000}{28}$ |
|  | = | 9,500 units per employee | 8,929 units per employee |

In this case, the actual productivity during June is high compared to the budgeted productivity, under both measures. An increase in productivity over budget means that more units were produced in one hour or by one employee. This will normally mean a reduction in costs, as the same number of units can be produced in fewer hours and therefore with reduced labour costs, machine costs and overheads.

If the labour cost is assumed here to be £10 per hour, the labour cost has actually increased in absolute terms from £44,000 per the budget to £48,000. If this figure had been considered alone, this may have been regarded as poor performance. However, the labour cost per unit has actually decreased from

$$\text{Budgeted} = \frac{44,000}{250,000} = £0.176$$

to

$$\text{Actual} = \frac{48,000}{285,000} = £0.168$$

and this is explained by the increased productivity.

Note that we have been considering measures that assess the performance of workers, and so have used labour hours here. The efficiency and productivity of machinery could be considered by replacing labour hours with machine hours. Although the variation in machinery performance may be expected to be less than that of labour performance, such a performance indicator would highlight if machinery was ageing or poorly maintained, and so becoming less efficient.

## HOW IT WORKS

Harris Engineering has a sales department which processes all orders for goods. A suitable performance target for the sales team might be sales orders per employee.

In June the six members of the telephone sales team processed 1,240 orders.

$$\text{Productivity per employee} = \frac{\text{Output} = \text{number of orders}}{\text{Number of employees}}$$

$$= \frac{1,240 \text{ orders}}{6 \text{ employees}}$$

$$= 207 \text{ orders per employee}$$

---

### Task 3

An advertising company budgeted for the production of 216 advertisements in the next quarter using 26 advertising executives. The actual performance in the quarter was only 188 advertisements produced by 22 executives.

What was the actual productivity of the executives (to 1 decimal place) compared with budget?

| | Productivity (per executive) |
|---|---|
| Actual | |
| Budget | |
| Favourable/(Adverse) variance | |

---

### Idle time ratios

A key performance measure that a production manager will be interested in, when assessing labour costs, is how much paid time is wasted as idle time. This is the difference between the actual hours that have to be paid to a worker, and the number of hours that are actually put to use in production ie hours paid versus hours worked. The absolute figure of idle hours for a department could be used as a performance indicator; an organisation would want this to be as low as possible, so would often budget for this to be zero.

The number of idle time hours can be multiplied by the labour rate (cost in £) to give a financial measure.

Alternatively this could be calculated as a ratio of the idle hours per employee:

$$\frac{\text{Total idle hours}}{\text{number of employees}}$$

If the actual performance is monitored, and the idle hours indicator is not zero, it may be that management take the decision to redeploy workers to other areas of the business such as the manufacture of alternative products.

It is important to note that idle time is not caused by workers working more slowly; it is caused by there being no work to do during this time, perhaps because of a materials shortage, a machine breakdown etc.

## Capacity

We said that increased productivity or efficiency is only one of the reasons why the labour force may have produced more units in a period than budgeted ie why their activity was higher than expected.

The other reason would be if the number of labour hours was actually more than budgeted. This could be because there were more employees available in this particular department, perhaps redeployed from elsewhere in the business, or because casual, seasonal staff have been employed. Alternatively, the increased capacity could be because overtime has been paid such that individual employees have themselves worked for more hours than budgeted in the period.

Simple performance measures relating to capacity are therefore:

- the total number of hours worked by employees in the period (or even more simply, the number of employees)

- the total number of overtime hours worked

- the number of labour hours (or overtime hours) worked per employee

- the number of hours worked by casual staff in the period.

We said that efficiency and capacity measures can relate to both labour and machines. Machine capacity is a particular issue for a capital intensive operation, which might include the following in its performance measures:

- the total number of machine hours in the period

- the number of hours lost through machine breakdowns

- number (or percentage) of machines in use per day. The percentage may be described as a machine utilisation rate, but you should always explain what you mean by a suggested measure clearly.

## Task 4

A manufacturing organisation had a budgeted output of 288,000 units planned for a 20 day period in October. 268,000 units were in fact produced.

There are 10 workers each guaranteed eight hours work a day for each of the 20 days. The budgeted output would be achieved by full use of this labour, with no overtime.

However, for two half days, the machinery used in production broke down and no units could be produced.

Suggest and calculate performance measures to explain why the activity was lower than expected.

## SERVICE ORGANISATIONS

In this chapter we have concentrated on performance indicators for manufacturing organisations. Performance indicators obviously also have to be calculated for organisations that provide a service rather than a tangible product, such as accountancy firms, a transport provider or a college of education.

Many of the performance indicators considered in this chapter will be relevant to service industries although they will need to be expressed slightly differently. For example, a unit might be a chargeable hour in an accountancy firm or a passenger mile in a transport provider.

Productivity will also be assessed in service organisations, adapted to suit their circumstances – in an accountancy firm it might be measured as the percentage of chargeable hours to total hours; in a college of education the number of students enrolled per lecturer; in a transport company the number of passengers transported per month.

When trying to assess the quality of its performance, such service organisations cannot look at 'defective units' but may use a variety of other performance measures. For example, an accountancy firm will monitor the number of clients that leave the firm for another firm, a transport provider will be concerned about delays on routes, a college of education will take particular note of the students' assessments of the lecturers.

Service organisations are sometimes the scenario in an assessment for a number of tasks. Use the information in the scenario and the techniques that you have learnt in this chapter to adapt performance indicators to the requirements of the organisation being considered.

---

## Task 5

Suggest a possible performance measure for an events planner (who plans weddings, parties and corporate events) to monitor the quality of his or her work.

---

## CHAPTER OVERVIEW

- Performance indicators can be calculated to summarise quality, wastage, efficiency/productivity and capacity – some of the performance indicators will be non-financial measures and some will be financial measures

- After the performance indicators are calculated, the actual and budgeted indicators must be compared and interpreted

- Measuring quality often involves measuring customer satisfaction with the goods or service  and measures may be non-financial eg % of customers who complain, or financial eg cost per customer of the customer service department

- Productivity can be measured as units produced per hour or units produced per employee

- Service organisations will also require performance indicators but they may be slightly different from those for manufacturing or retail organisations due to the nature of the organisation

## Keywords

**Performance indicators** – targets for operational performance

**Quality** – a measure of defectiveness or customer satisfaction

**Productivity** – a measure of how hard the employees are working

## TEST YOUR LEARNING

1   Suggest suitable performance measures for a supermarket manager to assess the performance of the cashiers.

2   Suggest a suitable performance measure for the quality of finished goods from a production line.

3   A bakery will throw away bread rolls made during the day if they have not properly risen. What performance indicators might the production manager use to monitor this?

4   A travel firm employs five sales representatives to sell holidays.

    Suggest an appropriate performance indicator to measure productivity against budget.

5   A pizza restaurant has three ovens, each with five shelves that can fit one pizza per shelf. Suggest an appropriate performance indicator relating to capacity.

# ANSWERS TO CHAPTER TASKS

## CHAPTER 1   Cost classification

**1**   Buys material for use in production – Purchasing department

Finds and secures new customers – Sales department

Ensures employees have the appropriate computer hardware and software – IT

Promotes the organisation's name, brand, products or services – Marketing

Manufactures products for sale – Production department

**2**   **Cost centres**

Purchasing department

Production department

Bottling/packaging department

Distribution/transport department

Maintenance department

**Profit centres**

Sales team

Merchandising/shop

**3**   Client entertaining at horse racing – Marketing department

Repair of security alarm system in offices – Administration department

Sick pay for production manager – Production department

Bonus for sales managers – Sales team

Depreciation of production equipment – Production department

**4 Fixed cost per unit:**

| Production level | Budgeted fixed cost per unit £ |
|---|---|
| 20,000 units | 5.00 |
| 40,000 units | 2.50 |
| 80,000 units | 1.25 |

**Working**

| Production level | | | Cost |
|---|---|---|---|
| 20,000 units | £100,000/20,000 | = | £5.00 per unit |
| 40,000 units | £100,000/40,000 | = | £2.50 per unit |
| 80,000 units | £100,000/80,000 | = | £1.25 per unit |

**5**

| Cost | Behaviour |
|---|---|
| Stores department costs which include £5,000 of insurance premium and an average of £100 cost per materials receipt or issue | Semi-variable |
| Machinery depreciation based upon machine hours used | Variable |
| Salary costs of lecturers in a training college where one lecturer is required for every 200 students enrolled | Stepped |
| Buildings insurance for a building housing the stores, the factory and the canteen | Fixed |
| Wages for production workers who are paid per unit produced with a guaranteed weekly minimum wage of £250 | Fixed then semi-variable* |

*This is fixed at low levels of activity because initially activity will have no impact on the cost. For example if workers are paid £1 for each unit each week with a minimum wage of £250, the cost will not have any variable behaviour until the 251st unit is produced (when it becomes semi-variable).

**6**

| Sales | Monthly salary £ |
|---|---|
| 4 sales | 880 |
| 8 sales | 960 |
| 15 sales | 1,100 |

**Working**

| Sales | Monthly salary | £ |
|---|---|---|
| 4 sales | £800 + (4 × £20) = | £880 |
| 8 sales | £800 + (8 × £20) = | £960 |
| 15 sales | £800 + (15 × £20)= | £1,100 |

**7**

| Costing method | Cost per unit £ |
|---|---|
| Absorption costing | 15.00 |
| Marginal costing | 10.00 |

**Workings**

**Cost per unit – absorption costing**

| | £ |
|---|---|
| Direct materials | 12,000 |
| Direct labour | 15,000 |
| Variable overheads | 23,000 |
| Fixed overheads | 25,000 |
| Total cost | 75,000 |
| Cost per unit = | £75,000/5,000 |
| = | £15 per unit |

### Cost per unit – marginal costing

|                     | £             |
|---------------------|--------------:|
|                     | £             |
| Direct materials    | 12,000        |
| Direct labour       | 15,000        |
| Variable overheads  | 23,000        |
| Total cost          | 50,000        |
| Cost per unit  =    | £50,000/5,000 |
|       =             | £10 per unit  |

**8**

| Overhead included in Product A | £5,000  |
|--------------------------------|---------|
| Overhead included in Product B | £26,000 |

### Workings

| Cost per inspection        | = | £74,000/370         |
|----------------------------|---|---------------------|
|                            | = | £200 per inspection |
| Overhead included in A's cost | = | £200 × 25        |
|                            | = | £5,000              |
| Overhead included in B's cost | = | £200 × 130       |
|                            | = | £26,000             |

## CHAPTER 2   Budgetary control systems

1   Authorisation and planning

2   The budget may reflect:

   – a reduced sales price per unit of existing product required to sell it if competitors' products are superior

   – reduced sales volume as the product becomes obsolete

   – corresponding reduced production budget

   – high research and development costs in relation to the new product

   – high advertising costs if the new product will be launched this year

   Note that only two suggestions were required.

BPP
LEARNING MEDIA

3    The budget committee should be made up of senior executives from all functional areas of the business plus the budget officer.

4    The finance officer is using an incremental method of budgeting by increasing the previous year's costs. This is inappropriate as the activities of the charity change from year to year, so the actual resources that have to be bought, including labour costs, or services which must be paid for, will vary significantly from the prior year. It is not just the cost of these that will vary because of inflation, but the charity's use of these resources. A more suitable alternative would be to use programme based budgeting. This would look at each of the projects being funded in turn, consider the resource requirement, and build a budget accordingly.

5    The company is using bottom up budgeting in order to create the budget. This might motivate the design team to work hard to achieve the budget because they feel part of the budget process, and believe that the targets set are realistic. However, the designer has built in budgetary slack in order to make the budget easier to meet. This will often have the outcome of causing favourable variances when actual costs are compared to the budget, even if there is no real improvement in performance.

6    The benefits are that all the managers of a department are motivated to achieve the firm's goals. It is of benefit to all managers if workload is spread between them. However, even if Sally works hard and achieves the targets set for her, she cannot receive her bonus if her colleagues do not work as hard. This is de-motivating.

     As the fee targets are set at the start of the year and not reviewed, the scheme could have a de-motivating effect, for example if staff leave and are not replaced but the departmental target does not take account of fewer available chargeable hours (which can be converted into fees).

     The staff who are not managers have no incentive to work hard as they cannot participate in the scheme.

7    As income is received and then spent on a quarterly basis, a suitable period for the budget to cover is a quarter. In reality, an annual budget may be drawn up which is split into quarters.

8    A forecast is an expectation of what might happen, whereas a plan is a deliberate commitment or intent.

## CHAPTER 3   Forecasting

1

| Opening and closing materials inventories | No |
|---|---|
| Production budget | Yes |
| Material quantity (kg) per unit | Yes |
| Material cost per kg | No |

The materials **usage** budget would use the production budget (number of units to be produced) and the material quantity (kg) per unit.

Note that the materials **purchases** budget would use the materials usage budget, together with the opening and closing inventory of materials, and the materials cost per kg.

2   Paper – revenue item as consumable

Service of fire alarm system – revenue item, no enduring benefit

Purchase of factory unit – capital item, enduring benefit

New motor for existing machine replacing broken one – revenue, no enhancement.

3   Salary rates for different types of employee (professional/non-professional)
Overtime hours worked
Overtime rates
Absentee levels
Idle time hours
Chargeable hours
Staff availability

**4**

| Information required | Source |
|---|---|
| Population figures for areas in the UK | Office for National Statistics |
| VAT rates | HM Revenue & Customs website |
| Possible sales prices achievable in the market place | Trade journal |

**5** Quota sampling would be the most appropriate method in this situation. Here a fixed number from each stratum of the population eg, male/female, different age groups etc, is chosen as the sample. Consumers will be interviewed until each quota has been satisfied.

**6** Sales volume forecast:

| Quarter | | £ |
|---|---|---|
| Quarter 1 | (248,000 × 1.03) × 0.65 | 166,036 |
| Quarter 2 | (248,000 × 1.03 × 1.03) × 0.85 | 223,638 |
| Quarter 3 | (248,000 × 1.03 × 1.03 × 1.03) × 1.30 | 352,295 |
| Quarter 4 | (248,000 × 1.03 × 1.03 × 1.03 × 1.03) × 1.20 | 334,951 |

**7** Forecast costs

| Quarter | £ |
|---|---|
| Quarter 1 | 374,487 |
| Quarter 2 | 458,214 |

**Workings**

Quarter 1     $346{,}700 \times \dfrac{177.9}{164.7} = 374{,}487$

Quarter 2     $394{,}500 \times \dfrac{191.3}{164.7} = 458{,}214$

**8** Variable cost per unit =

| £ | 6.00 |
|---|---|

Total fixed cost =

| £ | 23,000 |
|---|---|

**Workings**

|  | Units | £ |
|---|---|---|
| Highest level | 28,000 | 191,000 |
| Lowest level | 20,000 | 143,000 |
| Increase | 8,000 | 48,000 |

$$\text{Variable rate} = \frac{£48,000}{8,000}$$

$$= £6 \text{ per unit}$$

At highest level:

|  | £ |
|---|---|
| Variable cost 28,000 × £6 | 168,000 |
| Fixed cost (balancing figure) | 23,000 |
| Total cost | 191,000 |

**9**

|  | Dependent | Independent |
|---|---|---|
| Sales volume | ✓ | |
| Advertising costs | | ✓ |

On the basis that advertising affects the level of sales it can be assumed that the dependent variable is sales volume and the independent variable is advertising costs.

**10** Production costs:

| £ | 203,800 |
|---|---|

**Working**

Production costs $= 63,000 + (3.2 \times 44,000)$

$= £203,800$

**11**

| Month | Estimated sales units (000's) |
|---|---|
| 1 | 34.8 |
| 2 | 36.0 |
| 3 | 37.2 |

The first two years account for x = 1 to x = 24

Thus the x values in which we are interested are x = 25, 26, 27

x = 25 :    y = 4.8 + 1.2(25) = 34.8        ie 34,800

x = 26 :    y = 4.8 + 1.2(26) = 36.0        ie 36,000

x = 27 :    y = 4.8 + 1.2(27) = 37.2        ie 37,200

## CHAPTER 4   Budget preparation

1    Using an ideal standard for materials cost which allows for no material wastage will have a de-motivating effect on workers, as even with the most careful working they will never be able to achieve the materials usage reflected in this cost.

While the production manager is right to try to use the budget to improve the performance of workers, the budget must reflect realistic, although challenging, performance.    It should therefore use an attainable standard instead, which might be based on the materials usage of the most experienced (and presumably least wasteful) workers, and so will incorporate a small amount of wastage.

Additionally, if an ideal standard is used, such that material usage will always be greater than budgeted, this could lead to production stoppages if insufficient material has been purchased to meet the actual usage, and it is difficult to source more at short notice.

2    The correct answer is: ⎡ 3,300 ⎤ units

|  | Units |
|---|---|
| Sales | 3,500 |
| Less: opening inventories of finished goods | (800) |
| Add: closing inventories of finished goods | 600 |
| Production quantity | 3,300 |

3    The correct answer is: ⎡ 4,422 ⎤ units

|  |  | % | Units |
|---|---|---|---|
| Good units |  | 95 | 4,200 |
| Anticipated defective units | 4,200 × 5/95 | 5 | 222 |
| Required production | 4,200 × 100/95 | 100 | 4,422 |

**4** The correct answer is: ⟨85,556⟩ kg

|  |  | Kg |
|---|---|---|
| Kg required for production | 5 × 15,400 | 77,000 |
| Additional for normal loss | 77,000 × 10/90 | 8,556 |
| Required usage | 15,400 × 5 × 100/90 | 85,556 |

**5** The correct answer is:

£ ⟨327, 860⟩

| Litres |  |  |
|---|---|---|
| Materials usage |  | 124,000 |
| Less: opening inventory |  | (14,000) |
| Add: closing inventory | 14,000 × 1.15 | 16,100 |
| Materials purchases |  | 126,100 |
| Cost of purchases | 126,100 × £2.60 | £327,860 |

**6** The correct answer is: ⟨222⟩ hours.

| Standard time | 20 units × 10 hours | 200 |
|---|---|---|
| Additional time | 200 × 10/90 | 22 |
| Total time required | 20 × 10 × 100/90 | 222 |

**7** The correct answer is: ⟨60,000⟩ hours.

Hours required   12,000 × 6 hours × 100/120   60,000 hours

## CHAPTER 5 Preparing cash budgets

**1** The correct answer is:

£ ⟨366,000⟩

**Working - November receipts**

|  | £ |
|---|---|
| October sales (400,000 × 40%) | 160,000 |
| September sales (360,000 × 35%) | 126,000 |
| August sales (320,000 × 25%) | 80,000 |
|  | 366,000 |

**2**    The correct answer is:

| £ | 189,000 |
|---|---------|

**Working - October payments**

|  | £ |
|---|---|
| September purchases (260,000 × 75% × 60%) | 117,000 |
| August purchases (240,000 × 75% × 40%) | 72,000 |
|  | 189,000 |

**3    Cash budget – November**

|  | £ |
|---|---|
| *Cash receipts:* |  |
| Cash sales | 64,000 |
| Credit sales    November (238,000 × 40% × 98%) | 93,296 |
| October (216,000 × 60%) | 129,600 |
| *Total cash receipts* | 286,896 |
| *Cash payments:* |  |
| Purchases on credit | 144,000 |
| Wages and salaries | 80,000 |
| Overheads (65,000 – 15,000) | 50,000 |
| Dividend | 20,000 |
| *Total cash payments* | 294,000 |
| Net cash flow | (7,104) |
| Opening balance | (10,200) |
| Closing balance | (17,304) |

**4** The correct answer is:

£ | 109,025

**Working - October receipts**

|  | £ |
|---|---|
| October sales (150,000 × 10% × 97.5%) | 14,625 |
| September sales (100,000 × 50%) | 50,000 |
| August sales (120,000 × 37%) | 44,400 |
|  | 109,025 |

**5** The correct answer is:

£ | 1,687,500

**Workings**

**Production budget – August**

|  | Units |
|---|---|
| Sales | 45,000 |
| Less: opening inventory of finished goods | (4,000) |
| Add: closing inventory of finished goods | 6,000 |
| Production quantity | 47,000 |

**Purchases budget – for August production**

|  | Kgs |
|---|---|
| For production (47,000 × 5) | 235,000 |
| Less: opening inventory of materials | (40,000) |
| Add: closing inventory of materials | 30,000 |
| Material required – to be purchased the month before ie July | 225,000 |

**Purchases payment – August**

|  | £ |
|---|---|
| 225,000 kgs × £7.50 | 1,687,500 |

**6** The correct answer is:

$$£ \boxed{\phantom{xx}90,000\phantom{xx}}$$

**Working**

Closing receivables = opening receivables + sales – cash inflow

Budgeted sales = £24,000 − £18,000 + £84,000 = £90,000

## CHAPTER 6   Budget preparation – limiting factors

**1** The correct answer is $\boxed{22,000}$ units

**Working**

$$\text{Maximum production level} = \frac{165,000\,\text{kg}}{7.5\,\text{kg}}$$

$$= 22,000 \text{ units}$$

**2** The correct answer is $\boxed{4.3}$ hours per week

**Working**

| | |
|---|---:|
| Hours required 2,000 × 5.5 | 11,000 |
| Hours currently available 280 × 35 | 9,800 |
| Overtime hours required | 1,200 |

$$\text{Overtime per employee} = \frac{1,200}{280} = 4.3 \text{ hours per week}$$

## CHAPTER 7   Flexed budgets and variances

**1** The correct answer is:

$$£ \boxed{\phantom{xx}16,000\phantom{xx}}$$

**Working**

| | |
|---|---|
| At 120,000 units – 3 supervisors required – cost | =£12,000/3 |
| | =£4,000 each |
| At 180,000 units – 4 supervisors required – cost | =£16,000 |

**2** The correct answer is:

| £ | 18,290 |
|---|---|

**Working**

Cost per unit at 2,000 units = £15,800/2,000

= £7.90

Cost per unit at 3,000 units = £19,950/3,000

= £6.65

Therefore this is a semi-variable cost

| | Activity level | Cost |
|---|---|---|
| | units | £ |
| | 2,000 | 15,800 |
| | 3,000 | 19,950 |
| Increase | 1,000 | 4,150 |

| Variable element | = | £4,150/1,000 |
|---|---|---|
| | = | £4.15 per unit |

£

At 2,000 units:

| Variable element 2,000 units × £4.15 | 8,300 |
|---|---|
| Fixed element (bal fig) | 7,500 |
| Total cost | 15,800 |

At 2,600 units:

| Variable element 2,600 units × £4.15 | 10,790 |
|---|---|
| Fixed element | 7,500 |
| Total cost | 18,290 |

**3** Profit is higher under | marginal | costing

As inventory levels are falling profit will be higher under marginal costing.

(Note: Under absorption costing, more fixed overheads are brought forward from the previous period in opening inventory, than carried forward in closing inventory. There will thus be a net **additional charge** in this period.)

4 The casual worker is unskilled so may well have taken more time than the permanent worker, which would be expected to give an adverse variance. However the labour rate of the casual worker is probably cheaper leading to a favourable rate variance which more than compensates for any reduced efficiency. Alternatively, the casual worker may have been working more efficiently in an attempt to be taken on full-time.

*Tutorial note – you should have commented on the lower rate, but you may have missed the unskilled element. The third point is unlikely to be thought of by many candidates. The key with the discussion elements of the tasks in this area is that often the reasons for variances are unclear, but any logical arguments supported by the facts are likely to score well.*

5 The marketing overhead variance will be adverse because of the increased expenditure. There will be no effect on the sales variance, unless the selling price of the product is changed as part of the advertising campaign. Sales may increase over the level of the fixed budget due to increased volume, but since the flexed budget takes account of any change in volume, any variance is due solely to price changes.

6 If the business only pays its workers the minimum wage, then the variance is due, at least in part, to the increased labour rate compared with the standard being used, if the standard has not been updated to reflect this. The standard should be altered. However, this may not be the only reason for the adverse variance. The amount of the variance should be investigated compared to the level of increase of the minimum wage. Workers may be working less efficiently than budgeted.

## CHAPTER 8  Performance indicators

1 Quality performance indicators for a taxi firm:

- percentage of taxis arriving on time compared to total taxi trips made

- percentage of repeat customers compared to total customers

- survey results of customer satisfaction

- number of customer complaints

2 Assembly department performance measures re toy cars:

- number of wheels discarded per day
- number of wheels discarded as a percentage of total wheels used
- number of wheels discarded as percentage of toy cars made
- cost of wheels discarded per day

Note that the performance measures involving breaking wheels might involve machine or labour hours too (eg hours lost attaching wheels which break), as these are increased if time is spent attaching a wheel that then breaks, and so another wheel has to be attached. However, only two simple performance measures were required here.

**3**

| | Productivity (per executive) |
|---|---|
| Actual | 8.5 |
| Budget | 8.3 |
| Favourable/(Adverse) variance | 0.2 Favourable |

**Working**

| | Budget | Actual |
|---|---|---|
| Productivity | | |
| 216/26 | 8.3 per executive | |
| 188/22 | | 8.5 per executive |

**4** Possible performance measures include:

– Number of hours of idle time (and cost of this if labour rate were known)

– Number of hours worked (budget vs actual)

– Budgeted and actual units made per labour hour worked

– Number of hours of idle time = $2 \times 4$ (half day) $\times 10$ (number of employees who cannot work during this time) = 80 hours

The cost of idle hours would be found by multiplying the number of hours by the labour rate.

Number of hours paid/budgeted as worked = $10 \times 8 \times 20 = 1,600$ hours

Number of hours actually worked = $1,600 - 80 = 1,520$

Therefore, budgeted productivity = $288,000/1,600 = 180$ units/hour

Actual productivity based on hours actually worked = $268,000/1,520 = 176$ units/hour

Therefore the reduced activity is not only due to the machine breakdown giving rise to idle time, but the workers also worked less efficiently.

**5**    Number of new clients obtained by referral from past clients

Number (or percentage) of clients who book events again (repeat bookings)

Value of work from repeat bookings

Number of complaints by guests at the event (feedback from guests)

Number of complaints by client about event

**Answers to chapter tasks**

# TEST YOUR LEARNING – ANSWERS

## CHAPTER 1   Cost classification

**1**   The correct answers are:

Overtime costs of production workers – Production department
Depreciation of cars used by sales staff – Sales department
Training course for sales director – Sales department
Advertising posters – Marketing department

**2**   The cost behaviour demonstrated by this cost is   Semi-variable

**3**   The budgeted cost for supervisors is £ 60,000 (as three supervisors are needed to cover 270,000 units at a cost of £20,000 each).

This cost exhibits   stepped   behaviour.

**4**   The correct answer is: **True**.

| 10,000 units | Cost per unit | £43,600/10,000 | = | £4.36 |
| 12,000 units | Cost per unit | £52,320/12,000 | = | £4.36 |

As the cost per unit is the same at each level of production this would appear to be a purely variable cost.

**5**   The correct answers are:

|  | Fixed costs (£) | Cost per unit (£ to nearest 1p) |
|---|---|---|
| (a)  3,000 units? | 64,000 | 21.33 |
| (b) 10,000 units? | 64,000 | 6.40 |
| (c) 16,000 units? | 64,000 | 4.00 |

**Workings**

(a) Total fixed cost  $=$  £64,000
Fixed cost per unit  $=$  £21.33
£64,000/3,000

(b) Total fixed cost  $=$  £64,000
Fixed cost per unit  $=$  £6.40
£64,000/10,000

(c) Total fixed cost  $=$  £64,000
Fixed cost per unit  $=$  £4.00
£64,000/16,000

6  Cost of the production staff canteen

> Activity based charge to production cost centres

Redecorating reception area

> Allocate to administrative overheads

Machine maintenance

> Charge to production in a machine hour overhead rate

Sick pay for production workers

> Charge to production in a labour hour overhead rate

7  Since production is so machine-intensive, overheads should be absorbed on the basis of machine hours, so the overhead absorption rate = £180,000/30,000 = £6 per machine hour.

8

| | Cutting | Finishing |
|---|---|---|
| Reapportioned store overheads (£) | 80,000 | 20,000 |
| Overhead absorption rate (see working) | £1.45 per labour hour | £3.08 per labour hour |

| Costs per unit | GH (£) | JK (£) |
|---|---|---|
| Direct materials | 20.00 | 12.00 |
| Direct labour<br>(24.00 + 6.40)<br>(16.00 + 3.20) | 30.40 | 19.20 |
| Overheads<br>(4.35 + 3.08)<br>(2.90 + 1.54) | 7.43 | 4.44 |
| Total cost per unit | 57.83 | 35.64 |

**Workings**

Absorption rate

|  | Cutting<br>£ | Finishing<br>£ | Stores<br>£ |
|---|---|---|---|
| Allocated and apportioned overheads | 225,000 | 180,000 | 100,000 |
| Stores – reapportioned | 80,000 | 20,000 | (100,000) |
|  | 305,000 | 200,000 | — |

Total budgeted labour hours

| | | |
|---|---|---|
| (3 × 50,000) + (2 × 30,000) | 210,000 | |
| (1 × 50,000) + (0.5 × 30,000) | | 65,000 |

| Overhead absorption rate | £305,000 | £200,000 |
|---|---|---|
| | 210,000 | 65,000 |
| | £1.45 per labour hour | £3.08 per labour hour |

| *Cost per unit* | | GH<br>£ | JK<br>£ |
|---|---|---|---|
| Direct materials | | 20.00 | 12.00 |
| Direct labour – | Cutting | 24.00 | 16.00 |
| | Finishing | 6.40 | 3.20 |
| Overheads – | Cutting 3 × £1.45 | 4.35 | |
| | 2 × £1.45 | | 2.90 |
| | Finishing 1 × £3.08 | 3.08 | |
| | 0.5 × £3.08 | | 1.54 |
| Total cost per unit | | 57.83 | 35.64 |

**9** Overheads should be absorbed on an activity basis as follows:

Stores costs = £ | 437.50 | per | materials requisition |

Production setup costs = £ | 1,000 | per | setup |

Quality control costs = £ | 2,000 | per | inspection |

The budgeted cost per unit of LM is £ | 9.78 |

The budgeted cost per unit of NP is £ | 27.41 |

**Workings**

| | | |
|---|---|---|
| Stores cost | = | $\dfrac{£140,000}{320}$ |
| | = | £437.50 per materials requisition |
| Production setup costs | = | $\dfrac{£280,000}{280}$ |
| | = | £1,000 per set up |
| Quality control costs | = | $\dfrac{£180,000}{90}$ |
| | = | £2,000 per inspection |

| Product costs | | LM £ | NP £ |
|---|---|---|---|
| Direct materials | 50,000 × £2.60 | 130,000 | |
| | 20,000 × £3.90 | | 78,000 |
| Direct labour | 50,000 × £3.50 | 175,000 | |
| | 20,000 × £2.70 | | 54,000 |
| Stores costs | 100 × £437.50 | 43,750 | |
| | 220 × £437.50 | | 96,250 |
| Production setup costs | 80 × £1,000 | 80,000 | |
| | 200 × £1,000 | | 200,000 |
| Quality control costs | 30 × £2,000 | 60,000 | |
| | 60 × £2,000 | | 120,000 |
| Total cost | | 488,750 | 548,250 |
| | | | |
| Cost per unit | | £488,750 | £548,250 |
| | | 50,000 | 20,000 |
| | | = £9.78 | = £27.41 |

## CHAPTER 2   Budgetary control systems

1   A budget is a formalised numerical plan for the future actions of a business. Uses of a budget are:

Planning – the setting of a budget allows management to implement strategic plans.

Control – Management are also required to control the activities of the business and one method of doing this is to compare the actual result to the budgeted figures in order to report variances from budget.

Motivation – Given that the budget is used for control by monitoring performance, a budget can be used to motivate managers to improve this performance.

Additionally, budgets are used for authorisation of managers in terms of expenditure, and for co-ordination between the departments and functions of an organisation.

2   In order to determine the strategies that a business is to follow the senior management must first determine the overall strategic plan for the business. This is the medium- to long-term plan for where the business is going. Strategic plans may include elements such as growth in market share, maximisation of profit or growth by acquisition.

Once the overall strategic plan has been determined then management must decide how these strategic aims are to be met. This may require an in-depth analysis of the business, often by carrying out a SWOT analysis, which analyses the strengths, weaknesses, opportunities and threats to the business. Once this analysis has taken place then management can identify potential strategies that the business could follow. Finally the strategies that are most suitable to the business must be chosen.

3   The marketing costs shown in the budget for the next year may be greater than in previous years. Such overheads may include the costs of an advertising campaign or the costs of employing more marketing staff or a PR agency. The sales volume in the budget will be greater than in previous years. However, the sales price may have to be reduced to improve this sales volume.

Only two suggestions are required. In answering such tasks, think about the strategy, and how this would change how levels of income and cost are achieved.

**4**    In a bottom up system of budgeting the budget holders will typically be operational managers and they will have at least some input into the setting of the budget for the resource for which they are responsible. The degree of managerial input will depend upon the policy of the particular organisation, but in a typical system the manager may draft the initial budget. It will then be submitted to the budget committee and will be checked to ensure that it is in harmony with the other resource and production/sales budgets. There may well then be a period of negotiation between the budget holders and the budget committee until there is a compromise reached between what the budget committee wants and what the manager believes is feasible.

When all of the resource budgets have been agreed, the budget officer will produce the master budget made up of a budgeted income statement, a budgeted statement of financial position and a cash budget.

**5**    The draft budget is ready for review: the budget committee

The managing director needs help in interpreting the draft budget: the budget officer

**6**    The correct answer is:

| £ | 222,480 |
|---|---|

**Workings:**

£240,000 × 90%    =    £216,000    – reflects change in activity level

£216,000 × 1.03    =    £222,480    – reflects inflation

The budget figure would be £222,480.

**7**    Performance related pay is a system of offering managers or employees some form of bonus or other incentive if particular performance targets are met. It can be argued that performance related pay can help to ensure that there is goal congruence between the managers and the organisation; however, in order for this to happen, the system must have the following elements:

■    the target that is set must be perceived by the managers as attainable although it should also be challenging

■    the measurement of actual performance must be accurate

■    the managers must feel that they have control over all of the costs and/or revenues that are being compared to a target

■    the managers must not feel that meeting the target is dependent upon another manager's performance

- the rewards being offered by the performance related package must be desirable enough to motivate the manager to meet the target.

If any of these elements are not in place, then the performance related pay system may serve to de-motivate managers rather than fulfilling the aim of motivating the managers to meet the corporate goals.

## CHAPTER 3 Forecasting

1

| Information required | Source |
|---|---|
| Budgeted units of production per product | Production planning manager |
| Price of materials | Buyer |
| Sales brochure costs | Marketing Director |
| Mortgage interest on factory | Finance Director |

2 Time series analysis using moving averages or indexing can be used.

The limitations are that this assumes that the same trend will continue into the future. This is unlikely when changes in the external environment, the market for the product and product life cycle are considered.

3 The three main sources of information for sales forecasts are the sales personnel in the business, market research and time series analysis.

The key sales personnel of the business or the 'on-the-road salespeople' have the best first-hand knowledge of the current sales position and future potential sales. They may not necessarily be able to provide accurate forecasts of future sales but they should be able to provide an overview of the future situation and give any forecaster a feel for the future position.

Market research is expensive and probably only of particular use during the launch of a new product or the major modification of an existing product. This research will involve finding the opinions of potential consumers of the product through interviews, questionnaires or focus groups.

Time series analysis is a further way of forecasting future sales on the basis of historical sales, done by analysing past sales pattern to determine the trend of sales and any seasonal variations. The trend can then be extrapolated into future periods and the relevant seasonal variations applied in order to determine the forecast sales for the future

periods. Limitations are that a large amount of historical data is required, it assumes that the past is representative of the future and it may be hard to isolate cyclical changes due to the nature of the economy.

4    The correct answers are:

| Quarter 1 | 163,415 |
|-----------|---------|
| Quarter 2 | 129,809 |
| Quarter 3 | 102,477 |
| Quarter 4 | 185,739 |

**Workings**

Before extrapolating the sales from the Q4 20X1 figure, we need to strip out its seasonal variation to find the underlying trend value:

$$\frac{175,000}{1.25} = 140,000$$

This trend value can now be extrapolated as a basis for the required forecasts.

| Quarter 1 | Trend    | 140,000 × 1.015 | 142,100 |
|-----------|----------|-----------------|---------|
|           | Forecast | 142,100 × 1.15  | 163,415 |
| Quarter 2 | Trend    | 142,100 × 1.015 | 144,232 |
|           | Forecast | 144,232 × 0.90  | 129,809 |
| Quarter 3 | Trend    | 144,232 × 1.015 | 146,395 |
|           | Forecast | 146,395 × 0.70  | 102,477 |
| Quarter 4 | Trend    | 146,395 × 1.015 | 148,591 |
|           | Forecast | 148,591 × 1.25  | 185,739 |

5    The correct answers are:

| Quarter 1 | 176,400 |
|-----------|---------|
| Quarter 2 | 159,450 |
| Quarter 3 | 254,172 |
| Quarter 4 | 267,156 |

**Workings**

| Quarter 1 | 210,000 × 0.84 | = | 176,400 |
|-----------|----------------|---|---------|
| Quarter 2 | 212,600 × 0.75 | = | 159,450 |
| Quarter 3 | 215,400 × 1.18 | = | 254,172 |
| Quarter 4 | 217,200 × 1.23 | = | 267,156 |

6    Development stage
     Launch stage
     Growth stage
     Maturity stage
     Decline stage

7    A PEST analysis is based around considerations of political, economic, social and technological factors. The political factors will include any legislation such as minimum wage requirements that affect the business. The economic factors will include the current state of the economy, interest rates, inflation rates and foreign currency exchange rates amongst others. The social factors to be considered are social aspects of life that have an impact on the business's products such as changes in lifestyle, fashions and tastes etc. Technological factors will include changes in technology which affect not only the products demanded in the market but also the production methods.

8

|  | Jan | Feb | Mar | Apr | May | Jun |
|---|---|---|---|---|---|---|
| Forecast variable production costs £ | 17,036 | 18,831 | 21,201 | 18,713 | 19,083 | 19,775 |
| Forecast variable selling costs £ | 7,531 | 7,864 | 8,031 | 8,077 | 8,615 | 8,678 |

**Workings**

**Production costs**

|  | Jan | Feb | Mar | Apr | May | June |
|---|---|---|---|---|---|---|
| Production – units | 1,200 | 1,320 | 1,480 | 1,280 | 1,300 | 1,340 |
| Un-indexed cost £ (142.3) | 16,800 | 18,480 | 20,720 | 17,920 | 18,200 | 18,760 |
| Index | 144.3 | 145.0 | 145.6 | 148.6 | 149.2 | 150.0 |
| Indexed cost £ | 17,036 | 18,831 | 21,201 | 18,713 | 19,083 | 19,775 |
| | | | | | | |
| Sales – units | 1,250 | 1,300 | 1,320 | 1,320 | 1,400 | 1,400 |
| Un-indexed cost £ (121.0) | 7,500 | 7,800 | 7,920 | 7,920 | 8,400 | 8,400 |
| Index | 121.5 | 122.0 | 122.7 | 123.4 | 124.1 | 125.0 |
| Indexed cost £ | 7,531 | 7,864 | 8,031 | 8,077 | 8,615 | 8,678 |

**9**     The fixed element of production cost is estimated as £ ⎡169,000⎤

The variable element of production cost is estimated as £ ⎡3⎤ per unit.

The production cost for January which has a budgeted activity of 120,000 units is forecast as £ ⎡ 529,000 ⎤

The production cost for February which has a budgeted activity of 150,000 units is forecast as £ ⎡ 619,000 ⎤

The forecast production cost for ⎡ January ⎤ is the more accurate.

The January forecast is more accurate because the number of units (120,000) is within the range of activity levels used to calculate the variable costs and fixed costs (interpolation), whereas the figure of 150,000 units is outside that range (extrapolation). We cannot be sure that the costs will still behave in the same manner at an activity level of 150,000 units.

**Workings**

|  |  | £ |
|---|---|---|
| Highest level | 126,000 | 547,000 |
| Lowest level | 101,000 | 472,000 |
|  | 25,000 | 75,000 |

$$\text{Variable rate} = \frac{£75,000}{25,000} = £3 \text{ per unit}$$

Using highest level:

|  | £ |
|---|---|
| Variable cost 126,000 × £3 | 378,000 |
| Fixed costs (balancing figure) | 169,000 |
| Total cost | 547,000 |

January

|  | £ |
|---|---|
| 120,000 units |  |
| Variable cost 120,000 × £3 | 360,000 |
| Fixed cost | 169,000 |
| Forecast cost | 529,000 |

February

|  | £ |
|---|---|
| 150,000 units |  |
| Variable cost 150,000 × £3 | 450,000 |
| Fixed cost | 169,000 |
| Forecast cost | 619,000 |

**10** The correct answers are:

|  | Jan | Feb | Mar | Apr | May | Jun |
|---|---|---|---|---|---|---|
| Forecast store department costs (£) | 17,320 | 17,480 | 17,560 | 17,800 | 17,400 | 17,880 |

**Workings**

| Stores costs: | | £ |
|---|---|---|
| January | 13,000 + (0.8 × 5,400) | 17,320 |
| February | 13,000 + (0.8 × 5,600) | 17,480 |
| March | 13,000 + (0.8 × 5,700) | 17,560 |
| April | 13,000 + (0.8 × 6,000) | 17,800 |
| May | 13,000 + (0.8 × 5,500) | 17,400 |
| June | 13,000 + (0.8 × 6,100) | 17,880 |

**11** The correct answers are:

| Quarter 1 | 2,585 |
|---|---|
| Quarter 2 | 3,330 |
| Quarter 3 | 3,225 |
| Quarter 4 | 2,270 |

**Workings**

|  | Value of x | Trend | Seasonal variation | Forecast sales |
|---|---|---|---|---|
| Quarter 1 20X9 | 13 | 2,785 | – 200 | 2,585 |
| Quarter 2 20X9 | 14 | 2,830 | + 500 | 3,330 |
| Quarter 3 20X9 | 15 | 2,875 | + 350 | 3,225 |
| Quarter 4 20X9 | 16 | 2,920 | – 650 | 2,270 |

Value of X for Quarter 1, 20X9:

Quarter 1 20X6 =     1

Add: 3 years of 4 quarters = 12

So Quarter 1, 20X9 = 13

Trend for Quarter 1, 20X9

2,200 +(45 × 13) = 2,785

## CHAPTER 4   Budget preparation

1    Units of product

|  | Period 1 | Period 2 | Period 3 |
|---|---|---|---|
| Opening inventory | 1,140 | 1,200 | 1,350 |
| Production (bal fig) | 3,860 | 4,150 | 4,410 |
| Units required | 5,000 | 5,350 | 5,760 |
| Sales | 3,800 | 4,000 | 4,500 |
| Closing inventory | 1,200 | 1,350 | 1,260 |
| Units required | 5,000 | 5,350 | 5,760 |

**Workings**

**Closing inventory:**

Period 1        4,000 units × 30%   =   1,200 units

Period 2        4,500 units × 30%   =   1,350 units

Period 3        4,200 units × 30%   =   1,260 units

2    Units of product

|  | Period 1 | Period 2 | Period 3 |
|---|---|---|---|
| Units required (from test 1) | 3,860 | 4,150 | 4,410 |
| Actual production (rounded up) | 4,064 | 4,369 | 4,642 |

**Working**

Actual production needed = production units required × 100/95

3    The correct answers are:

- the materials usage budget in units is ⬚ 53,334
- the materials purchasing budget in units is ⬚ 51,846
- the materials purchasing budget in £ is ⬚ 248,861

**Materials usage budget – units**

Production requirements

| | |
|---|---|
| Period 1: 12,000 × 4 kg × 100/90 | 53,334 |
| Period 2: 11,000 × 4 kg × 100/90 | 48,889 |

**Materials purchasing budget – units**

| | |
|---|---|
| Material usage | 53,334 |
| Less: opening inventory | (18,600) |
| Add: closing inventory | |
| 48,889 × 35% | 17,112 |
| | 51,846 |

**Materials purchasing budget – £**

| | |
|---|---|
| 51,846 × £4.80 | £248,861 |

(Note: Amounts are rounded up to ensure sufficient availability)

4    The correct answers are:

The production budget for the quarter is $\boxed{43,334}$ units.

The labour usage budget for the quarter is $\boxed{164,858}$ hours.

**Workings**

**Production budget – units**

| | |
|---|---|
| Sales quantity | 42,000 |
| Less: opening inventory | (7,000) |
| Add: closing inventory | 8,334 |
| Production quantity | 43,334 |

**Labour usage budget – hours**

Hours required

| | |
|---|---|
| 43,334 × 3.5 × 100/92 | 164,858 hours |

**5** The correct answers are:

| Overhead cost £ | Quarter 2 | Quarter 3 |
|---|---|---|
| Light and heat | 76,896 | 85,680 |
| Maintenance | 82,090 | 90,325 |
| Leasing | 15,600 | 20,400 |
| Rent and rates | 21,000 | 21,000 |

**Workings**

Overhead budget – £

| | Quarter 2 £ | Quarter 3 £ |
|---|---|---|
| Light and heat | | |
| 16,020 × £4.80 | 76,896 | |
| 17,850 × £4.80 | | 85,680 |
| Maintenance (W) | | |
| (16,020 × £4.50) + £10,000 | 82,090 | |
| (17,850 × £4.50) + £10,000 | | 90,325 |
| Leasing | 15,600 | 20,400 |
| Rent and rates £84,000/4 | 21,000 | 21,000 |

Maintenance department costs working

| | Activity level | Cost |
|---|---|---|
| | 13,000 units | £68,500 |
| | 17,000 units | £86,500 |
| Increase | 4,000 units | £18,000 |

| Variable element | = | £18,000/4,000 units |
|---|---|---|
| | = | £4.50 per unit |

Fixed element

|  | £ |
|---|---|
| Variable element 13,000 units × £4.50 | 58,500 |
| Fixed element (bal fig) | 10,000 |
| Total cost | 68,500 |

**6** **(a)** **Production budget** ☐ 255 ☐ **units**

Production = sales + closing inventory – opening inventory

|  | Units | Units |
|---|---|---|
| Budgeted sales |  | 280 |
| Opening inventory | (30) |  |
| Closing inventory | 5 |  |
| Decrease in inventory |  | (25) |
| Budgeted production |  | 255 |

**(b)** **Materials usage budget** ☐ 1,785 ☐ **kg costing £** ☐ 89,250 ☐

| | |
|---|---|
| Budgeted production | 255 units |
| × usage per unit | × 7 kgs |
| Total budgeted usage in kgs | 1,785 kgs |
| × budgeted cost per kg | × £50 |
| Total budgeted usage in £ | £89,250 |

**(c)** **Labour cost budget £** ☐ 25,570 ☐

**Labour cost budget – grade O**

| | |
|---|---|
| Budgeted production | 255 units |
| × hrs per unit | × 2 hrs |
| Total budgeted labour hrs | 510 hrs |
| × budgeted cost per hr | × £15 |
| Budgeted labour cost | £7,650 |

**Labour cost budget – grade R**

| | |
|---|---|
| Budgeted production | 255 units |
| × hrs per unit | × 3 hrs |
| Total budgeted labour hrs | 765 hrs |

BPP
LEARNING MEDIA

Note that the budgeted labour cost is not dependent on the hours worked.

Budgeted labour cost = 16 × £280 × 4 weeks = £17,920

**Total labour cost budget** in £ = £(17,920 + 7,650) = £25,570

7   The correct answer is: ▭ 27,009 ▭ kg

| | | kgs | kgs |
|---|---|---|---|
| Material issued to production | (J: 450 × 25 kgs) | | 11,250 |
| | (K: 710 × 40 kgs) | | 28,400 |
| | | | 39,650 |
| Opening inventory | | (40,000) | |
| Closing inventory | | 27,359 | |
| Decrease in inventory | | | (12,641) |
| Purchases | | | 27,009 |

8   (a)  **Budgeted labour hours** ▭ 4,460 ▭

| | |
|---|---|
| Labour hours required for production of X (W1) | 2,100 |
| Labour hours required for production of Y (W2) | 2,360 |
| Total labour hours required | 4,460 |
| Basic hours available (W3) | 4,375 |
| Overtime hours | 85 |

**Workings**

1   Labour hours required = 420 units × 5 hours per unit = 2,100 hours

2   Labour hours required = 590 units × 4 hours per unit = 2,360 hours

3   Basic hours available = 35 hours × 5 weeks × 25 employees = 4,375 hours

(b)  **Cost of labour budget £** ▭ 44,812.50 ▭

| | £ |
|---|---|
| Basic wages during Period 7 (W1) | 43,750.00 |
| Overtime (W2) | 1,062.50 |
| | 44,812.50 |

**Workings**

Basic wages = £10 × 4,375 hours (from (a)) = £43,750

Overtime = overtime hours × £(10 × 125%) per overtime hour =
85 hours (from (a)) × £12.50 = £1,062.50

9    The correct answers are:

|  | Service 1 | Service 2 | Service 3 | Service 4 |
|---|---|---|---|---|
| Revenue budget (£) | 211,680 | 170,100 | 158,760 | 302,400 |
| Number of employees | 7 | 4.5 | 3.5 | 5 |
| Direct wages budget (£) | 94,080 | 75,600 | 64,680 | 117,600 |

**Workings**

(a)   Revenue budget

*Service*
1          £20 × 10,584 = £211,680
2          £25 × 6,804 = £170,100
3          £30 × 5,292 = £158,760
4          £40 × 7,560 = £302,400

(b)   No of employees required/department =

$$\frac{\text{Budgeted chargeable hours}}{35 \times 48} \times 100 / 90$$

*Service*
1          (10,584 × 100/90)/(35 × 48) = 7.0
2          (6,804 × 100/90)/(35 × 48) = 4.5
3          (5,292 × 100/90)/(35 × 48) = 3.5
4          (7,560 × 100/90)/(35 × 48) = 5.0

The business should employ the following staff:

| Service | Number of full time | Number of part time |
|---|---|---|
| 1 | 7 | 0 |
| 2 | 4 | 1 |
| 3 | 3 | 1 |
| 4 | 5 | 0 |
| Total | 19 | 2 |

(c)   Direct wages budget

| Service | | £ |
|---|---|---|
| 1 | £8 an hour × 7.0 employees × 35 hours a week × 48 weeks | 94,080 |
| 2 | £10 an hour × 4.5 employees × 35 hours a week × 48 weeks | 75,600 |
| 3 | £11 an hour × 3.5 employees × 35 hours a week × 48 weeks | 64,680 |
| 4 | £14 an hour × 5.0 employees × 35 hours a week × 48 weeks | 117,600 |

## 10   Budgeted operating statement (total absorption basis)

| | £ | £ |
|---|---|---|
| Revenue (25,000 × £6.50) | | 162,500 |
| Less cost of sales: | | |
| Direct materials<br>25,000 × 2kg × £0.75 | 37,500 | |
| Direct labour<br>25,000 × 6/60 × £12 | 30,000 | |
| Production overheads | 16,000 | |
| Cost of sales | | (83,500) |
| Gross profit | | 79,000 |

### Capital budget

| | £ |
|---|---|
| Capital purchase (car) | 20,000 |
| Total | 20,000 |

## CHAPTER 5   Preparing cash budgets

### 1   Forecast cash receipts

| | January | February | March |
|---|---|---|---|
| Budgeted cash receipts from sales (£) | 695,500 | 677,000 | 683,000 |

## Workings

|  | January £ | February £ | March £ |
|---|---|---|---|
| Cash sales (10% of sales figure) | 70,000 | 73,000 | 76,000 |
| Credit sales 40% × 720,000 | 288,000 | | |
| 40% × 700,000 | | 280,000 | |
| 40% × 730,000 | | | 292,000 |
| 45% × 750,000 | 337,500 | | |
| 45% × 720,000 | | 324,000 | |
| 45% × 700,000 | | | 315,000 |
| | 695,500 | 677,000 | 683,000 |

## 2 Forecast cash payments

|  | January | February | March |
|---|---|---|---|
| Budgeted cash payments for purchases (£) | 560,340 | 538,275 | 529,560 |

## Workings

Purchases

|  | October £ | November £ | December £ | January £ | February £ |
|---|---|---|---|---|---|
| 75% of sales | 592,500 | 562,500 | 540,000 | 525,000 | 547,500 |

| Cash payments | January £ | February £ | March £ |
|---|---|---|---|
| October purchases | | | |
| 592,500 × 15% | 88,875 | | |
| November purchases | | | |
| 562,500 × 65% | 365,625 | | |
| 562,500 × 15% | | 84,375 | |
| December purchases | | | |
| 540,000 × 20% × 98% | 105,840 | | |
| 540,000 × 65% | | 351,000 | |
| 540,000 × 15% | | | 81,000 |
| January purchases | | | |
| 525,000 × 20% × 98% | | 102,900 | |
| 525,000 × 65% | | | 341,250 |
| February purchases | | | |
| 547,500 × 20% × 98% | | | 107,310 |
| | 560,340 | 538,275 | 529,560 |

3    **Cash budget for the quarter ending 31 December**

|  | October | November | December |
|---|---|---|---|
|  | £ | £ | £ |
| *Cash receipts:* |  |  |  |
| Sales proceeds from equipment | 0 | 4,000 | 0 |
| *Cash payments:* |  |  |  |
| Wages | 42,000 | 42,000 | 42,000 |
| General overheads (W1) | 25,000 | 29,800 | 31,000 |
| New equipment | 0 | 40,000 | 0 |

**Workings**

**Working 1 – General overheads**

|  | October | November | December |
|---|---|---|---|
|  | £ | £ | £ |
| *September overheads* |  |  |  |
| (30,000 – 5,000) × 20% | 5,000 |  |  |
| *October overheads* |  |  |  |
| (30,000 – 5,000) × 80% | 20,000 |  |  |
| (30,000 – 5,000) × 20% |  | 5,000 |  |
| *November overheads* |  |  |  |
| (36,000 – 5,000) × 80% |  | 24,800 |  |
| (36,000 – 5,000) × 20% |  |  | 6,200 |
| *December overheads* |  |  |  |
| (36,000 – 5,000) × 80% |  |  | 24,800 |
|  | 25,000 | 29,800 | 31,000 |

4    The correct answer is: £270,000.

Proceeds = carrying amount + profits = £212,000 + £58,000 = £270,000.

## CHAPTER 6   Budget preparation – limiting factors

1

|  | Jan | Feb | Mar | Apr | May | June | Total |
|---|---|---|---|---|---|---|---|
| Materials required – kg | 2,600 | 3,100 | 3,000 | 3,100 | 2,800 | 3,200 | 17,800 |
| Material purchases | 3,000 | 3,000 | 3,000 | 3,000 | 3,000 | 3,000 | 18,000 |
| Excess/(shortage) | 400 | (100) | | (100) | 200 | (200) | (200) |

There is an overall excess in availability over requirements of 200 kg if 3,000 kgs are purchased each month. To minimise inventory levels, the shortages in February and April can be made up by buying only 200 kg more than is needed in January, so 2,800 kgs should be bought in January. In every other month 3,000 kgs should be bought. The shortage of 200 kg in June is made up by buying in May 200 kg more than is required for production in that month.

2 This appears to be a long-term labour shortage so the business should have two aims:

(a) to increase the availability of the required level of labour as soon as possible

(b) to attempt to lessen the problem in the short term before the additional labour becomes available.

The longer-term options in order to acquire more highly skilled labour are:

- to recruit additional highly skilled staff
- to train existing staff to this skill level

In the shorter term, until the recruitment or training reaps rewards, the options are:

- to increase the overtime worked by the existing employees
- to use agency workers
- to sub-contract the work
- to use finished goods inventory to satisfy sales demand
- to buy in the finished goods

3    As this is a short-term issue, the business could try the following:

- Use of material held in inventory – these could be run down in order to maintain production and sales.

- Use of finished goods held in inventory – in order to maintain sales in the short term, finished goods inventory can be run down even though production levels are not as high as would be liked

- Rescheduling purchases – if the amount of the material required is available in some periods but not in others, then the materials purchases could be rescheduled to ensure that the maximum use is made of the available materials.

4    The limiting factor is ┌──────────────┐ labour hours └──────────────┘

Material required for sales demand = 15,000 × 0.5 = 7,500 kg
Material available = 9,000 kg, so not a limiting factor
Labour required for sales demand = 15,000 × (24/60) = 6,000 hours
Labour hours available = 30 × 180 = 5,400 hours

Therefore, labour is the limiting factor, unless overtime can be paid.

5    The correct answer is:

| Product | Manufactured to maximise profit |
|---------|---------------------------------|
| Product A | |
| Product B | ✓ |

**Workings**

| Per unit | Product A | Product B |
|----------|-----------|-----------|
| Sales price £ | 13 | 8 |
| Direct materials £<br>2 × 2<br>1.5 × 2 | (4) | (3) |
| Direct labour £<br>0.5 × 10<br>0.25 × 10 | (5) | (2.5) |
| Variable overhead £ | (1) | (0.5) |
| Contribution £ | 3 | 2 |
| Contribution per labour hour<br>(£3/0.5)<br>(£2/0.25) | 6 | 8 |

Product B gives the greater contribution per labour hour and so should be the one produced.

## CHAPTER 7   Flexed budgets and variances

1   A fixed budget is prepared in advance of the budget period and serves as an overall plan of what the business is aiming for during the budget period. It ensures that all areas of the business are co-ordinated in their activities.

A flexed budget is prepared at the end of the budget period and is based upon the actual activity level during the period. It shows the standard cost of the actual production for the month and is used for control purposes, as the actual costs are compared to these standard costs to produce variances.

2   The correct answer is:

| | Budget | Flexed Budget | Actual | | |
|---|---|---|---|---|---|
| | 4,000 units | 3,600 units | 3,600 units | Variance | |
| | £ | £ | £ | £ | Fav/Adv |
| Sales 3,600 × £24 | 96,000 | 86,400 | 90,000 | 3,600 | Fav |
| Materials 3,600 × £4.50 | 18,000 | 16,200 | 15,120 | 1,080 | Fav |
| Labour 3,600 × £6.80 | 27,200 | 24,480 | 25,200 | 720 | Adv |
| Production overhead | 5,700 | 5,700 | 5,900 | 200 | Adv |
| Gross profit | 45,100 | 40,020 | 43,780 | 3,760 | Fav |
| General expenses (W) | 35,200 | 32,800 | 32,880 | 80 | Adv |
| Operating profit | 9,900 | 7,220 | 10,900 | 3,680 | Fav |

## Working – General expenses

Variable element of cost    =    £35,200 – £11,200

                         =    £24,000

Variable cost per unit       =    £24,000/4,000

                         =    £6 per unit

Cost at 3,600 units         =    3,600 × £6 + £11,200

                         =    £32,800

## 3 Operating statement: January

| | Flexed budget | | Actual | | |
| --- | --- | --- | --- | --- | --- |
| | 30,000 units | | 30,000 units | | Variance |
| | £ | £ | £ | £ | £ |
| Sales | | 90,000 | | 86,000 | 4,000 Adv |
| Materials | 24,000 | | 22,500 | | 1,500 Fav |
| Labour | 39,000 | | 41,200 | | 2,200 Adv |
| Production expenses | 5,600 | | 5,800 | | 200 Adv |
| Production cost | | 68,600 | | 69,500 | 900 Adv |
| Gross profit | | 21,400 | | 16,500 | 4,900 Adv |
| General expenses | | 15,000 | | 14,700 | 300 Fav |
| Operating profit | | 6,400 | | 1,800 | 4,600 Adv |

## Workings

### Sales

24,000 – standard selling price per unit    =    £72,000/24,000

                                          =    £3 per unit

28,000 – standard selling price per unit    =    £84,000/28,000

                                          =    £3 per unit

The sales revenue is thus strictly variable.

| | | | |
|---|---|---|---|
| 30,000 – standard sales income | = | 30,000 × £3 | |
| | = | £90,000 | |

**Materials**

| | | | |
|---|---|---|---|
| 24,000 – standard cost per unit | = | £19,200/24,000 | |
| | = | £0.80 | |
| 28,000 – standard cost per unit | = | £22,400/28,000 | |
| | = | £0.80 | |

The materials cost is thus strictly variable.

| | | |
|---|---|---|
| 30,000 – standard materials cost | = | 30,000 × £0.80 |
| | = | £24,000 |

**Labour**

| | | |
|---|---|---|
| 24,000 – standard cost per unit | = | £33,000/24,000 |
| | = | £1.375 |
| 28,000 – standard cost per unit | = | £37,000/28,000 |
| | = | £1.32 |

We may assume, then, that labour is a semi-variable cost.

*Semi-variable labour cost*

| | | |
|---|---|---|
| Increase in cost per unit increase | = | £4,000/4,000 units |
| | = | £1 per unit |
| Fixed element | = | £33,000 – (24,000 × £1) |
| | = | £9,000 |
| 30,000 – standard labour cost | = | (£1 × 30,000) + £9,000 |
| | = | £39,000 |

**Production expenses**

– fixed cost

**General expenses**

| | | |
|---|---|---|
| 24,000 – cost per unit | = | £12,600/24,000 |
| | = | £0.525 |
| 28,000 – cost per unit | = | £14,200/28,000 |
| | = | £0.507 |

We may assume, then, that general expenses are a semi-variable cost.

*Semi-variable general expense cost*

| Increase in cost per unit increase | = | £1,600/4,000 units |
| | = | £0.40 per unit |

| Fixed element | = | £12,600 – (24,000 × £0.40) |
| | = | £3,000 |

| 30,000 – labour cost | = | (£0.40 × 30,000) + £3,000 |
| | = | £15,000 |

## 4    Marginal costing budget

| | £ | £ |
|---|---|---|
| Sales | | 900,000 |
| Materials | 216,000 | |
| Labour | 324,000 | |
| Cost of production (54,000 units) | 540,000 | |
| Less: closing inventory (4,000 units) | (40,000) | |
| Cost of sales | | (500,000) |
| Gross profit | | 400,000 |
| Fixed production overhead | | (108,000) |
| Fixed general expenses | | (198,000) |
| Net profit | | 94,000 |

| Absorption costing profit | = | £102,000 |
| Marginal costing profit | = | £94,000 |

The difference of £8,000 is due to the difference in closing inventory valuation: £48,000 under absorption costing and £40,000 under marginal costing. This represents the share of fixed overheads carried forward in inventory under absorption costing $\left( 4000 \times \dfrac{108,000}{54,000} \right)$.

5    Budgeted fixed overheads = £1.90 × 240,000 = £456,000

Variance = £480,000 - £456,000 = $\boxed{£24,000}$ $\boxed{\text{Adverse}}$ .

**6** A controllable cost is one over which the manager of a responsibility centre has influence. If a manager's performance is to be judged, then it must only be judged on the basis of costs or revenues over which the manager has control. If uncontrollable costs are included then this could have a de-motivating effect on the manager.

**7** **REPORT**

| | |
|---|---|
| To: | Management Team |
| From: | Management Accountant |
| Date: | xx.xx.xx |
| Subject: | **Format of variance report** |

Following my meeting with the product manager last week, I have undertaken a review of the format of the variance report used throughout the organisation. I have concluded that, because of the way in which the information is presented, the report could be potentially misleading for users. I therefore recommend that the format be adapted as follows.

■ Information about volumes (hrs, kgs and so on) should be reported separately in order to make the report less confusing and easier to read and understand. All information on the monthly variance report, except that concerning production volumes, should be monetary.

■ The volume variances (those in hrs, kgs and so on) should be converted into monetary amounts in order that the financial implications of the variances are obvious.

■ Instead of calculating variances by comparing actual results and the original fixed budget results, actual results should be compared with budget results flexed to the actual production volumes. The flexed results provide a far more realistic and fair target against which to measure actual results. For example, the direct labour (£) variance is currently calculated by comparing the budgeted labour cost of producing 10,000 units with the actual labour cost of producing 9,905 units. A revised format should show a direct labour (£) variance calculated by comparing the actual direct labour cost with the budgeted direct labour cost of producing 9,905 units.

■ The report shows no flexed budget figures (the results which would have been expected at the actual production level achieved). A flexed budget column should therefore be included on the report.

- The report does not provide a narrative description of any known reasons for the variances. Explanations would increase the report's user-friendliness.

- The report should use the principles of exception reporting, highlighting the most important variances in order to direct management attention to areas where action is most urgently required.

- Controllable fixed costs (if they exist) should be included on the report and separately identified.

A recommended layout for the monthly variance report is shown in the Appendix to this report. An identical format could be used for the presentation of cumulative results to date.

## APPENDIX

## MONTHLY VARIANCE REPORT

|  | Original fixed budget Units | Flexed budget Units | Actual results Units | Total variance £ | % | Notes |
|---|---|---|---|---|---|---|
| Production volume | X | X | X |  |  |  |
| **Variable costs** |  |  |  |  |  |  |
| Direct material | X | X | X | X | X |  |
| Direct labour | X | X | X | X | X |  |
| **Total variable costs** | X | X | X | X | X |  |
| **Controllable fixed costs** | X | X | X | X | X |  |
| **Total costs** | X | X | X | X | X |  |

The notes column could be used to provide an explanation of the reasons for various variances occurring and/or to highlight important variances.

## 8    REPORT

| | |
|---|---|
| To: | Managing Director |
| From: | Accountant |
| Date: | xx.xx.xx |
| Subject: | November production cost variances |

One cause of the variances may have been the labour that was used in production for the month which was a more junior grade than normal due to staff shortages. This has given an overall favourable labour variance meaning the reduction in rate made up for any labour inefficiencies (extra hours) caused by using a lower grade. However, it may also have contributed to the high adverse materials variances if such staff caused more materials wastage.

For future months we should either ensure that we have enough of the normal grade of auction process.

The high adverse labour for production of this product or train the junior staff in the prod materials variance will have also been caused by an increase in the price of our materials. As it is believed that this is a permanent price increase by all suppliers, we should consider altering the materials standard cost to reflect this, otherwise each month we will have adverse materials variances.

The factory now has an additional rent cost which has presumably caused the adverse fixed overhead variance. If the additional inventory requirement and hence the additional rent is a permanent change then this should be built into the budgeted fixed overhead figure.

## CHAPTER 8   Performance indicators

**1**   Productivity measures include:

– Number of customers served per hour/day

– Number of customers served per cashier in a shift

– Value of goods processed through till per cashier or per hour

– Number of customers per queue at different times of day/different cashiers

Other performance measures may include:

– Number of calls made to supervisor per shift/per cashier.
– Number of customer complaints (if any) per cashier
– Time spent per cashier serving no customers (idle time)
– Cost of idle time as a percentage of cashier labour costs

*Tutorial note: remember to include simple, visual measures such as the number of customers in the queue.  These are not just a factor of the productivity of the cashiers but the demand of customers at particular times, but by knowing this, the manager can plan accordingly.*

**2**   Number of defective units

Cost of defective units

Percentage of production which is defective

*Note – only one of these measures was required*

**3**   Number of bread rolls thrown away per day/shift

Cost of bread rolls thrown away (ingredients, labour, machine costs of baking)

Percentage of bread rolls produced which are defective

**4**   Productivity could be measured in terms of the number of holidays sold per sales representative, or the number of holidays sold per day.

**5**   Number of ovens/shelves in use during a shift

Percentage of ovens/shelves in use during a shift

# INDEX

**A**bsorption costing, 15, 106, 188
Activities, 2, 3
Activity based budgeting, 45
Activity based costing (ABC), 16, 24
Additive model, 70
Attainable standards, 107
Authorisation, 37

**B**ase period, 75
Basic standards, 108
Bottom up budgeting, 46
Budget, 53
Budget committee, 41
Budget holders, 41
Budget manual, 40
Budget officer, 41
Budgetary slack, 47
Budgeted operating statement, 122
Budgeted statement of financial
    position, 122
Buying in, 174

**C**apital budgets, 58, 125
Capital expenditure, 58
Cash budgets, 122, 135
Cash flow forecast, 136
Centred moving averages, 69
Contribution, 173
Control, 36
Controllable costs, 202
Co-ordination, 36
Cost budgets, 56
Cost centre, 4
Cost driver, 24
Cost pools, 24
Cost unit, 2, 4, 6

**D**ata, 59
Defective output, 111
Dependent variable, 88
Direct costs, 6

**E**fficiency, 119, 129
External information, 60
Extrapolation, 87

**F**eedback, 203
Feedforward, 203
Fixed budget, 180
Fixed costs, 8, 83, 120
Fixed overheads budget, 57
Flexible budgets, 180
Flexed budget, 182
Forecasting expenditure, 80
Forecasting sales, 90
Forecasts, 50, 51
Full production cost, 13

**G**oal congruence, 47
Government statistics, 60
Gross profit margins, 143

**H**i lo method, 84

**I**deal standards, 107
Idle time, 117
Idle time ratios, 221
Incremental budgeting, 43
Indexing, 64, 75
Index number, 97
Indirect costs, 6
Information required for forecasting,
    59
Integrity of budgets, 126

Interdependence of variances, 196
Independent variable, 88
Internal information, 60
Interpolation, 86, 92
Investment centre, 4, 197
Irrecoverable debts, 153

**K**ey budget factor, 64, 108, 166

**L**abour cost budget, 56, 117
Labour shortages, 169
Labour usage budget, 56, 117
Lagged receipt/payment, 141, 144
Limiting factors, 166
Linear regression, 64, 87

**M**achine hours budget, 57
Marginal costing, 106, 188
Market research, 64, 65
Master budget, 42, 122
Materials purchases budget, 56,
    113, 149
Materials usage budget, 56, 113
Materials wastage, 114
Motivation, 37, 45, 202
Moving averages, 64, 67
Multiplicative model, 70

**N**ormal loss, 111
Net cash flow, 136

**O**perating statement, 122
Operational plan, 40
Overheads budget, 120

**P**erformance indicators, 212
Performance related pay, 48
PEST analysis, 74
Plan, 51
Planning, 36
Population, 96
Prime cost, 13
Product life cycle, 64, 72

Product mix, 172
Production budget, 56, 110
Production capacity, 170
Production facilities, 56, 120
Productivity, 218
Profit centre, 4
Programme based budgeting, 44
Purposes of budgeting, 36

**Q**uality, 214
Quota sampling, 66

**R**andom sampling, 65
Receipts and payments cash budget,
    136, 137
Relevant range, 8
Resource budgets, 56, 108
Responsibility accounting, 197
Responsibility centres, 4, 197
Retail price index, 60, 77
Revenue expenditure, 58
Rolling budgets, 42

**S**ales budget, 56, 108, 109
Sales revenue budget, 56
Sales forecasts, 64
Sampling, 64, 65
Seasonal variations, 64, 67
Semi-variable costs, 9, 84, 89, 120
Settlement discount, 141
Shortage of materials, 166
Standard costing, 104
Stepped costs, 9, 120
Strategic plans, 38
SWOT analysis, 39

**T**ime periods within a budget, 49
Time series analysis, 64, 67, 73
Top down budgeting, 46
Trend, 67

**U**ncertainties inherent in
    forecasting, 93

Variable costs, 7, 80, 120
Variable overheads budget, 57
Variances, 36, 104, 107, 179, 181

Zero based budgeting (ZBB), 43

**Notes**

# REVIEW FORM

## How have you used this Text?
*(Tick one box only)*

☐ Home study

☐ On a course_____

☐ Other _____

## Why did you decide to purchase this Text? *(Tick one box only)*

☐ Have used BPP Texts in the past

☐ Recommendation by friend/colleague

☐ Recommendation by a college lecturer

☐ Saw advertising

☐ Other _____

## During the past six months do you recall seeing/receiving either of the following?
*(Tick as many boxes as are relevant)*

☐ Our advertisement in Accounting Technician

☐ Our Publishing Catalogue

## Which (if any) aspects of our advertising do you think are useful?
*(Tick as many boxes as are relevant)*

☐ Prices and publication dates of new editions

☐ Information on Text content

☐ Details of our free online offering

☐ None of the above

**Your ratings, comments and suggestions would be appreciated on the following areas of this Text.**

| | Very useful | Useful | Not useful |
|---|---|---|---|
| Introductory section | ☐ | ☐ | ☐ |
| Quality of explanations | ☐ | ☐ | ☐ |
| How it works | ☐ | ☐ | ☐ |
| Chapter tasks | ☐ | ☐ | ☐ |
| Chapter Overviews | ☐ | ☐ | ☐ |
| Test your learning | ☐ | ☐ | ☐ |
| Index | ☐ | ☐ | ☐ |

| | Excellent | Good | Adequate | Poor |
|---|---|---|---|---|
| Overall opinion of this Text | ☐ | ☐ | ☐ | ☐ |

**Do you intend to continue using BPP Products?**  ☐ Yes  ☐ No

**Please note any further comments and suggestions/errors on the reverse of this page. You can e-mail your comments to: paulsutcliffe@bpp.com**

**Please return to: Paul Sutcliffe, Senior Publishing Manager, BPP Learning Media Ltd, FREEPOST, London, W12 8BR.**

**REVIEW FORM (continued)**

**TELL US WHAT YOU THINK**

Please note any further comments and suggestions/errors below.